Managing the
Data Warehouse

W.H. Inmon
J.D. Welch
Katherine L. Glassey

WILEY COMPUTER PUBLISHING

John Wiley & Sons, Inc.
New York • Chichester • Weinheim
Toronto • Singapore • Brisbane

Executive Publisher: Katherine Schowalter
Editor: Robert Elliott
Managing Editor: Micheline Frederick
Composition: Publishers' Design and Production Services, Inc.

This text is printed on acid-free paper.

Library of Congress Cataloging-in-Publication Data

0471-16310-4 (pbk)

Printed in the United States of America

10 9 8 7 6 5 4 3 2 1

Contents

Dedication

From Bill Inmon

> To my brother-in-law, Joe Foster, in hopes that someday he will learn to fish.

From J. D. Welch

> I would like to dedicate this book to: My mother, for obvious reasons; Arlene, for her loving support in the face of adversity; Ingvar, for his vision, leadership and friendship; and; Bill, for inviting me to go on, this wild ride, 'lo, those many years ago!

From Katherine Glassey

> To Yorgen, without his inspiration and support, I would not have begun this project. And I certainly could not have completed it were he not such an extraordinary and devoted father to our children.
>
> Also my thanks to Kris Laskowski, and to Kathy Waite who pitched in and supported the team brilliantly when I was "on the down side of the curve."

Preface

In the beginning there were simple systems of automation. Then came database systems and online systems. In a very short time the computer had found its way into the warp and woof of corporate life. From no computers in the 1950s to millions of computers of every size in the 1980s, the world of technology has exploded beyond anyone's belief at a rate that seemed to be impossible.

The early systems of computation were designed to run the day-to-day transactions of the corporation. Immediate clerical decisions were the focus of these pioneering systems. With the advent of the first systems came a by-product of data. The data reflected the activities that were transpiring and grew as time passed and business was conducted.

Soon, the amount of work required to maintain the applications mounted, to the point that 95 percent of the program design and development work being done by a shop was dedicated to maintenance. At the same time that the maintenance burden was growing, the end users were becoming frustrated with the inability of the Information Systems (IS) organization to respond to their need for information. In case after case, end users knew that the data they needed was available. Yet, in each case, the IS department gave one reason or another why the data could not be accessed. End users felt abandoned and frustrated.

Then, data warehouse was created. Data warehouse took the by-product transaction data and organized and stored the data so that the end user could get his or her hands around it. At last the data was available for end-user informational processing.

Data warehouse represented a fundamental shift in the conception of information systems and introduced some important new concepts:

- Data should be integrated across the enterprise.
- Summary data had a real value to the organization.
- Historical data held the key to understanding data over time.
- Metadata played a very important role in that infrastructure.
- Maintaining the accuracy of that historical data over time while also providing what-if capabilities required by a flexible architecture.
- Data-mart processing could not be done successfully without a proper foundation of building the data warehouse first.

In addition to solving some very important problems for the corporation, the creation of the data warehouse relieved the application programmer from the burden of trying to do informational processing from the legacy systems environment. The backlog of application and system maintenance—for the first time—became manageable.

But the real momentum for data warehouse began when people realized that available information in the data warehouse could be used for competitive advantage. This information supported the corporation's ability to attract and keep market share, lower expenses, and raise revenues. These attributes elevated data warehouse to the forefront of information systems.

Thus, data warehouse had great promise for both the technician and the business person. It is no wonder that data warehouse has gone from rogue concept to conventional wisdom in a very short time.

The rise of data warehouse created the need for management of a discipline that a few years ago did not exist—data warehouse administrator or DWA. Part data administrator, part database administrator, some end user, a little systems programmer, a lot of application programmer and designer—the DWA is the focus of an entirely new world.

This book is on managing the data warehouse, primarily from the perspective of the DWA. The many issues and challenges—some predictable, some unpredictable—that face the DWA are the main focus.

This book is part of a series of books on data warehouse and related subjects. The first book, *Building the Data Warehouse*, addresses the larger issues of architecture and design that surround the data warehouse. Now in its second edition, *Building the Data Warehouse* had the distinction of starting the entire data warehouse movement.

The second book in the series, *Using the Data Warehouse*, addresses what to do once the data warehouse is built. In addition, it introduces the idea of a larger architecture that can be called the corporate information factory.

The third book in the series is *Building the Operational Data Store* which discusses the notion of data warehouse in the operational environment. While data warehouse is purely an informational architectural structure, there is still a need for information in the operational environment. Integrated, collective information is created and managed in the operational data store.

This fourth book in the series is for those who must make a data warehouse environment work once the environment has been built.

This book has two important focal points:

1. Identifying the important issues needed for successful data warehouse administration.
2. Addressing what the issues of administration are.

Some of the topics covered include

■ monitoring data warehouse activity;
■ monitoring data warehouse data;

- administering data warehouse security;
- metadata management administration;
- selecting and managing end-user tools;
- administering the data warehouse or data mart interface;
- data warehouse refreshment;
- managing growth in the data warehouse environment; and
- managing summary data.

This book is for data warehouse administrators and anyone desiring success in data warehousing. It will appeal to data administrators, database administrators, designers, developers, and decision support systems (DSS) analysts. In addition, managers of data warehouse environments will find this book to be invaluable.

The authors would like to thank many people for the many different kinds of support—moral, editorial, and so on—they have received.

Special thanks to

Jim Ashbrook, Prism Solutions

Arnold Barnett, Barnett Data Systems

Debra Columbana, Prism Solutions

Cheryl Estep, Chevron Corp.

Claudia Imhoff, Intelligent Solutions

Melba Inmon, Forest Rim Technologies

Cynthia Schmidt, Prism Solutions

Judy Teson, Prism Solutions

Ed Young, D2K

John Zachman, Zachman International

WHI/JDW/KLG

Monitoring Data Warehouse Activity

The data warehouse **administrator**—the "DWA"—is an **organizational disciplinarian** who has appeared with the advent of data warehousing and decision support systems (DSSs). The DWA is responsible for the ongoing success of the data warehouse once it becomes functional.

The DWA must understand the many skills of his or her team:

- Database designer, who designs and builds the data warehouse.
- Data modeller, who integrates a new data warehouse with an existing one.
- Developer, who puts new integration and transformation programs in place.
- Politician, who competes for resources necessary for the building of the data warehouse.
- Systems manager, who selects hardware and software for the building of the data warehouse.
- Systems programmer, who handles capacity planning and tuning for the data warehouse.
- End user, who must understand the problems of the financier, sales manager, actuary, engineer, etc.

In some cases the DWA must not only understand these skills, but be able to perform them. In short the DWA is responsible for an entirely new environment supporting decision-making that is crucial to the success of the corporation. Of the many facets to the job of data warehouse administrator, this book will outline the most important and obvious.

MONITORING WAREHOUSE ACTIVITY

The most fundamental act of the data warehouse administrator—once the data warehouse is built—is to monitor the activity inside the warehouse. This activity can be classified into two categories:

- DSS access of data by the end user.
- System function needed for the loading and management of the data inside the data warehouse.

In one sense the job of the DWA is simple: There is no online high-performance transaction response time to worry about. However, the DWA must worry about huge amounts of data—volumes of data never before seen by any database administrator. The simplicity of the data warehouse environment from a functional perspective is offset by the need to manage truly gargantuan amounts of data.

While online update is not a concern of the DWA, there still is a need for good DSS response time. (Although, in truth online transaction response time is quite a bit different from DSS transaction response time, as shall be discussed.)

Without knowing what is going on inside the data warehouse, there is no effective way to manage the warehouse. Before *any* other activity is undertaken, the DWA must be able to measure and keep records of all activity inside the warehouse. Although there are many good reasons why an activity monitor for the data warehouse is necessary, perhaps the most compelling is that, as data grows in the data warehouse environment, proportionately less of the data is used. Figure 1.1 illustrates this irony.

For example, in the first year the data warehouse, it may contain 10 GB (gigabytes) of data. In that earliest year, 100 percent of the data is used by DSS analysts. In year two the warehouse grows to 50 gigabytes of data, but less than 90 percent of the data is being used by the DSS analysts. In year three there are now 100 gigabytes of data in the warehouse and less than 70 percent of the data is used. In year four the data warehouse grows to 250 gigabytes of data, but the actual amount of data accessed in the data warehouse on something approaching a "regular" basis has dropped below 50 percent.

This phenomenon of the increasing size of the data warehouse and the simultaneous decreasing use of the data presents a real challenge to the DWA. On the one hand, each year the DWA goes to management with a request for more storage and more processing power to use that storage. The costs for this processing power grow significantly larger every year. However, each year the end users actually access—as a percentage of the total data—less and less data. Does it make sense to add storage every year when less of the storage is being used? Of course, it does not make sense.

Furthermore, the cost of the requests for storage and processing power is not trivial. The volumes of data that are being considered and the machines used for processing are very significant and do not constitute a rounding error on the corporate budget.

There are several reasons why the data warehouse is made up of so much data. First, the data warehouse contains a robust amount of history. Prior to the data warehouse, historical data was treated as an afterthought in the corporation. Data warehouse entails the formal recognition of the importance of historical data and its rigorous treatment. With the historical data come correspondingly large volumes of data.

The second reason for so much data is that the data warehouse contains summary data as well as detailed data. While detailed data can be planned for, summary data is often created spontaneously—as part of the end user's "discovery" process. But summary data requires space and processing power, just as the detailed data does. This coexistance of both detailed and summary data is an example of "managed redundancy," which will be discussed in greater detail in Chapter 11.

Fig 1.1 suggests a simple cure. Why not purge unneeded data over the years? At the end of each year, look inside the data

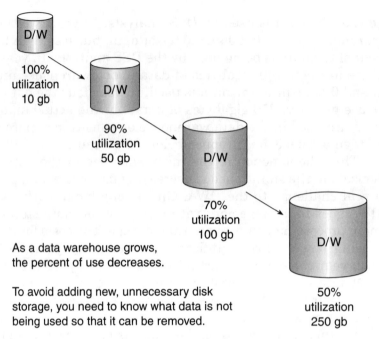

100%
utilization
10 gb

90%
utilization
50 gb

70%
utilization
100 gb

As a data warehouse grows,
the percent of use decreases.

To avoid adding new, unnecessary disk
storage, you need to know what data is not
being used so that it can be removed.

50%
utilization
250 gb

Figure 1.1 Why do I need a data warehouse activity monitor?

warehouse and determine what data has been used and what data has not been used, then purge the unaccessed data. Unneeded data can be removed from the data warehouse environment or moved to hierarchical storage where it can be retrieved at a later time if needed. This simple idea is really quite a good one. But in order to implement the idea, it is necessary to first know what data is and is not being used by the DSS analysts. If data that is being used is purged, then the end user has reason to complain. If unused data is allowed to remain in the data warehouse, then there is waste.

What Data in the Data Warehouse Is Being Used?

Determining data use is deceptively complex. It is not sufficient to know what tables of data are being accessed, because there may be only one record in a table that is being accessed. A much lower level of granularity is needed to determine use. In order to effectively purge data from the data warehouse, the DWA must know

■ What rows of data are/are not being accessed.
■ What columns of data are/are not accessed.
■ In some cases, what occurrences of data are being accessed.

Once data use is determined, then the DWA can be very selective in determining what data stays inside the data warehouse and what data goes.

In addition, a statistical inference can be made. Suppose that some pieces of data are being used only once or twice in a year, while other pieces of data are being used many thousand times per year. The DWA may want to investigate the circumstances for use of the infrequently used data. If this data is not being used for a very critical process, then the DWA may well want to remove the data from the data warehouse, even though it has some limited use. If, however, it is infrequently accessed but for critical business purpose, the DWA may decide to leave that data in the data warehouse.

In order to do all of this, it is presupposed that data can be monitored so that the use of the data can be measured down to a very fine level. An activity monitor is required for effective management of the bulk of data that flows through the data warehouse.

Who Is Using the Data Warehouse?

This is a second important question the DWA faces, as illustrated by Figure 1.2. Some users do not access the data warehouse very often; others access it frequently and regularly. When the telephone rings and the DWA answers, how does the DWA know what is going on inside the data warehouse? How does the DWA know whether he or she is talking to someone who seldom uses the data warehouse, or someone who uses the data warehouse as a regular part of the business? Knowing the usage profile of the end user is crucial in order to prioritize the urgency with which questions are answered. To answer the question concerning use of the data warehouse, an activity monitor is needed.

Figure 1.2 Who is doing the bulk of the activity?

What Is the Response Time?

Suppose the DWA gets a telephone call asking for an explanation of response time. The end user says that response time today is terrible. How does the DWA know whether the end user is portraying response time accurately or whether the user is just having a bad day? Figure 1.3 depicts the dilemma of not knowing what is going on in terms of response time at the end-user's terminal.

In order to determine whether response time really is bad or adequate, an activity monitor is needed. Quantification and measurement of results over a lengthy period of time are required to evaluate what is really happening.

What Kind of Activities Are Being Submitted?

The type of activity that is being submitted to the data warehouse is also of great interest to the DWA, as illustrated in Figure 1.4. Some users are submitting very large queries, while others are submitting small queries. The makeup of the work-

Figure 1.3 Who is getting good or bad response time?

load going into the data warehouse is of great importance in determining why the data warehouse is performing as it is. The DWA needs an activity monitor to be able to quantify just how much the workload varies from one user to the next.

Occurrences of Activity

In addition to the makeup of the workload, the number of queries, and the perceived response time from the data warehouse environment, the DWA must see how the workload has varied over time, as shown in Figure 1.5. Figure 1.5 shows that throughout

Figure 1.4 Who is doing what kind of activity?

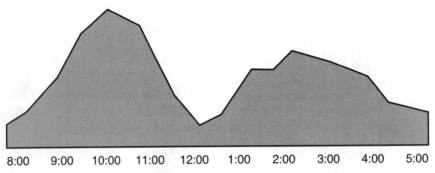

Figure 1.5 When is activity occurring?

the day the workload is very variable in the data warehouse environment. When the workload has great peaks and valleys, the DWA can take any one of several corrective actions:

■ Charge more for peak period processing.
■ Educate users to submit long running queries over night rather than at peak times.
■ Augment the end users' access tool(s) with a "governor" that only returns a sample set of data instead of the "full" return set.
■ Create a "sample" environment where queries can be done without going against the whole body of data during peak period processing, and so forth.

In short, once the DWA is apprised of exactly what is going on at different times of the day in the data warehouse environment, he or she can act to counterbalance the time sequencing of the workload. But without quantification and measurement of the activities in the data warehouse, the DWA is at a loss to effectively manage the environment.

An initial question to pose is: Just how much does the workload in question vary from the norm? In other words, is today's result really any different from any other day's result, and if so, by how much? Figure 1.6 shows how this very important question might be answered.

The figure shows the importance of monitoring activities over a lengthy period of time and creating a composite measure-

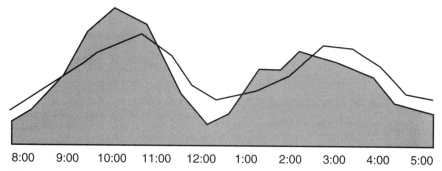

Figure 1.6   How does current activity vary from average activity?

ment—a *benchmark* measurement. The benchmark measurement can then be used to tell if something unusual is going on in the system or whether it is "business as usual."

Not only do details need to be created and aggregated for a single day, but also data and details that measure the activity inside a data warehouse environment over time need to be collected. Figure 1.7 shows how data needs to be telescoped. The

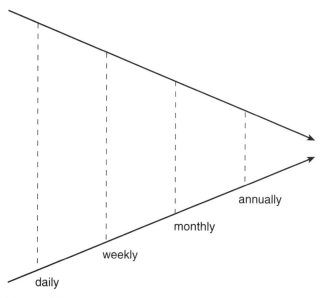

Figure 1.7   In order to see the larger picture, activity data must be "telescoped" over time.

"telescoping" of data collected as part of the activity monitor process is necessary for the following reasons:

- Trends do not become apparent unless looked at over a lengthy period of time.
- When looking at total resource use, it is important to look at aggregate numbers for periods of time other than a day—in other words looking at total use for a week, month, quarter, and so on is important.

The telescoping of data over time provides the foundation needed to make both micro and macro observations as to the activities and the resource utilization of the data warehouse.

GRANULARITY OF THE ACTIVITY MONITOR

The granularity of the data monitor is one of the most important aspects of the software. Figure 1.8 shows the granularity that is required for an activity monitor. In order to accurately measure the activity that the DWA needs, the activity monitor must be able to measure activity at the

table level,

table/column level, and

the table/column/occurrence level.

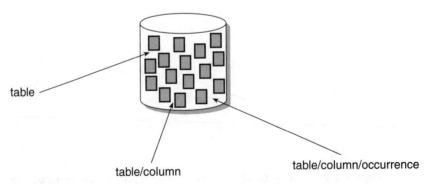

Figure 1.8 Data needs to be monitored at different levels of granularity.

Any granularity measurements made at a h... granularity than this will not allow the DWA to dete... actly what data can be removed from the data warehouse. the other hand, the granularity of the activity analysis must be carefully considered because it is easy to get carried away and say that *all* activity monitoring must be at a very low level. The problem is that when *all* activity is monitored at the lowest level possible, the overhead of monitoring rises significantly. The best resolution is for the DWA to monitor most data warehouse data at the highest level possible (that is still meaningful) and to monitor only selected tables at the lowest level necessary.

As an example, suppose the DWA has 200 tables to monitor. The DWA monitors 190 of the tables at the table level and 10 of the tables—the most troublesome and critical tables—at the table/column and the table/column/occurrence level.

CHARGEBACK AND ACTIVITY MONITORING

One of the most important features of a data warehouse environment is that of *chargeback* that lets the end user know about the cost of using the data warehouse. Without chargeback, the end user has no way of knowing just how much data is being processed at the work station. However, with chargeback, the end user becomes aware of the resources that are being consumed.

Figure 1.9 shows that end users need to be made aware of the costs of doing data warehouse processing. An activity monitor creates the foundation for doing chargeback by collecting details of use. The DWA then selects an algorithm that determines the cost. The algorithm takes into consideration many different aspects of the end user's workload profile:

- When a query was submitted.
- How big the query was.
- The priority of the query.
- The number of other queries that have been submitted.
- Whether the query could be run overnight.
- The time of the week/month the query was submitted.
- The data the query was submitted for and so on.

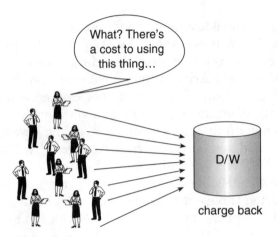

Figure 1.9 When users push back on the cost of the data warehouse, it is nice to be able to say—in a quantified manner— what the use of the data warehouse was.

Based upon the many factors that the DWA deems relevant, the algorithm is used to determine the chargeback to the end user.

AN ACTIVITY MONITOR—WHY NOT ANY OTHER MONITOR?

The notion of monitoring a system is not new. Monitors of various descriptions have been in existence for a long time. The very earliest monitors were for hardware devices. Next came monitors for online transaction processing (OLTP) systems. Then there were database monitors.

Each of the monitors had its place in the development of modern information systems. And each of the earlier monitors has some overlap—however small—with the monitor for the activity that occurs in a data warehouse. However, data warehouse activity monitoring requires a fresh and unique approach. There are many differences between a data warehouse activity monitor and an online transaction monitor, for instance. Figure 1.10 shows some of those differences.

A data warehouse activity monitor is for DSS processing only. Therefore, there is no need to worry about update process-

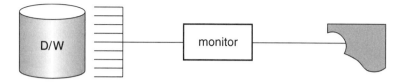

A data warehouse monitor
- is for DSS only
- is for the data warehouse administrator, not the systems programmer
- measures data usage at a very granular level—at the work station/ table/column
- has a DSS understanding of transactions
- is not cluttered by unnecessary and irrelevant measurements
- contains an historical perspective of measurements
- is DBMS-independent
- is operating system-independent
- uses SQL as the lingua franca

Figure 1.10   How is the data warehouse activity monitor different from any other kind of monitor?

ing or deadly embraces. Update contention is not an issue. The data warehouse activity monitor is built solely for the data warehouse administrator and is peculiar to that administrator's needs. The data warehouse activity monitor needs to be able to measure the use of data at varying degrees of granularity which are determined by the data warehouse administrator. It must be able to go to a very fine degree of granularity when needed—down to the table-column-occurrence level. The transactions that are measured are DSS transactions, not OLTP transactions.

There is a fundamental difference between a DSS transaction and an OLTP transaction: DSS transactions are extremely undisciplined in terms of resource use whereas OLTP transactions are extremely disciplined. Because of this difference in discipline, the workload that characterizes the DSS environment is very irregular while the OLTP workload is reasonably regular and predictable in its size and shape.

The DSS monitor should not be cluttered by unnecessary and irrelevant measurements that were important in the OLTP environment. The data warehouse activity monitor contains both a current and an historical measurement of important variables.

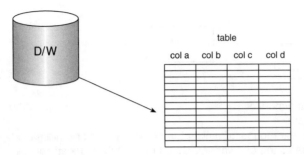

Figure 1.11 The monitor needs to track activity down to the table/column/ occurrence level of granularity.

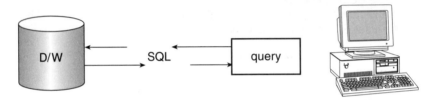

Figure 1.12 Measurements must be trapped at the SQL level.

The monitor also needs to be database management system (DBMS) and operating system-independent if it is to have widespread applicability and use. Because of this need for independence, SQL serves as the lingua franca for capturing and measuring warehouse activity. Figure 1.11 shows that the data warehouse activity monitor needs to be able to track data warehouse activity down to the table-column-occurrence level of granularity. Figure 1.12 illustrates the trapping of activity by the data warehouse activity monitor at the SQL level.

DIFFERENCES BETWEEN DSS AND OLTP

While there are many differences between the OLTP and the DSS environments, the most significant as far as the data warehouse activity monitor is concerned, is that of the difference between transactions and the resources used by those transactions, as shown in Figure 1.13. In Fig 1.13, an OLTP transaction is seen to

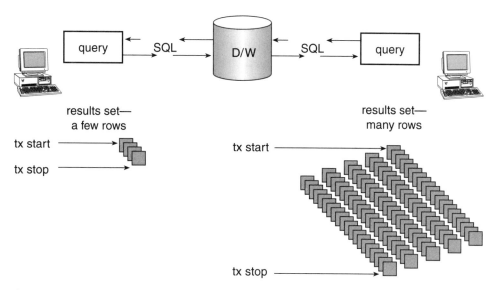

Figure 1.13 DSS transaction response time requires that two transaction response times be measured—the response time from the moment of the launch of the query to the moment the first results are returned and the response time from the moment of the launch of the query to the moment the last of the results are returned.

consume very few resources; it looks at very few rows of data. Furthermore, *all* OLTP transactions will look at a limited amount of data. Based upon this pragmatic definition of a transaction, an OLTP transaction is one that uniformly uses very few resources. As a result of this discipline, there is consistently good response time in the OLTP environment; two to three seconds is the norm.

The DSS transaction environment is quite different. Here, a transaction may look at *many* rows of data. It is not unheard of for a DSS transaction to require the access of 1,000,000 rows of data or more. On the other hand, some DSS transactions may not require the access of more than a handful of rows, much like an OLTP transaction. Because of the number of rows that may be accessed by a DSS transaction (otherwise known as the *result set*), two transaction response time measurements are required: transaction start time and transaction stop time.

Transaction start time for DSS transactions is the length of time from the initiation of the transaction until the *first* of the data is returned to the workstation; transaction stop time is the length of time from the initiation of the transaction until the *last* of the data is transmitted. In the case of a large DSS transaction, there may be a considerable amount of time from the start to the stop of the transaction.

Note that this definition of start and stop time is foreign to the OLTP environment. Since there are only a few units of data that are accessed by each transaction in OLTP, there is no need for making a distinction between the start of result set transmission and its stop.

MEASURING DSS PARAMETERS OF ACTIVITY

While DSS response time is certainly one important measurement that must be trapped by the data warehouse activity monitor, it is hardly the only parameter. The full set of parameters that needs to be trapped by the data warehouse activity monitor is described in Figure 1.14.

A request is the issuance of an SQL call to the data warehouse server. An access is the result of that SQL call. There are two other parameters which may or may not be captured by the activity monitor—non-SELECT SQL activity and non-SQL activity. Non-SELECT SQL activity is SQL activity that may be run in the data warehouse environment other than the access of data. Non-SQL activity may also be run, such as e-Mail. These other parameters are a catch-all that includes all other system activity.

```
table requests
table/column requests
table accesses
table/column accesses
table/column/occurrence access
non SELECT activity
non SQL activity
transaction start measurement
transaction stop measurement
```

Figure 1.14 The parameters of SQL needed to be trapped for analysis.

WHAT THE MONITOR REPORTS

There are *many* permutations and combinations of reports that can be made using the suggested parameters. Indeed the DWA needs to whittle down the possibilities for reporting into the five or six reports that are most relevant to managing the data warehouse environment.

One of the possibilities for an activity monitor report is seen in Figure 1.15. This report matches the number of rows returned in the result set on a system-wide basis spread across the days of the week. It reveals on what day of the week there is the most activity, as measured by the number of rows that have been accessed. A variation of the same report is seen in Figure 1.16.

The Figure shows the same report compared to the average activity. The DWA can use the data warehouse activity monitor to produce the reports which show just how much variation there is between the current week and the average week.

Any number of variables can be measured and correlated, once the raw data has been collected. Figure 1.17 shows one such possibility. Here, the DWA has collected different kinds of data and placed them on the same monthly scale to determine whether there is any correlation between them.

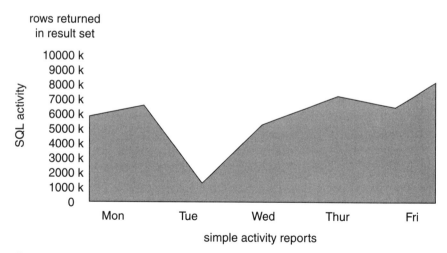

Figure 1.15 Monitor reports: On what day does the most or least SQL activity occur, and by how much?

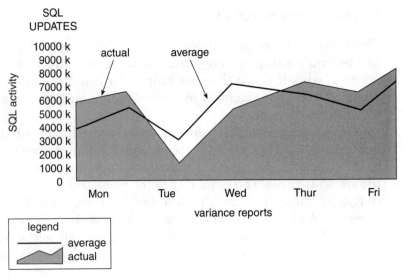

Figure 1.16 Monitor reports: How much has this week's update activity differed from the normal or average week?

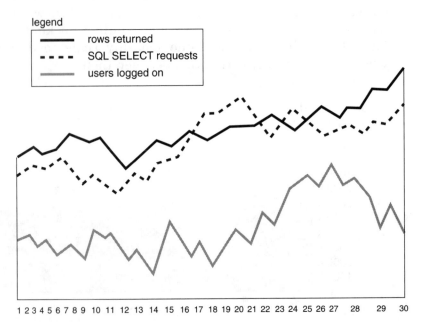

What is the correlation, if any between:
- The number of users logged on and the number of rows being returned in a result set?
- The number of users logged on and the number of SQL SELECT requests that are being made?

Figure 1.17 Monitor reports: monthly multivariate report.

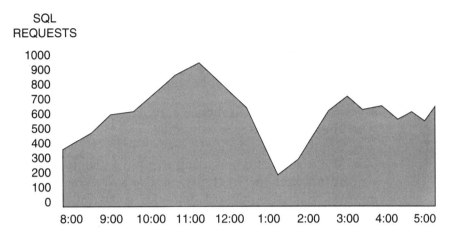

Figure 1.18 Monitor reports: When is the busiest time of day? By how much?

Another very typical report that assumes importance to the DWA once the activity monitor is up and running is the measurement of the busiest time of day by the submission of SQL requests, as shown in Figure 1.18. Yet another variation of the reports that are possible with the data warehouse activity monitor is a description of what subject areas are the most popular and the least popular, as shown in Figure 1.19.

Figure 1.19 Monitor reports: What subject areas are the most and least popular?

ADMINISTERING THE DATA WAREHOUSE ACTIVITY MONITOR

There are several activities the DWA needs to do in order to properly administer the data warehouse activity monitor:

- Install the data warehouse activity monitor.
  - Make sure space is available.
  - Create the needed data sets.
  - Make sure the operating system is compatible with the data warehouse activity monitor software.
- Make sure the network transfer software is installed and functional.
- Determine which work stations should be monitored.
- Determine which workstations will be monitored at the data warehouse server.
- Periodically install new releases of the software.
- Determine which tables should be
  - monitored at all,
  - monitored at the table level,
  - monitored at the table/column level,
  - monitored at the table/column/occurrence level.
- Decide whether other network activity will be monitored.
- Decide what reports are necessary.
- Create benchmark data
  - hourly,
  - daily,
  - weekly,
  - monthly,
  - annually.
- Designate one workstation as the DWA controller.
- Make sure that not too many reports and not too much low-level data has been specified.
- Determine how data will be rolled up over time—hourly, daily, weekly, monthly, etc.
- Determine whether data will be collected by department, location, etc.
- Determine what data will be stored at a system-wide level and at a workstation level.
- Determine the archival strategy for all data, and so forth.

SUMMARY

One of the basic activities of data warehouse administration is that of monitoring the activity that flows through the system. There are many good reasons why monitoring data makes eminent sense:

- To determine exactly what data is being accessed in the data warehouse by the DSS analyst.
- To determine what kind of queries are being submitted.
- To determine what kind of response there is.
- To be able to contrast current activity against a baseline of activity to determine whether things are actually good or bad.
- To create a telescope of activity over time.
- To be able to look at system activity at multiple levels, depending on the criticality of a table, and
- To do chargeback.

The data warehouse activity monitor is very different from other monitors in that it manages an entirely different environment. Transactions in the DSS environment are quite different from other transactions that are found in the OLTP environment.

Monitoring Data Warehouse Data

2

The first mandatory activity for the data warehouse administrator is the monitoring of the activity that goes on inside the data warehouse. The DWA must know what users are doing, what data is being accessed, and how the system is responding to the workload in order to properly do the job of data warehouse administration. But, as important as activity monitoring of the data warehouse is, it is hardly the only important activity. The monitoring of the data in the data warehouse environment is the next important activity for the DWA.

MONITOR DIFFERENCES

At first glance, there may appear to be little difference between the monitoring of activity and the monitoring of data. In fact, there are very major differences. Consider what an activity monitor does. It:

- Determines who is using the data warehouse.
- Measures when the warehouse is used.
- Accounts for response time in the warehouse.
- Profiles the workload flowing through the data warehouse.

■ Identifies what data is being used.

A data monitor for the data warehouse environment does something altogether different. It:

■ Measures how many records of data there are in the warehouse.
■ Calculates and stores the growth pattern of those records.
■ Measures "profiles" of data that are meaningful to the DSS analyst and the DWA.
■ Calculates and stores the growth pattern of those "profiles."
■ Checks on the validity of the data to determine that there is a high degree of quality of data in the data warehouse.
■ Is used to create *threshold* values for the profiles that have been identified.

Each of these functions will be explained in depth later in this chapter. Figure 2.1 outlines the major functions of monitoring data in the data warehouse.

There are some major functional differences between the activity monitor and the data monitor in the data warehouse, yet both complement each other. While both monitors are important,

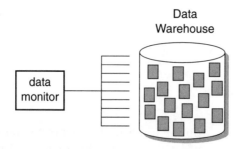

What is in the warehouse now?

What growth has occured in the warehouse?

What profiles are there?

What thresholds are there?

What is the quality of the data?

Figure 2.1   Major functions of monitoring a data warehouse.

one monitor without the other is inadequate for effective data warehouse administration.

FROM THE DSS ANALYST PERSPECTIVE

In order to understand why a data monitor is important, consider the DSS analyst who must use the data warehouse. The DSS analyst submits a query one day only to find that the query has used an inordinate amount of resources—the query has accessed 50,000,000 rows of data! The DWA and the DBA tell the DSS analyst that there should be no more submission of queries that size unless the query is cleared by both of them.

The DSS analyst—in good faith and desiring to be a good corporate citizen—tries to abide by the guidelines set down by the DWA and the DBA. But one day the DSS analyst wants to use the data warehouse in a way that it hasn't been used before. The DSS analyst prepares a query. Immediately before the launch of the query, the DSS analyst stops to consider if this query will access a huge amount of data and might need the permission of the DWA.

The DSS analyst has a dilemma. How does the DSS analyst know—before submitting a query—whether the query has the potential of accessing a huge amount of data? What the DSS analyst needs is something that tells how much data of what type there is in the data warehouse *before* a query is submitted. If there are only 5,000 rows that the analyst will be looking at, then the DSS analyst does not need any approval from the DWA. But if there are 100,000,000 rows of data that possibly will be scanned by the query, then the DSS analyst will definitely want the DWA and the DBA to check out the query before it is submitted.

Therefore, there needs to be an organized, quantified, up-to-date profile of the data that is in the data warehouse that is available to the DSS analyst *before* any questionable query is submitted. That profile and survey of data inside the warehouse are created by the data warehouse data monitor.

Consider another scenario. A data warehouse has been in existence for a while. It has had data placed in it for a number of years. The data warehouse is also large. One day the DSS analyst goes to the DWA and says: "I think there is something wrong here. I did a survey of all our male and female employees. The data warehouse said there were 510 males and 613 females that worked for our company. But the total employee count is 1,386. I don't see where 510 + 613 adds up to 1,386. Can you tell me what is wrong here?"

The DWA agrees that something is amiss and examines the queries done by the DSS analyst; the DSS analyst has submitted queries that look like

```
SELECT data        SELECT data
FROM EMPFILE       FROM EMPFILE


WHERE SEX = 'M'    WHERE SEX = 'F'
. . . . . . . . . . . . . .    . . . . . . . . . . . . . .
```

On the surface it would appear that the survey would have been comprehensive, covering each of the employees exactly once. The DWA then digs deeper into the issue and finds that in the very early days of the data warehouse that there was a load program that inserted data into the data warehouse differently than the way data is loaded today. The DWA discovers for a short period of time that data has been loaded so that

```
males = '1' and females = '0'
```

When the DSS analyst looked for males = 'M' and females = 'F,' the analyst discovered the most recent employee records. But there were a few records representing an employee that did not have either representation; accordingly, those records were not counted as part of the employee population.

The DWA has just uncovered *dirty data* in the data warehouse. In order to achieve a higher quality of data in the data warehouse, a simple audit of data must be done. The vehicle for this audit is the data warehouse data monitor.

BASIC FUNCTIONS

The basic function of a data warehouse data monitor is that of creating simple counts of data, as seen in Figure 2.2. The moni-

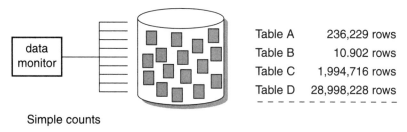

Simple counts

Figure 2.2 Creating simple counts of data.

tor in this figure looks at each table and simply counts the rows of data in the table. There is no distinction made between the data of one type and data of another type in the table. Each row or each record simply tallies once in the counter.

This simple count is very useful for a general determination of the size of a table. This broadbrush approach is a good start. However, the nature of data warehousing is that tables grow rapidly. Almost as soon as the data warehouse data monitor tallies the table counts, those counts are out of synch with reality. Therefore, simple counts must be done frequently (depending on the growth rate of the table, every month, every quarter, etc.). The growth of the tables in the data warehouse can be measured over time by combining the results of multiple executions of the data warehouse data monitor. Figure 2.3 shows a representation of how simple counts can be combined over time.

Data Profiles

Data profiles are fundamentally different from simple counts of data in that profiles go into the data warehouse and examine the

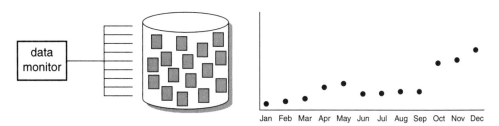

Figure 2.3 Tracking of simple counts over time.

contents of the data to determine what data of what type is there. The DWA determines what profiles are going to be useful to track. Common profiles might look like

- insurance policies where there is cross-coverage of auto and homeowners,
- insurance policies where there have been no claims in the past two years,
- insurance policies where the policy is older than five years, etc.

or

- sales of parts costing more than $20 per unit,
- sales of home improvement stock,
- sales made on weekends,
- sales made in the summer,
- sales of items bought by credit card, etc.

Figure 2.4 shows some simple profiles.

customers since 1980	5,887
customers since 1985	10,885
customers since 1990	12,862
customers since 1995	18,882
accts < 1,000	109,002
accts < 5,000 & > 1,000	13,339
accts < 25,000 & > 5,000	2,982
accts > 25,000	559
employees uncompleted high school	27
employees high school education	76
employees with bachelors	217
employees with masters	24
employees with PhD	3
employee salary < 20,000	12
employee salary < 40,000 & > 20,000	107
employee salary < 60,000 & > 40,000	186
employee salary < 80,000 & > 60,000	26
employee salary > 80,000	16

Figure 2.4 Profiles of data.

The DWA selects the profiles in anticipation of helping the DSS analyst manage the workload. If it is likely that the DSS analyst community is going to be interested in a cross-cut of data, then the DWA specifies it. In addition, by examining the profiles the DWA can determine where the growth is occurring inside the data warehouse.

Note that the profiles are not mutually exclusive. A given row of data can contribute to any number of profile counts. For example, the record for a single insurance policy may be for homeowners where there never has been a claim made and where the policy is older than five years. Depending on how the DWA defines the profiles, the record may belong to any number of profiles.

The DWA may specify the profile categories so that they do not overlap and form a complete picture of the profiles of data. In Figure 2.4, in the profile for accounts, an account would fit into one and only one profile of data. Exactly how the profiles are defined and whether there is overlap is strictly up to the DWA.

Of course profiles can be created over a lengthy period of time. Figure 2.5 shows that multiple measurements of profiles have been taken and gathered together over time. The perspective of profiles over time provides not only a look at what is going

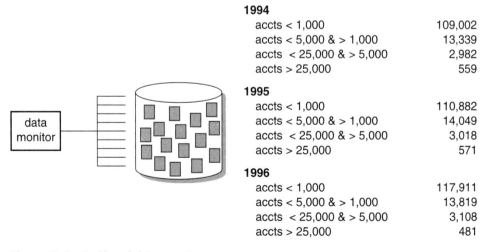

1994	
accts < 1,000	109,002
accts < 5,000 & > 1,000	13,339
accts < 25,000 & > 5,000	2,982
accts > 25,000	559
1995	
accts < 1,000	110,882
accts < 5,000 & > 1,000	14,049
accts < 25,000 & > 5,000	3,018
accts > 25,000	571
1996	
accts < 1,000	117,911
accts < 5,000 & > 1,000	13,819
accts < 25,000 & > 5,000	3,108
accts > 25,000	481

Figure 2.5 Profiles of data over time.

on right now in the data warehouse, but, also how trends have been developed over time.

While the primary use of the profile data is for the DSS analyst controlling query activity and for the DWA to monitor what is occurring inside the data warehouse, there is another secondary use of the profile data. The profile data itself can be useful for the DSS analyst in terms of doing analysis. In other words, the DSS analyst can turn to the profiles—especially the profiles of data over time—in order to actually do DSS analysis. In the normal circumstance, the DSS analyst looks to the data warehouse for raw data for analysis. Such is the case for ad hoc and spontaneous analysis. But occasionally the DWA has tracked the data the DSS analyst needs as part of the profile collection and assimilation. In this case, the DSS analyst is free to use what data has already been collected.

Thresholds of Data

A simple count of rows is achieved by merely tallying how many rows there are in a table. A profile is created when the DWA specifies that a certain type of data is to be tallied. But it is possible to do more with data than tally it; you can add or otherwise calculate actual values in the data warehouse. Such a calculation is called a *threshold* value.

A threshold is created when the DWA specifies a type of data (just as the DWA did for a profile) and a calculation to be made once the qualification of the data is met. As an example of a threshold, the DWA might specify that the total salaries be calculated for all men that work for a company. While the data warehouse data monitor looks through the human resources file for men, it calculates the total salaries that men are making from the same record. As another example of a threshold, when the data warehouse data monitor is run against the claims file for an insurance company looking for all claims that are older than six months, the DWA indicates that the total amount of the claims be specified. In yet another example of a threshold, the data warehouse data monitor is running against the sales file and the DWA specifies that for all sales greater than $5,000 the data warehouse data monitor calculate the net sale (sale amount – (commission + tax)).

The ingredients of a threshold are

■ a specification of a data qualification, and
■ a formula specifying what can be calculated once the qualifications of data are met.

Figure 2.6 describes some examples of typical thresholds.

In this figure the DWA has specified the qualifications so that they form a continuous representation of the data in the warehouse. The formula is a simple one—the summarization of all balances of the data that qualifies. Of course, the formula for calculation could be much more complex than a simple summarization. There is no limitation on the formula that is specified as the threshold other than that the data that is needed for calculation be available at the time of monitoring.

Like profiles and simple counts, thresholds can be monitored over time. Figure 2.7 shows some examples of thresholds that have been created and collected to represent a set of threshold values over time.

Threshold values have many purposes in the world of DSS. One value is to inform the DSS analyst of what is going on in the data warehouse insofar as values are concerned. Another value is to track trends over time. While profiles primarily serve the purpose of informing the DSS analyst how best to formulate queries, thresholds are best used in the actual DSS process itself.

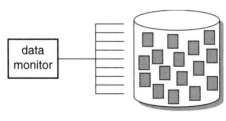

total balance for accts < 1,000	12,998,001
total balance for accts < 5,000 & > 1,000	13,009,992
total balance for accts < 25,000 & > 5,000	8,992,299
total balance for accts > 25,000	109,998,992

Figure 2.6 Thresholds of data.

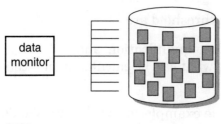

1994

total balance for accts < 1,000	12,998,001
total balance for accts < 5,000 & > 1,000	13,009,992
total balance for accts < 25,000 & > 5,000	8,992,299
total balance for accts > 25,000	109,998,992

1995

total balance for accts < 1,000	32,008,117
total balance for accts < 5,000 & > 1,000	18,992,227
total balance for accts < 25,000 & > 5,000	7,911,992
total balance for accts > 25,000	201,887,281

1996

total balance for accts < 1,000	27,817,227
total balance for accts < 5,000 & > 1,000	13,871,772
total balance for accts < 25,000 & > 5,000	5,998,171
total balance for accts > 25,000	231,981,177

Figure 2.7   Thresholds of data over time.

Data Quality

Once the data warehouse is built, how does the DWA actually know what is contained in the data warehouse? A good way for the DWA to find out is to actually set parameters to test the values in the warehouse. Figure 2.8 exhibits a simple form of testing for quality of data.

In Figure 2.8 the DWA has asked the data warehouse data monitor to look for records where gender is specified in other than an "M" or an "F" manner. Upon finding data that so qualifies, the DWA then specifies what identifier is needed to tell the DWA which record contained tainted data. Unlike a profile or a threshold where there is one output from all of the monitor processing, for audit and quality monitoring there can be many outputs, or none, if no data is found that qualifies.

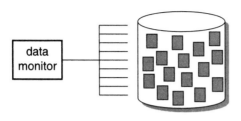

Which employee records have a sex designator other than "M" or "F"?

Howard Jackson	1
Mary Smith	Y
Bill Jones	1
June Lewis	Y
Tom Young	1
Larry Jones	X
Sue Gray	0

Figure 2.8   Data quality issues.

The ability to audit the quality of data can take one of two forms:

1. Look at all records for a specified condition.
2. Look at only qualified records for a specified conditions.

The only condition to be satisfied is that the data that is needed to qualify data and the data on which the specified condition is tested must be easily available as the data monitor passes through the data warehouse.

As some examples of quality control auditing, a DWA may specify any of the following:

■ Look for all records where gender not = 'M' or 'F'.
■ When part number is alphabetic, look for all records where unit of measure (U/M) not = "carton" or "box" or "unit" or "tin."
■ When region = "sw" or "ne", then look for sales code not = "qi" or "am" or "ou" or "pk."
■ Look for all records where sales amount is not numeric.

The line between conventional DSS and traditional monitoring blurs in the face of threshold calculations. Nevertheless, there are distinctions between the two; Figure 2.9 focuses on those differences.

Other Uses of a Data Warehouse Data Monitor

While simple counts, profiles, thresholds, and quality control of data are the normal use of a data monitor, it can be used for

Data Monitor	DSS
Regular measurement	Measurement done spontaneously
Combinations of measurements done concurrently	Measurement done individually
Examination of a single record	Multiple record types able to be examined
Definition of measurement is static	Definition of measurement is fluid
No overhead of doing measurement	Tremendous overhead of doing measurement

Figure 2.9   How does a data monitor differ from standard DSS?

other purposes as well (even if those purposes are secondary to the primary use of the data monitor). One of the incidental uses of a data monitor is that of gathering data during the passage of the data warehouse. Figure 2.10 shows the data monitor used as a data-gathering mechanism. The circumstances in which the

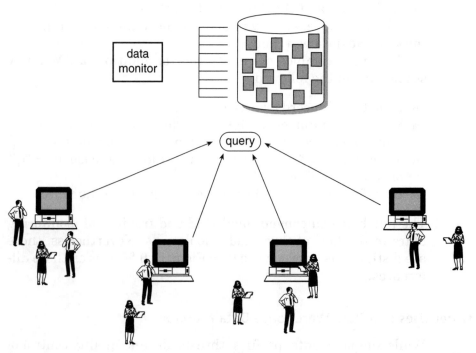

Figure 2.10   Using a data warehouse data monitor.

data warehouse data monitor can be used as a tool for gathering data are:

■ Where the DSS analyst gathers data in a predictable fashion.
■ Where the gathering of data can be scheduled.
■ Where the data that is gathered is contained in a single row (i.e., the row that is being monitored).

These conditions are somewhat restrictive. There will be many cases where the DSS analyst will want data under other conditions. When that is the case, the data warehouse data monitor cannot be used for gathering data. However, when the DSS analyst does want data under the conditions identified, then the data warehouse data monitor becomes a very efficient and convenient vehicle by which to gather data.

THE CHALLENGE OF MANAGING LARGE VOLUMES OF DATA

The essence of a data warehouse is large volumes of data. For a variety of reasons, data warehouses accumulate more data than any other type of architectural construct of information systems. The large volumes of data that are normal for the data warehouse pose a special problem to the DWA.

The first thing the DWA does is to schedule the monitoring of the data warehouse on a table-by-table basis. Some tables will require more frequent monitoring than other tables. Of course, the entire data warehouse is not monitored on an all-at-once basis. Breaking the monitor process up into a separate monitor of different tables is only the first step in managing the data monitor process.

Because of the large volumes of data that will exist in one or more tables, the DWA must carefully schedule the actual monitoring of the warehouse so that there will be no disruption to the regular work that goes on with the data warehouse. This means that the data monitor is run after hours or on weekends, during the times when there is little DSS processing occurring. In addition, there usually is no need to schedule a data monitor execution frequently. Scheduling a monitor execution every month usually suffices for most tables. Figure 2.11 shows the infrequent scheduling of the data monitor.

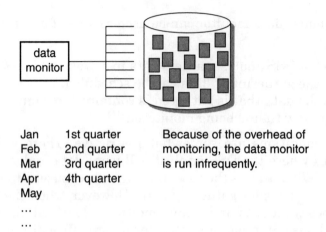

Jan   1st quarter   Because of the overhead of
Feb   2nd quarter   monitoring, the data monitor
Mar   3rd quarter   is run infrequently.
Apr   4th quarter
May
...
...

Figure 2.11   Scheduling the monitor for execution.

But, even with scheduling the monitoring infrequently during off hours and with the scheduling of the monitoring on a table-by-table basis, the DWA still faces a challenge because of the volume of data that exists in the largest tables found in the warehouse. In the face of these huge amounts of data, there is a need to reduce the amount of time any given execution of the data warehouse data monitor requires. The best way to reduce the time required for monitoring the largest tables is to break up the data warehouse monitor run into a series of smaller programs for the largest tables. In other words, if it requires eight hours to monitor the largest table in the data warehouse, then the program that does the monitoring needs to be broken up into a series of coordinated smaller programs. Each of the smaller programs will monitor a subset of the data found in the table. As a case in point, if there were eight programs instead of one, the data monitor process could occur in one hour rather than eight hours. Breaking up a long monitor process into a coordinated series of smaller programs yields many advantages.

Sectors

How then is such a coordinated break-up achieved? The easiest way is to break the large table that is to be monitored into a series of *sectors*. A sector is purely a logical division of a table. The DBA is the person who decides what is to be sectored and what is not to be sectored.

Some examples of the sectoring that can be assigned by the DBA might look like the following:

Example 1	*Part Number Table*
Sector 1	parts starting with "A00000" to parts ending in "F999999"
Sector 2	parts starting with "G00000" to parts ending in "S99999"
Sector 3	parts starting with "T00000" to parts ending in "Z99999"

Example 2	*Human Resources Table*
Sector 1	names starting with "Aaronson" and ending with "Guinasso"
Sector 2	names starting with "Haynes" and ending with "Robertson"
Sector 3	names starting with "Samuels" and ending with "Zachman"

In these above cases, the sectors created by the DBA are designed to be inclusive of all the data in the table and are nonoverlapping. The DBA did not necessarily have to specify the sectors that way. The sectors could have been designed so that some data was not included in the sector definition. Or the DBA could (at least in theory) have specified the sectors so that there was overlap among the sectors. (Even though overlap is theoretically possible, it makes no sense to do it.)

It makes sense that the definition given by the DBA is inclusive and nonoverlapping. The point is that the DBA is free to define the sectors as desired and can define as many sectors as needed. The examples show that the DBA has chosen three sectors. Over time the DBA will want to change the sector definition as the data itself changes. The number of sectors starts out small, but as the data warehouse grows, the DBA defines more sectors in order to break the data into finer pieces.

Once the DBA has defined the sectors, the data warehouse data monitor is able to create a monitor program for each sector, as shown in Figure 2.12. After the programs are run for each sector, the results are consolidated to give the appearance of a single program that has been executed. The results of the execution are saved so that an historical record can be made and the changes in the database can be tracked over time.

The sector monitors can be run in a parallel environment, as seen in Figure 2.13. Here, the sectors have been defined so that there is a correspondence between the sector definition and the parallelization of the data. In other words, the DBA has defined the sector so that one sector monitor runs against data controlled by one parallel processor, the next sector runs against data found only in the next parallel processor, and so forth. In doing so, the data warehouse data monitor can be run quite efficiently against a large table that has been parallelized.

In any case, once a large data warehouse data monitor program has been broken into sectors, the different monitors can be run independently. Figure 2.14 shows that the monitor program for sector 4 is run first; then the monitor for sector 3 is run; finally, the monitors for sectors 2 and 1 are run.

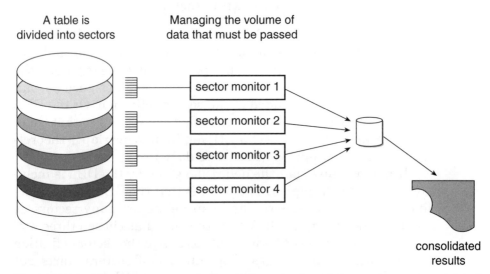

Figure 2.12 The sectors are monitoring independently and the results are consolidated to appear as if only one program were run.

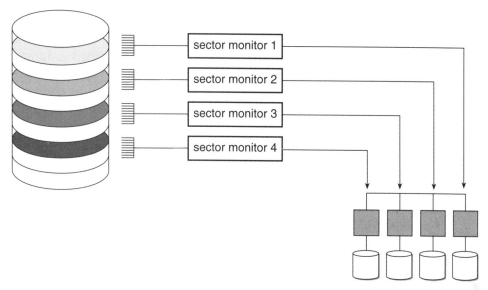

Figure 2.13 Sectors may be defined to correspond to the parameters of parallelization.

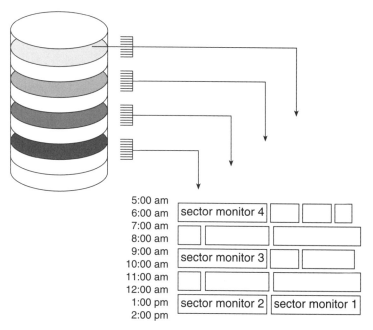

Figure 2.14 The sector monitors can be scheduled for independent execution.

The ability to create sectors in the definition of a large table of the data warehouse environment that needs to be monitored has many benefits. The monitor programs can be run independently, the sectors can be defined to correspond to the structure of the parallelization of the data, and the sectors can be changed over time as the characteristics of the data warehouse change.

ADMINISTERING THE DATA WAREHOUSE DATA MONITOR

The DWA needs to specify many different things in the set-up and ongoing administration of the data warehouse data monitor. Some of the more important activities are:

- Determine which tables in the data warehouse need to be monitored.
- Decide which tables will need sectoring.
- Decide how to sector those tables that are large.
- Determine the frequency of monitoring.
- Allocate space for system data sets.
- Load the monitoring software onto the data warehouse server.
- Schedule the different programs.
- Confer with the DSS analysts to determine:
  - What profiles are useful.
  - What thresholds are useful.
  - What data needs to be audited.
  - What needs to be done with the results of auditing, etc.

COMPLEMENTARY NATURE OF MONITORING SOFTWARE

The function provided by the data warehouse data monitor is complementary with the function provided by the data warehouse activity monitor. Figure 2.15 symbolically relates the complementary nature of these products.

The activity monitor looks at what is happening in terms of activity and the data monitor looks at the data warehouse from the perspective of the data inside the warehouse. Both monitors

Figure 2.15 The data warehouse data monitor and the data warehouse activity monitor are designed to work hand-in-hand in a complementary fashion.

provide a current perspective and a perspective over time. While the picture painted by one or the other monitor is most interesting, in order to paint a complete picture the DWA needs both monitors.

SUMMARY

The data warehouse data monitor is software that looks at the insides of the data warehouse. The data warehouse data monitor looks at

- simple counts of rows of data;
- profiles of data, looking inside the warehouse at the specifics of the contents of the warehouse;
- thresholds of data, where more than simple counts are made of qualified data inside the warehouse; and
- audits, where records that do not conform to prescribed parameters are identified.

In addition to forming a current picture of counts, profiles, thresholds, and audits, the data warehouse data monitor provides an historical picture of the contents of the data warehouse.

One of the biggest challenges the DBA faces is that of managing the volumes of data that are found in the data warehouse. One way is to sector the data in the data warehouse and produce a separate monitor program to monitor each sector. In such a manner, the data warehouse can be monitored in a parallel fashion.

Managing Security in the Data Warehouse

3

Data warehouse is peculiar: In most cases, there is a tremendous effort made to build the data warehouse with no thoughts of security at the moment of construction. After the first few iterations of the data warehouse are built, the DSS analyst community becomes thoroughly enamored of the warehouse. Only after the warehouse has been built and running for a while does it dawn on the users and the administrators of the warehouse that there might be data in the warehouse that merits protection. Indeed, in some cases some data in the data warehouse presents a liability.

SECURITY AS AN ISSUE

Some of the cases where security can become an issue in the face of data warehousing are:

- Where financial data resides in the warehouse.
- Where personal medical information resides in the warehouse.
- Where human resource and salary information reside in the warehouse, and so forth.

Consider the case where financial information is kept in the warehouse. The warehouse represents a place where consolidated, integrated financial information is gathered. Furthermore, the data is organized so that it is easy to get to. Suppose a company had a rogue financial analyst who decided to "do the books" for the corporation a week or two before the company made its public declaration as to the financial state of the company. The data warehouse greatly enables the rogue financial analyst to determine the financial state of the corporation. If the company will be making or losing more money than expected, then the analyst can use that information in the stock market to make money on private financial information that is not publicly known. Such an occurrence is both unethical and illegal, and no corporation wishes to engage in such activity, but the data warehouse invites such nefarious activity.

Consider another case. A health insurance company stores information about its insurees in a data warehouse. The medical information is available for the DSS analysts to work on. However, one day someone through the Internet starts to access data from the health care data warehouse. Does the health insurance company want an outsider to have access to personal medical information about its insurees? There is an ethical and a legal exposure for which the health insurer is libel. While the data warehouse opens the door to many possibilities and opportunities, there is an exposure to sensitive data that must be considered as well.

RECOGNIZING THE NEED FOR SECURITY

There is then a very strong case to be made for security in a data warehouse environment. It is up to the DWA and the organization's security administrator to take the lead in recognizing these security needs and be proactive in the creation and administration of the infrastructure required for the protection of sensitive data in the warehouse.

A standard reply to the questions about security in the data warehouse is that there are already security measures in place. After all, doesn't the DBMS have its own security? Indeed, the DBMSes that will house the data warehouse data do have their

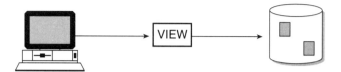

Figure 3.1   Standard VIEW-based database security.

own built in security. The problem is that DBMS security is VIEW based and designed for the operational environment, not the DSS environment. In VIEW-based security, the DWA or the security administrator defines what data can be seen and manipulated through a VIEW defined by the administrator. Figure 3.1 shows that standard DBMS security is VIEW-based.

In VIEW-based security, there is the assumption that the DBA knows what is going to be done with the data once it is accessed. The VIEW is then created to accommodate the known activity that will be done. The problem is that in a DSS environment the end user does not know what he or she is going to be doing with the program or transaction, much less the data that will be involved. The DSS analyst cannot sit down and tell the DWA or the security administrator what will transpire. The very essence of DSS is *not* knowing what will occur once the end user has access to the data in the data warehouse. Because the DBA cannot know what activity or line of thought the end user will be engaging in, DBA cannot create a VIEW to accommodate the end user. Figure 3.2 illustrates the limitations of VIEW-based security.

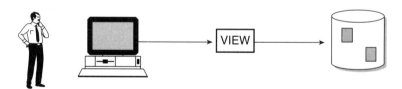

Assumptions for VIEW-based database security:
- We know what the end user wants to see.
- The end user wants to see the same type of thing every time.
- We can create VIEWs as fast as the end user can dream up ways to look at data.

Figure 3.2   Limitations for VIEW-based security.

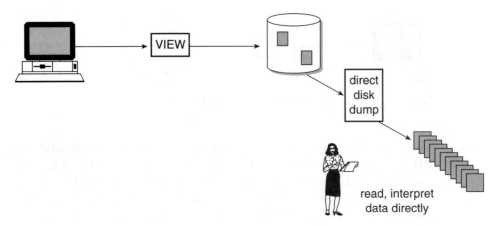

Figure 3.3 If a system programmer wants to do a direct disk dump of the data, then VIEW-based security does nothing.

The second problem with VIEW-based DBMS security in the data warehouse environment is that VIEW based security is easily bypassed. An end user merely has to do a direct disk dump of data, then reformat the data to tell what the contents are. VIEWs do nothing to prevent an interpretation of data once the data is dumped outside the control of the DBMS. Figure 3.3 shows the technique of dumping data outside of the DBMS and interpreting the data independently.

A third problem with VIEW-based security is that the data to be secured is exposed as the data moves up and down the line. While the data that is cleared by the VIEW may well end up at the proper address, as the data flows from the server to the client (or vice verse), the line transmission is subject to unauthorized access. VIEW-based security does little or nothing then for network transmission.

Using DBMS Grants for Security

An alternative to using views to implement security is to take advantage of the function of the DBMS to *grant* different rights to different users. None of the end-users of the data warehouse should be granted the right to *update* data or *insert* rows into the data warehouse. The question is, should all users be granted the right to *select* data from every table in the data warehouse?

Particularly sensitive data could be partitioned into a separate set of tables, and only those users who were authorized by management would then receive a select grant for those tables. In this way, a simple, native security feature of the DBMS can be used to prevent unauthorized access to sensitive data in the data warehouse.

The technique does, however, present a different problem for the data warehouse DBA. In many cases, the data that must be secured is part of an overall subject area, the remaining data for which is not sensitive. Separating the sensitive data from the rest of the subject area's data is relatively simple. However, in order for the sensitive data to be of value to the authorized users, some nonsensitive data has to be redundantly stored with it. At a minimum, the same key values need to be replicated for the sensitive and nonsensitive data. This is an example of *managed redundancy,* which will be discussed at greater length later in the book.

A FUNDAMENTAL LEVEL OF SECURITY

For a very low level of security, it is necessary to encrypt the data as it is written into the data warehouse. If the encryption is done as the data is captured, the data is secure as it passes down the line going into the data warehouse server. Once the data is encrypted and stored in the data warehouse, the data is then accessed on an authorized basis only. Figure 3.4 shows how data is encrypted in the data warehouse environment.

In Figure 3.4, a value of "abc" is read by the load process. The value "abc" is converted to a value of "xyz" by the encryption routine at the moment it is read. The value "xyz" then passed down the line and is loaded into the data warehouse.

At a later point in time, when an unauthorized user desires to read the data, there is no disruption with the access process. The data in the warehouse can be read by anyone. But when an

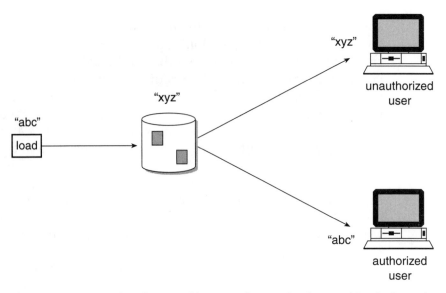

Figure 3.4 Encrypting data provides a much more fundamental level of security.

unauthorized access takes place, the data is sent to the unauthorized user as "xyz." When an authorized user desires to read the data, the data is decrypted and the actual results of "abc" are displayed to the end user. Once the data is retrieved and decrypted, the authorized end user is free to do anything with the secured data, as seen in Figure 3.5.

What security is provided by the encryption or decryption of data in the data warehouse environment? The first and most obvious security is that of not allowing unauthorized end users to see secured data. At the same time, the authorized end user is not prevented from looking at data in the data warehouse, nor is the unauthorized end user prevented from seeing data which has no security requirements.

The next level of security that is achieved by encryption and decryption of data in the data warehouse is protection from unauthorized dumping and interpretation of data. Figure 3.6 shows that if encrypted data is dumped, it is dumped in an encrypted state. The end user still needs the decryption routine to be able to make sense of the dumped encrypted data, even though the data has been removed from the database.

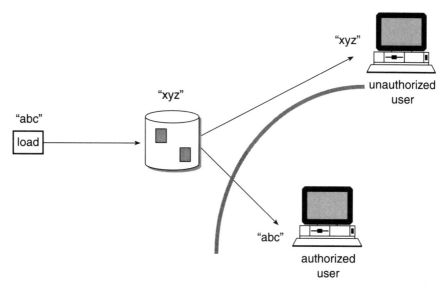

Figure 3.5 Once the data is retrieved and decoded, the end user can do anything desired to the data, in as free-form a fashion as desired.

The third level of protection afforded by encryption of data is protection from unauthorized access during the transmission process. With encrypted data, unauthorized access can occur during transmission, but there is no harm unless the user that accesses the data has the decryption code.

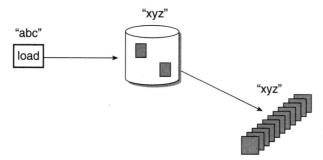

Figure 3.6 A direct dump can be done against the data in the warehouse, but the systems programmer still has no idea what the data means.

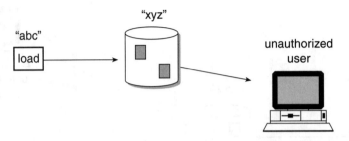

Some of the possibilities for returning data to an unauthorized user:

"xyz"—raw encoded data
"xyz"/encoded—raw endoced data with indicator
null—no data whatsoever

Figure 3.7 Returning encoded data to an unauthorized user.

States of Presentation to the Unauthorized User

The data can be presented to the unauthorized end user in one of several states. Figure 3.7 shows some of the common possibilities.

One way to present the unauthorized user with encrypted data is to display the raw data—the "xyz" value. Another way is to have the "xyz" values presented along with some indication that the values are, in fact, encrypted. A third possibility is to have no data at all presented to the unauthorized end user. Any or all of these approaches may be used for managing the presentation of secured data to the end user.

Encryption Possibilities

The data can be encrypted in many ways. Figure 3.8 shows some of the common possibilities. One possibility for encryption is to encrypt a column of a table. In this case, all occurrences of data for the column are encrypted. The next possibility is to encrypt the entire table. The third possibility is to encrypt only selected rows. Each of these cases has its own advantages and disadvantages.

The first case, where the column is encrypted, is the most common case. The security administrator knows that all occurrences of a column will be encrypted. The administration is straightforward.

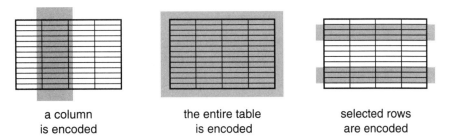

a column
is encoded

the entire table
is encoded

selected rows
are encoded

Figure 3.8 Some possibilities for the encoding of data in a warehouse.

The second case, where all the columns in a table are encrypted, is extremely rare and seldom employed. The reason for this is that when all columns are encrypted, the column or columns that make up the key of the table are encrypted as well. In almost all but the most unusual of cases, encrypting the key(s) of a table is a very bad idea because the individual occurrences of data in the table cannot be located. When the keys of a table are encrypted, there are only two ways to locate data in a table:

1. Access the entire table, decode each key that has been accessed, then select the desired keys.
2. Know before you start the search the value of each key you want to look at and encrypt each value you want to look at to see if there is a match in the warehouse.

Both of these approaches are awkward, inefficient, and unusable in anything but the most unusual of circumstances.

The third case, where only selected rows of data are encrypted, is a less common form of encryption, but one that is occasionally useful. To understand why there might be a problem here, consider a table where a person's age was encrypted some of the time, but not encrypted the remainder of the time. The table contains a few records that look like this:

Amy Johnson	age	36
Ben Johnson	age	28
Cal Johnson	age	97781 (encrypted)
Dave Johnson	age	71165 (encrypted)

Ed Johnson	age	47
Frank Johnson	age	27
Joe Johnson	age	11098 (encrypted)
Ken Johnson	age	52

Now suppose an unauthorized user did a query against the data that looked like this:

```
SELECT AVERAGE AGE
FROM HRTABLE
WHERE LASTNAME = "JOHNSON"
```

The result would show that the average age of employees named Johnson was 33,779 years old! Of course, such a result is preposterous. What has happened is that encrypted data has been freely mixed with unencrypted data and the result is chaos. For this reason then, great care must be taken when mixing separate rows of data, some of which may contain encrypted data and some of which may not.

Multiple Encryption Algorithms

Another possibility for defining encryption in the data warehouse environment is to have some rows encrypted by one algorithm and other rows encrypted by another algorithm, as seen in Figure 3.9. The usefulness of this approach to encryption is that data representing different types of categories can be placed in the same warehouse. For example, data encrypted under algorithm A may represent customers in Ohio, data encrypted under algorithm B may represent customers in Kentucky, and data encrypted under algorithm C may represent customers in Indiana. All customers may appear in the same data warehouse, but there will be different encryption algorithms applied based on the locale the customers represent. In such a case, end users in Ohio can look at Ohio data only, end users in Kentucky can look at Kentucky data only, and end users in Indiana can look at Indiana data only. Of course, the same caveats apply to mixing encrypted and unencrypted data in the same warehouse.

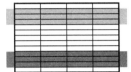

Figure 3.9 Some rows are encoded with one encoding algorithm and other rows are encoded with another algorithm.

The Encryption Algorithm

The encryption algorithm is a complex piece of code, as shown in Figure 3.10. The encrypting algorithm must exhibit several properties:

- The data, once encrypted, must be able to be decrypted.
- The encryption algorithm must produce a pattern that is not readily discernible.
- A given unencrypted value must encrypt into a single decrypted value.
- A given encrypted value must be decrypted into the original unencrypted value.
- The execution of the encryption algorithm must be efficient.

These conditions apply to any form of encryption.

In addition, the encryption algorithm for the data warehouse must exhibit some other unusual properties:

- Field characteristics must be preserved (i.e., if a field is numeric in its unencrypted form, then its encrypted form must be numeric).
- Length characteristics must be preserved (i.e., if a field that is unencrypted is n bytes in length, then the encrypted field must be n bytes in length).

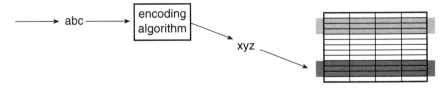

Figure 3.10 There are many considerations in choosing an encoding algorithm.

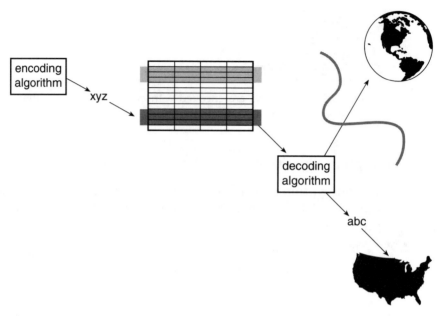

Figure 3.11 One of the issues is the availability of encoding and decoding algorithims outside the United States.

Although these two properties are not standard properties of encryption, they are absolutely essential.

Encryption on a Worldwide Basis

Another important consideration of encryption and decryption is the ability to legally cross international boundaries, as depicted in Figure 3.11. The algorithm shown in the figure can be used freely within the borders of the United States. However, the algorithm cannot be legally transported outside of the United States. This is an important consideration that must be dealt with before an algorithm is selected.

DECRYPTING THE DATA

Data can be decrypted in one of several places once the system has determined that an authorized user has requested the data. The two most common places for decryption to occur are:

- at the data warehouse server after the data has been accessed and before the data has left the server for the end user's workstation, or
- at the end user's workstation.

Doing the decryption at the server before transmission to the end user necessarily implies that there is a security exposure during transmission. The other choice—that of doing the decryption at the workstation level—requires that the decryption algorithm be passed down the line.

Ostensibly, this passage of the decryption algorithm represents a network exposure, except decryption algorithms work by requiring a *key*. The key for a given column is not passed up or down the line, but remains at the work station, thereby minimizing the exposure to security (see Figure 3.12).

Managing Decryption Keys

The keys that are required to enable the decryption algorithm are managed as their own separate entity and require their own protection. The keys can be encoded or locked in data *blobs*. In addition, the keys can be changed en masse periodically to ensure that casual access to a system will not result in an exposure. Figure 3.13 shows the practice of changing the keys to the different columns of data en masse.

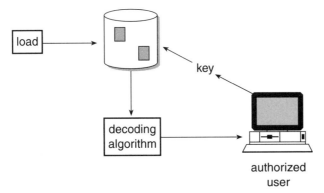

Figure 3.12 A typical interaction that enables the data to be decoded.

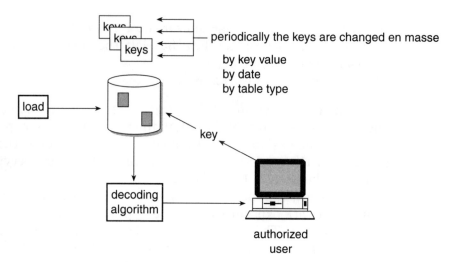

Figure 3.13 Changing decoding keys.

Workstation or End-User ID Authorization Keys

The keys to authorization—which are different than the keys to column decryption—can be protected in a like manner, and created by workstation or by end-user id, as shown in Figure 3.14. There are several issues that relate to whether the keys are created by workstation or by end-user id. Both approaches have their advantages and disadvantages.

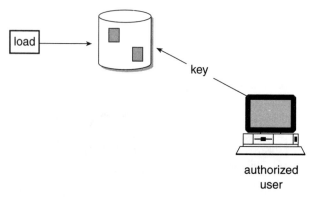

Figure 3.14 Keys can be created by workstation or end-user id.

The advantage of creating workstation keys is that the workstation key is *hard-wired* into the actual device that is receiving the data. In this sense, the data arriving at the workstation is very protected. However, *anyone* may be behind the workstation, so the physical protection of an authorized workstation becomes its own issue. In addition, once the workstation is authorized by an appropriate person, there needs to be some mechanism to deauthorize the workstation once the authorized person leaves the premises.

The advantage of an end user id is that it is transferable across multiple workstations. The system does not care what workstation a person is at when an end-user id is used for authorization. However, if the end-user id is stolen (or if someone is a lucky guesser), then the end-user id can be used by anyone and there is no security. As in the case of workstation authorization, there needs to be some mechanism to deauthorize the workstation once the authorized person is through with his/her session.

Decryption and Software Packages

One of the most important issues of encryption and decryption in the data warehouse environment is that of working cooperatively with software packages, such as access and analysis packages. Figure 3.15 illustrates the need for doing decryption of data before the data reaches the software package.

If the encrypted data were to reach the software package, it would be too late to do decryption. The software package takes over management of the data once the data enters its domain. There is no guarantee that the encrypted data could ever be isolated and manipulated before it was used once the software package gains control of the data. For this reason then, it is necessary to do whatever decryption is going to be done before the data reaches the software package handling the query. It does not matter whether the data is decrypted at the server and shipped down the line or whether the data arrives at the end-user workstation and is decrypted there before passing into the hands of the access and analysis software.

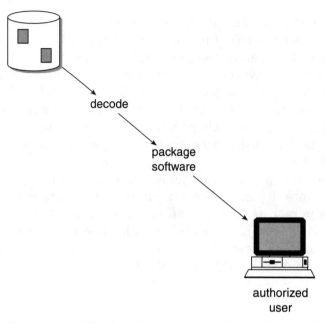

decode

package
software

authorized
user

Figure 3.15 The decoding needs to be done before the data reaches the package software in order to keep the encryption transparent.

CLEARING THE TERMINAL

However encryption and decryption are handled, there needs to be a clearing of the terminal at the end of the authorized session, as shown in Figure 3.16. Data in the session and the decryption algorithm need to be cleared. In addition, it is useful to clear authorization keys.

The clearing may occur as a result of

- the end user proactively sending a message that causes a clearing;
- time passing between the last activity of the end user and an "alarm clock" going off, which causes a clearing;
- an automatic clearing every n minutes;
- a prescribed time for a session ending;
- more than one of the above, etc.

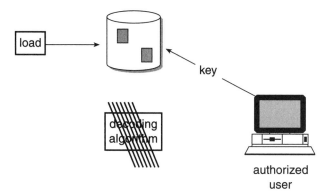

Figure 3.16   At the end of the authrorized session the terminal id cleared.

However it is accomplished, the workstation needs to be automatically cleared when an end user terminates the authorized session.

THE OVERHEAD OF ENCRYPTION AND DECRYPTION

One of the most important issues concerning encryption and decryption as a means of security is resource consumption. Figure 3.17 illustrates the overhead of encryption and decryption in the data warehouse environment.

The first issue raised by security overhead is whether input/output (I/O) is being consumed. In general, I/O is *not* consumed to any great extent by data warehouse security because length preservation is maintained by each field that is encrypted. No block splitting will be required. Encryption and decryption algorithms can be applied at the moment of block reads, so that there usually is no reason for an I/O to be caused just for the purpose of security. In other words, security processing can be attached to existing reads and writes, so that no new and unnecessary reads and writes will have to be done.

The major overhead that is consumed by data warehouse security is CPU cycles. Encryption and decryption undoubtedly require CPU cycles (as opposed to I/O). But even CPU cycles can be minimized by moving the encryption and decryption to the workstation, where there are many more free cycles for processing

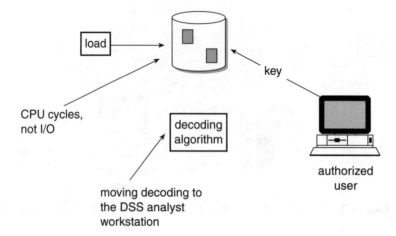

While there is overhead associated with security using encryption and decryption, the overhead is minimized by

• using CPU cycles not I/O cycles at the data warehouse server;
• moving decoding activity down to the DSS analyst workstation.

Figure 3.17 Overhead of encryption and decryption.

than there are at the data warehouse server. If the overhead of encryption and decryption becomes a problem, then fewer columns and rows can be encrypted as a last resort.

LIMITING DBMS PROCESSING

One of the major considerations of doing encryption and decryption is the limitations imposed by the insertion of encrypted data into the database. Figure 3.18 suggests the limitations that are imposed after the load process has occurred.

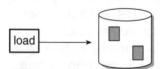

Figure 3.18 Once data has been loaded into the data warehouse in an encoded manner, no DBMS activity can be run against the data other than simple retrieval.

In Figure 3.18 data is loaded into a data warehouse. During the load process some of the data is encrypted. Once the data is encrypted, nothing can be done to the data other than access it. For example, suppose three records are loaded into the data warehouse:

Unencrypted Data

record 1	Ace Hardware	part A23	qty	4500
record 2	Jones Supply	part M50	qty	360
record 3	Wilson Goods	part A23	qty	109

Encrypted Data

record 1	Ace Hardware	part T6Y	qty	981108
record 2	Jones Supply	part IU7	qty	877298
record 3	Wilson Goods	part T6Y	qty	009187

Once the data is loaded into the warehouse in an encrypted fashion, the fields that are encrypted cannot be accessed in any other way than by key of the record. For example, it does a programmer no good to issue an SQL statement to the effect.

```
SELECT *
FROM HARDWARE
WHERE PART > C65
```

or

```
SELECT AVERAGE QTY
FROM HARDWARE
WHERE SUPPLIER = ACE HARDWARE
```

The data, once encrypted, cannot be manipulated by standard query after it is placed into the data warehouse. To be used, the data must be decrypted if there is to be any meaning to the queries that will be run.

This limitation—*not being able to do any database activity other than pure access by key once placed into the data warehouse*—must be understood by the DWA and the security administrator. There is an important tradeoff to be made here. A

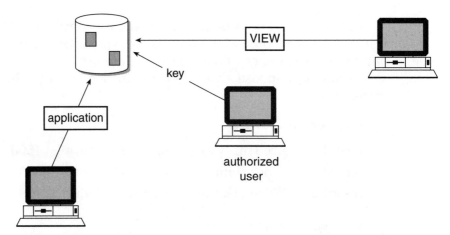

Figure 3.19 More than one type of security can be used for the data warehouse.

high level of security can be achieved by encrypting and decrypting data, but there are some features that are given up when that option is chosen.

Of course, there can be multiple levels of security within a data warehouse. Encryption and decryption are not the only choices. The DWA and the security administrator can employ multiple levels and types of security depending on the needs of the end user and the organization. Figure 3.19 shows that different types of security can be employed—all at the same time— for the data warehouse environment.

ADMINISTERING SECURITY

There are numerous activities that are required of the DWA and/or the security administrator in the administration of security:

- Deciding what level of security is needed.
- Deciding what encryption algorithm will be used.
- Deciding what data will be encrypted:
  - Encryption by column.
  - Encryption by row.

- Encryption by column and row.
- Multiple encryption algorithms, used in the same table.
- Deciding what users will have access to what data.
- Deciding what response the end user will have:
  - Will the end user see encoded data?
  - Will the end user see encoded data and a flag that states that it is encoded?
  - Will the end user not see any encoded data?
- Where will the decoding algorithm be executed,
  - at the data warehouse server;
  - at the end-user workstation.
- How often will the keys be changed en masse?
- Who will have access to the security keys?
- How will auditing be done?
- How will encoding and decoding algorithms be handled in foreign countries?
- How will workstations be cleared at the end of a session?
- What will be the basis of authorization
  - workstation id, or
  - end-user id.
- Resolve what libraries the encoding and decoding algorithms reside in.
- Determine where VIEW-based security is appropriate.
- Determine where application-based security is appropriate.
- Determine how security will be changed should there be a breach, etc.

SUMMARY

Data warehouse requires special security for data relating to financial transactions, personal medical records, and human resources data, such as salary information. Standard database security is VIEW-based. This is inadequate for data warehouse security for the following reasons:

1. VIEW-based security can be bypassed by a direct dump of data.
2. VIEW-based security requires that the activities of the end user be a known commodity before the activity is begun.

3. VIEW-based security does not protect data as it moves up and down the lines of transmission.

The most secure way to protect sensitive DSS data is by encryption and decryption. By encrypting and decrypting data as it moves in to and out of the data warehouse, the problems presented by VIEW-based security are solved.

Encryption and decryption of data warehouse data have their own set of considerations. The primary consideration is that once data is encrypted and placed in the data warehouse, then *nothing* can be done to the data until it is decrypted. For this reason, it makes no sense to encrypt keys in the data warehouse under normal circumstances.

Decrypted data can be presented to the end user in one of several ways:

- As decrypted data.
- As decrypted data with a notification that the data is encrypted.
- No presentation at all for decrypted data.

More than one encryption algorithm can be used for the same data in a table if the data needs to be partitioned.

Administering the Data Warehouse Data Model

The data warehouse data model needs to be administered over time, just as other parts of the data warehouse environment. Operational environment changes require maintenance of the data warehouse data model. For example, if the DSS analyst decides to add a new subject area, the data warehouse data model needs maintenance. If the departmental analyst decides to explore a new area, the interface between the current level detail and the data mart needs to be maintained.

In short, there are many circumstances under which the data model needs to be managed and maintained over time. Building the data model at the outset of the development of the data warehouse effort, then abandoning the model thereafter, does not do justice to the need for integration in the world of DSS processing.

THE DATA WAREHOUSE DATA MODEL

The data warehouse data model—like the operational data model—consists of some basic components:

Entities

Relationships

Definitions

Keys

Attributes

Foreign key relationships

Domains of values

Subgroupings of data, and so forth.

The components of the data model are designed to meet the decision support needs of the organization. Figure 4.1 shows the contents of the data warehouse data model.

As a rule, the data warehouse data model is built from the corporate data model that is built, in turn, to satisfy the larger, more general-information needs of the corporation. The data warehouse data model is derived from the corporate data model to satisfy the DSS needs. Some of the activities of derivation that are done in going from the corporate data model to the data warehouse data model are:

■ Removing purely operational data from the corporate data model.
■ Making sure that every unit of data has an element of time (year, month, day, etc.) attached to it.
■ Adding in appropriate derived data to the data warehouse data model.
■ Doing stability analysis to the data warehouse data model.
■ Treating data relationships as artifacts of the relationship, and so forth.

The corporate data model is made up of several levels of modelling. Figure 4.2 shows the high-level data model, the mid-level

entities
relationships
keys
attributes
foreign key relationships
definitions
subgrouping of data

Figure 4.1 The data warehouse data model.

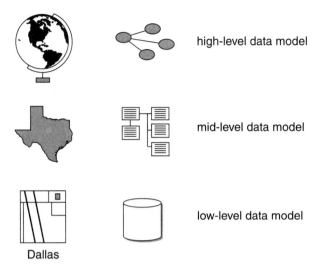

high-level data model

mid-level data model

low-level data model

Dallas

Figure 4.2   There are different levels of data modelling.

data model, and the low-level data model. Just as there is a relationship between a globe, a map of Texas, and a street map of Dallas, Texas, so there is a relationship between the high-level data model, the mid-level data model, and the low-level data model.

A globe is useful for showing *all* the components of the earth, such as the oceans and continents, in their relative positions. But the globe is not useful for showing how to get from Washington to New York. The map of Texas shows a great deal more specific detail than the globe; it shows how to get from Wichita Falls to Port Arthur. But the map of Texas is woefully incomplete compared to the globe. The street map of Dallas, Texas shows how to get from the Dallas airport to downtown Dallas. In that regard the map of Dallas is very detailed, but it is very incomplete in that there are many, many roads and places in Texas and the world that do not appear on the map.

The different levels of data modelling have the same relationship to each other. The high-level model is good for showing what all the components of the model are, but says little in detail about the model. The mid-level of the model is good for a degree of detail, but it describes only part of the total model. The low-level data model is at an even lower level of detail and describes an even smaller part of the data model.

WHERE THE MODEL APPLIES

The data warehouse data model applies to the current level of detail of the data warehouse. Any implication of the data model for the data mart or the bulk data is purely coincidental. Figure 4.3 shows where, architecturally, the data warehouse data model applies.

The data warehouse data model applies to the current level of detail only. It does not apply to the data-mart level, nor the bulk storage level of data. Instead, the detail that forms the backbone of the entire data warehouse, DSS environment is shaped by the data model. Sometimes the data that exists at the current level detail is called *atomic data*. The atomic data is as granular as data can get in the DSS environment. As such, the atomic data is at the bedrock of the analysis that occurs. Since the structure and shape of the bedrock data is determined by the data model, it is very important that the data warehouse data model be created properly.

The different levels of the data model apply in a very prescribed manner to the overall design of the data warehouse, as shown in Figure 4.4. As the figure shows, the high-level model forms the basis for the mid-level model, the mid-level model forms the basis for logical database design, and the low-level model forms the basis for physical database design, as the structure of the data warehouse is described to the database management system.

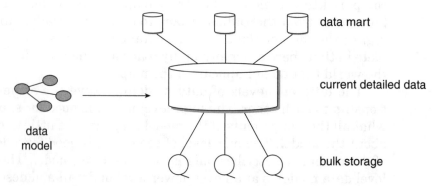

Figure 4.3 The data warehouse data model applies to the current level of detail.

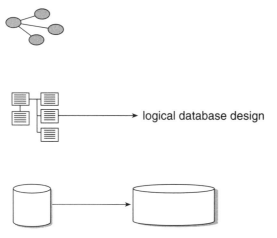

logical database design

Figure 4.4 The physical database design is done directly from the low-level design; the logical database design is done from the mid-level design.

Between logical database design and physical database design are a plethora of design activities and considerations, such as:

■ Considerations of the granularity of data.
■ Partitioning of data to manage the volumes of data to be found in the data warehouse.
■ Design of arrays of data into the structure.
■ Introduction of redundant data when performance warrants.
■ Preparation for the indexing of data.
■ Merging of tables when appropriate and so forth.

DATA-MART DATA MODELS

In looking at the larger architecture of the data warehouse, it is a natural question to ask, "What about the need for a data model for the data mart?" In some cases, a data model for a data mart makes sense; in other cases, it does not. Figure 4.5 suggests the possibility of a data model for the data mart.

Where the data mart reflects very basic data that arrives in the data mart regularly and is used as a basis for much other calculation and analysis, then a data-mart data model makes sense.

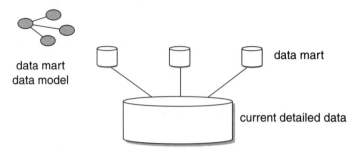

data mart
data model

data mart

current detailed data

Figure 4.5 What about a departmental data model?

However, if multidimensional processing is the primary activity of the data mart, then a data model probably does not make sense. (Or if a data model is created in this case, then the data model will be a very simple one.) With multidimensional software, it is easier to create the definition and calculation on-the-fly from the predefined structures than it is to formally model the data.

If the data mart contains summarized data almost exclusively and if that summarized data is constantly changing, then a data model probably does not make sense. Finally, if the data mart is very small and informal, then a conventional data modelling effort probably is a waste of time.

INTERFACES

Although they are not considered as a normal part of the data model, the interfaces between the operational environment and the current level of detail, and the interfaces between the current level of detail and the data marts also warrant attention as candidates for modelling and capturing as part of the metadata infrastructure. Figure 4.6 shows these important interfaces.

The interfaces are an important part of the infrastructure from a modelling and a metadata standpoint. The interfaces profoundly shape the data that resides in the mart. The data-mart data is usually summarized or at least customized to meet the peculiar needs of a department or group of end users. Because the interfaces determine what data passes from one environ-

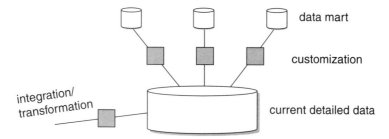

Figure 4.6 The interfaces loading data into data warehouse and into the data marts are important as well.

ment to another and because the interfaces shape the data in the data mart, there is a need to keep careful track of the interfaces. The larger picture of the data models and the interfaces as they integrate within the architecture is depicted in Figure 4.7.

The data warehouse is at the center of iterative DSS design and development. As such, the entire environment shown in Figure 4.7 is subject to change. At no point in time can the architecture depicted in this figure be considered static. The values and the structures of data within the architecture are constantly

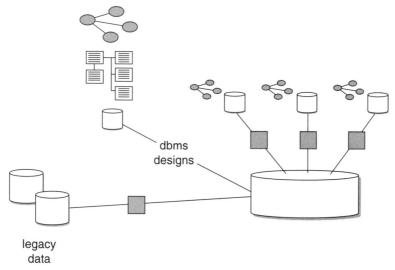

Figure 4.7 The larger picture of metadata and data models.

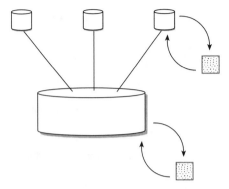

Figure 4.8 Iterative development occurs at both the current level of detail and the data mart.

changing, as long as iterative processing is occurring. Indeed, one of the measures of success is just how much the environment changes.

Iterative development occurs at both the data mart and the current level of detail, as seen in Figure 4.8. The deeper, more profound development occurs at the atomic level of the data warehouse. Here, the explorer does analysis. The more predictable DSS analysis is done at the data-mart level. In any case, iterative analysis occurs at both levels and with it comes change, constant change, to the DSS infrastructure.

As changes occur, they are affected almost immediately against the data (at least, they are affected as quickly as the volume of data will allow.) As the changes are made to the physical structures of data, those changes are retro-reflected backward into the data warehouse data model infrastructure. Figure 4.9 shows the retro-reflection backward. The figure shows a wide variety of changes, some at the data-mart level and others at the atomic level.

One of the interesting aspects of the changes that are shown in Figure 4.9 is that some of the changes have a very large ripple effect while other changes have almost no ripple effect whatsoever. Some changes that occur at the data-mart level cause a disruption all the way back to the original corporate data model. As an example of a very disruptive change, consider the alteration of the key structure of the most basic unit of data for a cor-

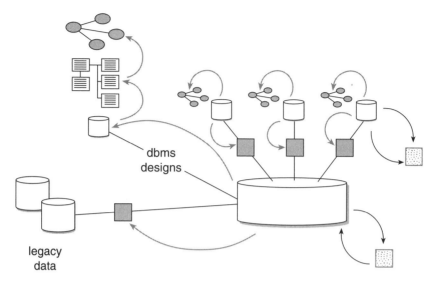

Figure 4.9 There is a feedback loop from the changes made during iterative development and data model.

poration. For a manufacturer this might be a part number; for a retailer this might be a SKU designation; for a bank this might be an account number; and so forth. Such a change will echo throughout the entire infrastructure.

But profound changes are uncommon (thankfully!). Much more likely is a change that has a very negligible ripple effect. For example, in a data mart, a DSS analyst wants to alter the way sales are calculated based on the end of the month. Instead of using the actual end of the month, the DSS analyst wants to change the department's view to look at the sales month as ending on a prescheduled corporate calendar. Such a change will hardly be noticed outside the department.

Minor changes are common. Given the infrastructure described in Figure 4.9, the changes can be absorbed with a minimal impact.

How exactly are physical changes to be retro-reflected back into the data model? Should the changes be reflected into the data model at the moment in time when they are actually made?

From a practical standpoint, it is not possible that with every change to the data warehouse, the data modeler goes back and makes the change to the data model. Instead, a better approach is to periodically review what changes have been made, then go back and retro-reflect the set of changes into the data models for a specified time period. A frequency of every six months or so is recommended.

Using computer-assisted system engineering (CASE) technology or other modelling technology is a very convenient way to store and present the data models. With automation of modelling, periodic comparison can be made. Without some form of automated modelling, maintaining the models over a lengthy period of time is difficult to do.

SUMMARY

The data warehouse data model is created from the corporate data model and consists of keys, attributes, entities, relationships, definitions, and so forth. The data model for the atomic level of the DW consists of three levels: a high-level data model, a mid-level data model, and a low-level data model. Each level of modelling has its own purpose.

The data warehouse data model applies to the current level of detail, the atomic level. The physical database design is done from the low-level modelling. Data marts may or may not have a data model, depending on the size and stability of the data mart. Also, because of the iterative nature of data warehouse development, there is a need to retro-reflect changes into the model on a regular basis.

Managing Metadata in the Data Warehouse

The heart of the architected environment is the data warehouse; at its nerve center is metadata. Without metadata, the data warehouse and its associated components in the architected environment are merely disjointed components working independently and with separate goals. In order to achieve harmony and unity across the different components of the architected environment, there must be a well-defined and disciplined approach to metadata.

THE METADATA INFRASTRUCTURE

The infrastructure of metadata is complex because metadata serves several agendas at the same time. The separate agendas are often at cross-purposes with each other. The infrastructure of metadata that the metadata manager administers must

- recognize the need for commonality of metadata across different environments and enable metadata to be shared among the different components of the architected environment, and

■ recognize the need for local autonomy in each environment, allowing metadata to be managed locally with no interference or consideration from other users outside the immediate environment.

At first glance these goals appear to be contradictory.

As an example of the first goal, suppose a database designer has designed a table based on a data model. The database designer is well-advised to share the intelligence of the design with the developer. In turn the developer is well-advised to share his or her perspective of the design with the end user, and so forth. This continuity of design, development, and use of data is achieved through the exchange of metadata. A certain degree of sharability of metadata is needed among the different communities of designers, developers, and users, if there is going to be any continuity of thought.

But sharability is not the only goal of the metadata infrastructure. As an example of the second goal, consider the end user who is executing Lotus 1-2-3 at a workstation. Does the end user need to tell anyone else what analytical work is being done at the workstation? Does the end user need authorization from some higher authority to do analysis—to create formulas, to create data elements—with the spreadsheet? Of course, the end user does not need to ask anyone's permission to create and manipulate a spreadsheet. But the end user is creating and destroying metadata as fast as the spreadsheet changes. In this case, the DSS analyst needs complete control over the metadata at his or her disposal. There needs to be local, autonomous control of metadata across the metadata infrastructure.

As another example of the need for local, autonomous control of metadata, consider a developer who, at the end of the working day, has created a partial design of a data warehouse. The developer intends to resume work tomorrow where work stopped today. Does the developer need anyone or any mechanism telling him or her that the metadata must be placed in a particular library? Of course not. The developer may come in tomorrow and throw away all work that has been done today. The developer needs to have complete and autonomous control over metadata as it relates to development, while the development process is a work in progress. Any interference in the process of using, creating, and manipulating metadata is unwarranted and disruptive.

Other Goals for the Metadata Infrastructure

The two goals for metadata—sharability and autonomy—are seemingly incompatible and contradictory. But in order for the metadata infrastructure to be successful, both goals must be achieved. In addition to meeting these goals, metadata must be able to

- be distributed across the network of metadata objects that make up the infrastructure, and
- be technologically compatible and available to the local metadata environment.

As an example of the first of these goals, consider different components of the architected environment—an operational environment, a data warehouse, and an on-line analytical processing (OLAP) environment. The operational environment is an MVS mainframe environment running IMS and VSAM. The data warehouse environment is a Tandem environment running Non-Stop SQL. And the OLAP environment is on a Sun Workstation under UNIX using Informix. The MVS IMS/VSAM environment needs to be able to distribute metadata to the Tandem Non-Stop SQL environment. The Tandem Non Stop SQL environment needs to be able to receive metadata and distribute metadata to the Sun UNIX Informix environment. Therefore, the metadata infrastructure must be able to transmit metadata cross the different technological environments.

At the same time, metadata needs to be used interactively in each environment. In the MVS IMS/VSAM environment, metadata must be able to be gathered interactively and used as part of the development process. In the Tandem and the Sun UNIX environments, metadata must be available to and interactive with the DSS analyst.

Like the previous goals for metadata, these two goals—to be able technologically (1) to distribute metadata across different platforms and (2) to use metadata interactively within the platform—must be fulfilled, even though they appear to be diametrically opposed. Although, the metadata infrastructure is full of contradiction, it is easy to view it with only a single set of objectives. The metadata infrastructure that is created ends up satisfying only a single set of objectives.

Repository

An example of a narrow-minded view of the metadata infrastructure is the *repository* perspective of metadata that emphasizes the sharability of metadata. All metadata is collected in a central location and is managed centrally in the repository. By having centralized control of metadata, a high degree of sharability is achieved. But centralized management of a broad and complex metadata infrastructure environment simply has proven to be unworkable. While some metadata does need to be collected and managed centrally, many components of metadata do not belong in a centralized repository environment. A centralized repository approach is fine in theory, but does not work in practice. The problem with the centralized, repository approach is that there is little or no allowance made for the need for local autonomous control of metadata.

Everybody Do Your Own Thing

The flip side of the centralized repository perspective is the *everybody-do-your-own-thing* approach to metadata. In this approach to a metadata infrastructure, metadata is highly decentralized and there is a tremendous amount of local autonomy. Metadata is created and controlled throughout the architected environment in many small and local environments. There is no cohesion between the environments—no uniformity of metadata, no sharability of metadata, no exchange of metadata, and so forth. While each local environment is quite satisfied with its own immediate needs and wants, there is a tremendous loss of economy of scale and there is no discipline or uniformity of metadata across the environment. The everybody-do-your-own-thing approach to metadata is as impractical and unsound as the centralized repository approach. Both approaches need to have their best parts woven into a unified infrastructure of metadata and their worst parts discarded.

A UNIFIED APPROACH TO METADATA INFRASTRUCTURE

This chapter describes a *modern* approach to a metadata infrastructure that fulfills *all* the objectives of metadata in equal measure. The notion of a metadata infrastructure begins with the architected environment, as described in Figure 5.1.

Components of the Architected Environment

The components of the architected environment are:

■ The operational environment.
■ The transformation layer.
■ The operational data store (ODS).
■ Current detailed data of the data warehouse.
■ The lightly summarized data-mart portion of the data warehouse.

For an in-depth discussion of the architected environment, refer to Chapter 3 in *Building the Operational Data Store*.

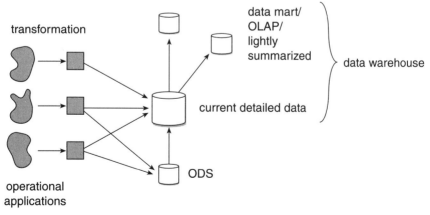

Figure 5.1 The architected environment.

The architected environment has different components that serve very different purposes in the information systems environment. There are different users throughout the different parts of the architecture, as shown in Figure 5.2.

The clerical community doing day-to-day transaction processing is the user at the operational level. The corporate executive making tactical corporate decisions is the user of the ODS. The DSS analyst exploring for patterns and trends that have heretofore gone undetected is the user of the current detailed data. Executive management and the DSS analyst community are the users at the data mart/OLAP level. Each of the users has his or her own agendas and expectations as to what makes his or her own environment successful.

Each of the different components of the architecture has its own technological hardware foundation. The operational foundation is often a mainframe. The ODS is often some form of massively parallel processing (MPP) technology. The current level of

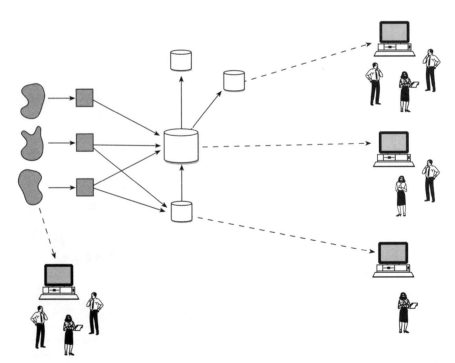

Figure 5.2 There are different users throughout the architected environment.

detail may be MPP technology or symmetrical multi-processing (SMP) technology. The data-mart level is served by client-server technology. There are exceptions to these technological foundations, of course. Very different technology is optimal for each component.

In addition to the different components of the architected environment being served by different hardware platforms, the architected environment is also served by different software technologies. The operational environment often contains a great deal of high-performance transaction processing. The ODS environment contains a mixture of high-performance update and DSS sequential processing. The current level of detail of the data warehouse is based around software that serves large amounts of data and supports exploration of the data. The data mart/OLAP environment supports immediate access and exploration of data. From a software perspective, there is a wide diversity of technologies that are found scattered across the architected environment.

In order to achieve any unification across these hardware platforms and software technologies, there needs to be an infrastructure of metadata that allows the different components of the architected environment to be related. Figure 5.3 illustrates the infrastructure of metadata across the architected environment.

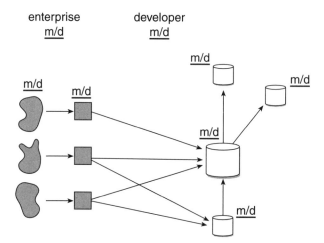

Figure 5.3 The different kinds of metadata.

Metadata—the Composition

Figure 5.3 shows each component of the architected environment with its own private and unique store of metadata. There is metadata for

the operational environment;

the integration and transformation layer;

the ODS;

the current detailed portion of the data warehouse;

the data mart;

the developer environment; and

the enterprise modeller.

Each of these components of the architected environment has some metadata residing at its environment. The metadata that resides at each component is quite different from the metadata that resides at some other component. Typically, the contents of metadata that reside at each level look like:

- Operational
  - COBOL 01/02 layouts
  - Index specifications
  - Physical characteristics of data
  - Control blocks specifications
  - Programming specifications
- Transformation layer
  - Source-to-target specifications
  - Conversion outline
  - Merge specifications
  - Resequencing arrangements
- ODS
  - Source-to-target identification
  - Frequency of update delineation
  - COBOL 01/02 layouts
- Current level of detail of the data warehouse
  - COBOL 01/02 layouts
  - Source-to-target identification
  - Versioning

- Metrics
- Refreshment schedule
- Business-technical cross-reference
- Alias cross-reference
- Data-mart level of the data warehouse
  - Source-to-target identification
  - Physical structure
  - Indexing
  - Business-technical cross-reference
- Enterprise modeller
  - Data model
  - System of record identification
  - Subject-area groupings of tables
  - Strategic plan-data model cross-reference
- Developer
  - Physical structure layouts
  - Data model-database design cross-reference
  - Source-target specification

At the same time, there are some areas of overlap and some uniqueness for each of the different components of the metadata infrastructure spread across the architected environment.

DISTRIBUTING METADATA ACROSS THE ARCHITECTED ENVIRONMENT

Having metadata spread across the architected environment is an exercise in futility if there cannot be communication between each of the components of metadata. Figure 5.4 depicts the need for the intercomponent communication of metadata across the architected environment.

The figure suggests that there is an interchange of metadata objects throughout the infrastructure of metadata. No one component is allowed to sit in isolation. Communication occurs with those components where there is a need for exchange.

Of particular importance is the availability and interactive use of metadata at the end-user level, as shown in Figure 5.5. At the end-user level—where the "rubber meets the road"—the

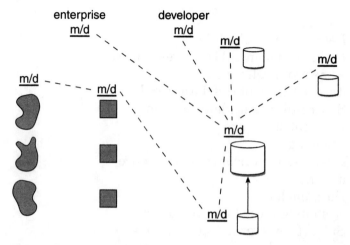

Figure 5.4 How the different components of metadata are networked.

payback for building the architected environment is achieved. Metadata is extremely useful for the end user doing DSS analysis. The DSS analyst can find out

- what files contain data of a certain type;
- where data came from;
- what conversions have been done to data;
- what other data is related to a unit of data;
- the impact of making changes, etc.

Most importantly, the DSS analyst can engage the metadata interactively in the query formulation process by selecting portions of metadata and using them in the creation and formulation of queries. There is then an extremely important role for metadata in the analysis and discovery process.

METADATA IN THE OPERATIONAL ENVIRONMENT

Figure 5.5 shows that metadata is most useful in the ODS and the data warehouse environment for the interaction with the DSS analyst. But, isn't metadata useful as well in the operational and developmental processes? Why are the ODS, current level of detail of the data warehouse, and the data-mart level of the data warehouse the only components shown in Figure 5.5?

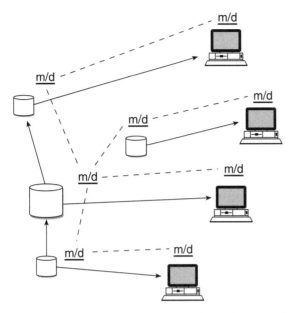

Figure 5.5 Metadata extends to the end-user workstation.

Metadata is certainly useful in the operational world. But consider the operational world from the standpoint of the user— the clerical community. The clerical community executes the same transactions repeatedly, day after day. The first time a clerk learns a process, the metadata attached to the process is quite useful to the clerk. But after the clerk has executed the process for a week, the clerk starts to take the metadata for granted due to familiarity with the transaction that is being executed. It is like driving to work each morning: The first few times you drive to work you pay attention to the road signs, but after driving to work many times, you don't. You know they are there and you obey them, but you do not focus on them as you drive to work.

Now consider the world of DSS analysis. The essence of the DSS analyst's job is in uncovering worlds that have never been examined; he or she is constantly looking for something new and different. As such, the DSS analyst makes constant use of metadata, since metadata is the place where the search for new information begins. The metadata never is taken for granted in the world of DSS. Just as a motorist who lives in Chicago and is traveling to

Phoenix must pay careful attention to the road signs while passing through Gallup, New Mexico, so he or she doesn't end up in Albuquerque, the DSS analyst must be attentive to metadata.

There is a big difference in the day-to-day significance of metadata to the DSS analyst versus the clerical community. The clerical community really does not make interactive use of metadata, while the DSS analyst community makes extensive and regular use of metadata. It is for these reasons then that the ODS, current level of detail, and the data mart are included in the diagram in Figure 5.5.

But at the workstation, there is more than one variety of metadata. Figure 5.6 shows metadata that needs both to be

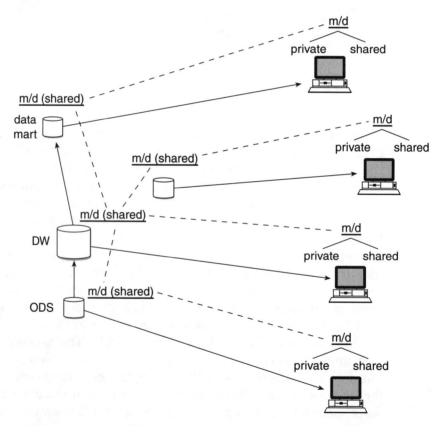

Figure 5.6 At every DSS analyst level there is a need for private and shared metadata. Other terms for private and shared metadata are local and global metadata.

ODS	shared	ODS DSS analyst	private shared
Data warehouse	shared	Data warehouse DSS analyst	private shared
data mart	shared	data DSS analyst mart	private shared

Figure 5.7 The kinds of metadata for the DSS environment.

shared and to remain locally controlled at the workstation. The figure shows the two varieties of metadata at the end-user delivery level. The shared metadata

- is created and maintained elsewhere, but is used at the workstation; or
- is created and maintained at the workstation, but has use outside of the organization where the workstation resides.

The metadata that is local to the workstation and requires autonomous control is created, maintained, and used solely at the workstation.

The metadata that exists at the ODS, current level of the data warehouse, and the data mart/OLAP environment is almost exclusively shared metadata. The metadata that is transported to those environments, and created and maintained there is meant for the entire organization. As such it is shared metadata.

There is local metadata in other parts of the metadata infrastructure as well. The developer has his or her own local metadata, the enterprise modeller has his or her own local metadata, and so forth. Figure 5.7 outlines the different kinds of metadata for the DSS environment. Each kind of DSS metadata will be described in the following sections.

ODS Shared Metadata

The metadata that is shared at the ODS environment is shown in Figure 5.8. In the ODS shared metadata environment there is basic structural information which is needed to describe to the

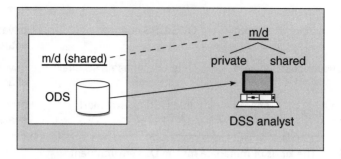

ODS shared metadata:

- structural description
  - internal relationships
  - keys
  - attributes
- sources of data
- metrics
- definitions
  - business term or technical term
  - alias
  - standard definition

Figure 5.8 Typical ODS metadata.

DSS analyst how to get to the ODS data. The ODS also requires source information, as well as metrics. The metrics describe how much of what type of data there is. The metrics are crucial to the ODS environment because of the need to control resource use in order to achieve good and consistent response time. Definitions are an important part of the ODS metadata environment because the DSS analyst needs to make distinctions between the types of data found in the ODS.

ODS DSS Analyst Shared and Local Metadata

The types of metadata found in the ODS DSS analyst environment are depicted by Figure 5.9. The ODS DSS analyst typically operates on a workstation. As the data is downloaded to the ODS DSS analyst workstation, the metadata that is sharable can be downloaded as well, or the metadata can be downloaded by itself to the workstation. The ODS DSS analyst can formulate a query

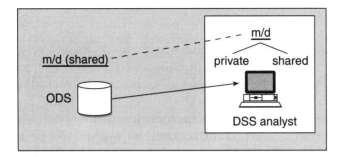

ODS shared metadata:

- structural description*
  - internal relationships
  - keys
  - attributes
- sources of data
- metrics
- definitions
  - business term or technical term
  - alias
  - standard definition

ODS DSS analyst provate metadata:

- dynamically defined or calculated data*
  - content
  - structure
  - calculation
  - time of calculation
  - visibility of results
    - accessibility of calculations

*Applies exclusively to the department of ODS DSS analyst is working for.

Figure 5.9 There is very little difference between ODS metadata and ODS metadata and ODS DSS analyst metadata other than that the ODS DSS analyst metadata is owned by the department doing the calculation and ODS metadata is owned by everyone.

at the workstation and send it to the ODS processor for execution. In any case, whether the ODS data is downloaded to the workstation or whether the query is formulated at the workstation and executed on the ODS processor, the ODS DSS analyst has access to his or her own supply of metadata.

The ODS DSS analyst metadata consists of shared and local (i.e., private) metadata. Shared DSS analyst metadata contains information as to the structures of data the ODS analyst can access, sources of data, and definitions of data. The local ODS DSS analyst metadata consists of dynamically calculated or defined data and any other data the ODS DSS analyst might use in doing an analysis.

Data Warehouse Shared Metadata

The metadata found in the data warehouse is exclusively shared. If there is any place where a classical repository of metadata might be found, it is here. Typically, the shared metadata found in the data warehouse contains the elements found in Figure 5.10. Shared data warehouse metadata contains basic structural information and source information, as well as metric information, schedule of refreshment information, versioning, definitions, developer related information, and security information.

Metric information is especially useful in the data warehouse because of the large volumes of data that are found there. If the end user is going to take care with the submission of queries, the

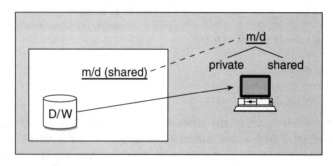

Data warehouse shared metadata:

- structural description
  - keys
  - attributes
  - snapshot parameters
- sources of data identification
- metrics
- refreshment cycle
- versioning
- definitions
  - business or technical cross-reference
  - alias
  - standard definitions
- developer
- relationship to data model
- security levels

Figure 5.10 Elements of shared metadata in the data warehouse.

use of metrics is essential so that the end user can know what to expect before the query is submitted. Refreshment information is useful because the end user needs to know how current the information is. The last time a table was refreshed is an extremely useful piece of information for the DSS analyst. *Versioning* refers to the capability of keeping track of structural changes over time. As metadata changes, it is necessary to keep track of those changes because the data warehouse will contain a robust amount of historical data. Developer-related information allows the physical design to be connected to the high-level data models produced at the enterprise level. Security information is necessary for the establishment and maintenance of the security infrastructure.

The data warehouse shared metadata is normally built as a part of the data warehouse, on the same platform as the warehouse. In addition, the shared metadata may or may not be available in the software technology that houses the data warehouse.

Data Warehouse DSS Analyst Shared and Local Metadata

The metadata that is used by the DSS analyst using the data warehouse is normally housed on the DSS analyst workstation. Of course, the DSS analyst may go to the data warehouse to retrieve metadata and bring it to the workstation. However, there will be metadata at the workstation waiting for use by the DSS analyst.

Figure 5.11 outlines the types of metadata found at the data warehouse DSS analyst workstation. There are two kinds of metadata found here—shared and local (i.e., private). The shared metadata is very similar to the metadata found on the data warehouse except that the shared metadata resides at the workstation. In addition to the standard shared metadata, there is unique metadata such as local definitions, local calculations, and work-in-progress checkpoint information as well. The local definitions apply to the department that the DSS analyst works for and are shared among the members of the department. The local DSS data warehouse metadata applies to the immediate tasks of analysis that the DSS analyst is doing.

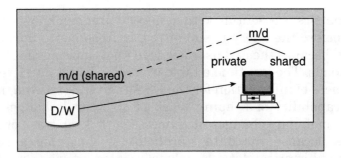

Data warehouse DSS analyst
shared metadata:

- structural description*
  - keys
  - attributes
- selection processing
  - selection criteria
  - time of selection
- refinement
  - resequencing
  - restructuring
  - reformatting
  - summarization
- access tool parameters and syntax
  - local definition
  - local calculations
  - refreshment cycle
  - wip checkpoint

Data warehouse DSS analyst
private metadata:

- Whatever the problem at hand demands,
  note that metadata is stored in support
  of heuristic DSS analysis.

*Applies to the department that the analysis is being done for.

Figure 5.11 Types of metadata at the data warehouse DSS analyst workstation.

Data Mart Shared Metadata

The data mart or OLAP environment requires its own metadata. All of the metadata at the data-mart level, like the metadata at the data warehouse level, is shared. The data-mart level is designed to suit the needs of a given department, whereas the data warehouse is designed to support the needs of the entire organization.

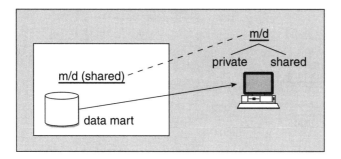

Data mart shared metadata:

- structural description
  - keys
  - attributes
  - snapshot parameters
- source of data identification
- selection
  - selection criteria
  - selection procedure
- refreshment cycle

Figure 5.12 Contents of metadata at the data mart.

Figure 5.12 identifies the contents of metadata that might be found at the data mart. It contains structural information, source information, selection information, and refreshment cycle information.

Data Mart DSS Analyst Shared and Local Metadata

Once the data passes from the data mart into the workstations being serviced by the data mart, metadata is passed as well. The data mart DSS analyst is similar to the DSS analyst found at the data warehouse, with a few exceptions:

- The data mart DSS analyst looks at smaller amounts of data.
- The data mart DSS analyst looks at data with a departmental flavor, whereas the data warehouse DSS analyst looks at data with a corporate flavor.
- The data mart analyst looks at data on a much more predictable basis than the data warehouse DSS analyst who fre-

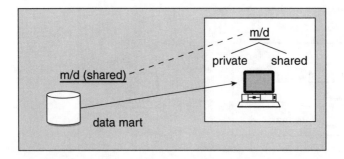

Data mart DSS analyst
shared metadata:

- structural description*
  - keys
  - attributes
- selection processing
  - selection criteria
  - time of selection
- dimensions available
- access tool parameters and syntax
- local definition
- local calculations
- refreshment cycle
- wip checkpoint

Data mart DSS analyst private metadata:

- Whatever the problem at hand demands, note that metadata is stored in support of heuristic DSS analysis.

*Applies to the data mart that the analysis is being done for.

Figure 5.13 Metadata at the data-mart level for the DSS analyst workstation.

quently does exploration. Figure 5.13 shows the typical metadata found at the data-mart level for the DSS analyst workstation.

Common threads that flow through the ODS, data warehouse, and data mart are: structural information, sourcing information, and certain other information found throughout the environment. However, there are some distinct differences between the environments. The best way to characterize the differences is in terms of the questions and issues that are being addressed at each level, as illustrated in Figure 5.14.

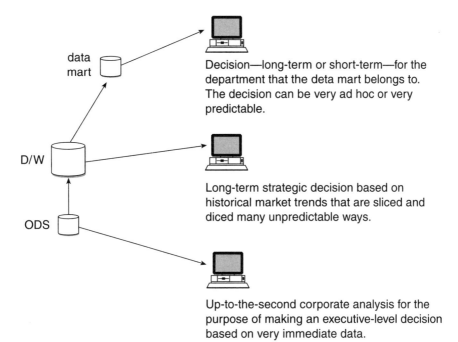

Figure 5.14   Metadata at the different levels is needed to support different kinds of decisions.

Different Types of Decisions Made in Different Places

As Figure 5.14 shows, the ODS analyst is making up-to-the-second corporate decisions. The DSS analyst using the data warehouse is doing exploration, for the most part. The result of the explorations will be long-term decisions. The data-mart DSS analyst is making ad hoc or predictable decisions, with a departmental flavor.

JUSTIFYING METADATA

The metadata infrastructure for the architected environment is complex and requires implementation over multiple technologies. There is no question that a complete implementation of the metadata infrastructure is expensive. And, when there is an expense, there is always the question, how is the expense justified?

The easiest way to justify the resources for the metadata infrastructure is to use an analogy. Suppose that a parent comes home in the evening to find his or her child struggling over a report that has been assigned in school. The parent asks if the child needs help doing the report.

It turns out that the report is on subatomic particle movement focusing on photons and mesons. The parent is taken aback because he or she does not have a working knowledge of this subject. In short order the parent and the child head for the local public library.

At the library they start their search for material for the report. How do they efficiently find the information they need? One approach is to start with the first book in the library and look to the next book. After all the books on the shelf are searched, the next shelf is searched. Then the next rack is searched and so forth. In such a manner the parent and the child would eventually find the material they need.

But such a search is foolish, because most books in the library have no information about subatomic physics. A much more rational way to proceed is to go to the card catalog and look up appropriate *subjects*. This way, the parent and child can quickly determine the location of books that will have information about the desired subject. The task in this analogy becomes even more daunting if the child were to try to find the necessary information on the internet without the aid of an online search service.

In many ways the corporation is like the public library. It is large, complex, and contains a wealth of information. It owns a wealth of data, just as the library owns a wealth of books. Figure 5.15 makes the analogy between the corporation and the library.

Consider how a report is generated in the corporation. When an analyst wants to find information for a new report or a new analysis, he or she tries to find some person who knows where the data might be to build the desired report: an old programmer, an old database administrator, an old end-user liaison. On a good day, the analyst actually finds such an individual.

However, people do not make a good substitute for a card catalog. Over time people forget, are promoted, or change jobs. As people age and as the volume and complexity of data rises in the

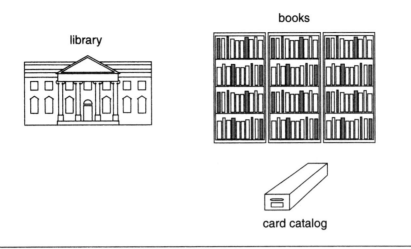

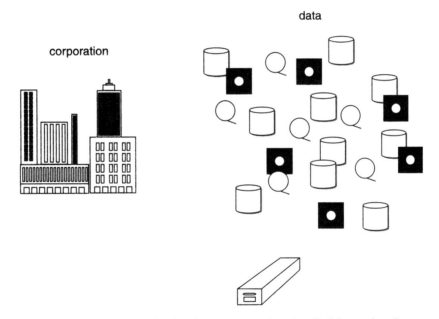

Figure 5.15 The card catalog for the corporate data is called "metadata."

corporation, people become increasingly less adequate for the purpose of finding information.

In order for an organization to become a world-class information processing organization, there is a need for a card catalog. In the world of information systems that card catalog is called metadata.

DATA WAREHOUSE AND METADATA

The data warehouse has its own special need for metadata. One of the characteristics of a data warehouse is that it contains information over a lengthy period of time. Five to 10 years worth of information is a possibility for a data warehouse. There are several implications concerning the management of data over a lengthy period of time. One is that 5 to 10 years worth of data requires a large volume of storage. The other implication is that the structure of data changes. Figure 5.16 shows the implications of storing data over a lengthy period of time.

One year there is one understanding of product and customer; the next year there is another understanding of product

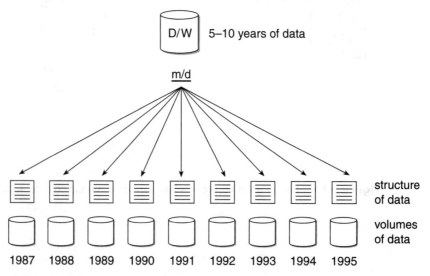

Figure 5.16 Metadata is used to keep track of structural changes over time.

and customer. As these understandings change from the business perspective, the underlying data structure changes as well. Over a 10-year time frame there will be many changes to the historical data that is collected in the data warehouse. It is the metadata that keeps track of these changes over time. This feature of metadata is called *versioning*. With versioning, a DSS analyst can look backward in time and tell what the prevailing conditions were at the moment in time desired. But the real value of metadata is not yet obvious.

Consider a DSS analyst who builds a report for 1995. The analyst shows the report to management and management is enthusiastic, to the point that management asks for the same report for 1990. Since there is 1990 data in the warehouse, the DSS analyst has no problem in producing a new report for that year.

The DSS analyst completes the report and gives it to management, expecting more kudos. But management—to the DSS analyst's surprise—is very uncharitable. The DSS analyst is puzzled and asks management why. The manager explains that the DSS analyst has placed some unbelievable data into the hands of management. Figure 5.17 depicts this scenario.

Management points out that the analyst has reported revenues of $50,000,000 in 1995 and $10,000 in revenue in 1990. Management says that the DSS analyst must have things wrong and questions the credibility of the entire analytical effort.

Context and Content of Historical Data

The DSS analyst is disappointed, but before giving up, he or she points out some things to management:

- In 1990, the definition of what a product was is quite different than the way a product is defined in 1995.
- In 1990, the marketing territories of the company were arranged quite differently than they were in 1995.
- In 1990, the accounting basis was different than the basis in 1995.
- In 1992, there was a merger of companies that changed things quite dramatically.

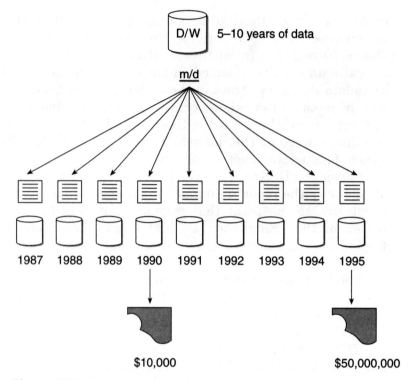

Figure 5.17 Reports are generated for data that is five years apart.

■ In 1994, there was a large reorganization of the company.
■ In 1990, basic calculations were made with a formula that was quite different than the same type of formula in 1995, and so forth.

Figure 5.18 shows the differences that the DSS analyst points out to management.

Now that management focuses on the DSS analyst's points, management is pleased with the results of the reports. The DSS analyst has used the *context* of information over time to explain the *content*. When data is stored over time, it is not sufficient to store the content: The context of information is as important as the content in being able to understand and interpret the information.

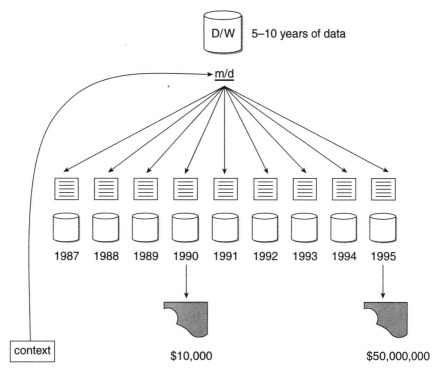

Figure 5.18 Existing systems are adequate for managing the content of data; but, in order to manage data over time, it is necessary to manage the context of data as well—otherwise the content of data makes no sense.

The context of information is stored and managed in metadata over time. It is the usefulness of context that wins the day for the DSS analyst. Once management understands the content and the context of information over time, then management is able to make informed decisions.

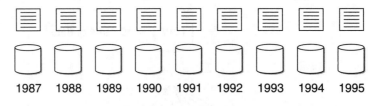

versioning of metadata

Figure 5.19 Keeping a continuous record of the history of metadata.

Versioning and Metadata

The ability of metadata to be tracked over time is called versioning, as illustrated in Figure 5.19. As an example of the importance of versioning of metadata, consider that a data warehouse will have a rich amount of historical data in it. Five to 10 years worth of data is reasonable for many organizations. When a DSS analyst looks at data that is seven years old, how does he or she know what the context of the data is? How does the DSS analyst know that on August 13, 1989 the source of the products table was file ARJ-56? How does the DSS analyst know that on November 12, 1991 the accounting data was calculated using an accrual method rather than a cash method? How does the DSS analyst know that on July 19, 1994 the key of part number was converted to 10 digits from 6 digits? The answer is that with versioning the DSS analyst knows as of a moment in time the context of data.

METADATA AT THE WORKSTATION

One of the most important uses of metadata is its capability to be used for interactive dialog with the access tools, as shown in Figure 5.20. The DSS analyst has accessed the metadata and done the preliminary analysis that sets the stage for a query. Once the analyst has in mind what needs to be queried, the next step is the actual formulation of the syntax of the query. By having the metadata syntax on hand, the DSS analyst ensures that the syntax will be formulated as crisply as possible. In other words, the DSS analyst has insured that there will be few if any syntax errors in the formulation of the query by having interactive access to the metadata.

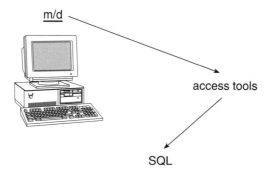

Figure 5.20 One of the most important used of metadata at the DSS analysts workstation is that of forming the basis of query formation.

But query formulation is only one important use of interactive metadata. One of the most intriguing uses of metadata at the end-user workstation is the possibility of the DSS analyst doing queries and analysis against the metadata itself, as shown in Figure 5.21. The figure shows that there are all sorts of possi-

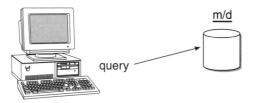

- Where is the data element,—QTYONHAND— found?
- What is the source of EMPLTAX?
- How has BALONHAND been converted from its origination in the operational environment?
- If a change occurs in CURRBAL, what source systems are affected?
- There is a data element in the source system called XVT-235J. If there is a change made in the source system, what data warehouse data elements are affected?
- The business person calls it CURRENT BALANCE. What does the technician call it?
- The finance department calls it RECEIVABLE. Is it the same thing in the marketing department?

Figure 5.21 The metadata is able to be queried in its own right.

bilities for the DSS analyst to use metadata in interactive analysis at the workstation. Metadata is particularly useful for the early stages of DSS analysis where the DSS analyst is trying to determine what the framework for the DSS analysis will be.

DATA MART AND METADATA

The source of all corporate data that flows into the departmentalized data mart is the current detailed data of the data warehouse. As such, the current level of detail represents corporate data and the data mart represents a departmental perspective of the same data.

There is a fair amount of processing that occurs as the data moves from the current level of detail to the data mart, as seen in Figure 5.22. The metadata that is captured in this progression is a little bit different than the metadata captured elsewhere. It

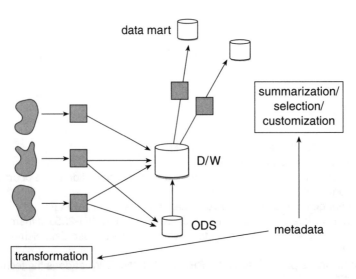

Figure 5.22 Metadata needs to include both the transformation from the operational environment to the data warehouse and ODS environment and the selection/summarization/customization process that occurs as data passes from the data warehouse to the data mart and OLAP environment.

- describes what data is selected,
- describes how the data is summarized, and
- describes how the data is customized to meet the needs of the department that owns the data mart.

In a sense the metadata captured at this point is really meta-process information, as opposed to metadata information, because the information is about process not data.

In order for the data mart analyst to accurately and effectively use the information in the data mart, he or she must know what processing has occurred as the data flowed from the current level of detail into the data mart. The processing that has occurred *qualifies* the data-mart data. Any analysis of data-mart data must be aware that this qualification has occurred.

THE METADATA INFRASTRUCTURE

One of the challenges of the metadata infrastructure is that it must be built and maintained across a wide diversity of technological platforms and software technology, as shown in Figure 5.23. The operational environment is composed mostly of transaction processing technology. The data warehouse environment is composed of parallel technology. The developer environment is typically CASE-oriented. The enterprise environment is CASE-and/or repository-oriented, and the data mart environment is OLAP-oriented. Each of these environments is very different from the others. Yet in order to create and maintain the metadata infrastructure, each of these environments must be addressed. Either metadata must be extracted from the technology found in each of these environments where metadata is created, or metadata must be created as part of the infrastructure in each of these environments and managed interactively there, or both.

In addition to the challenge of managing the metadata infrastructure, there must be an exchange of metadata objects throughout the metadata infrastructure, as seen in Figure 5.24. The objects that are shared are those that are moved from one environment to the next.

In order to be able to make use of the shared meta objects that are passed from one environment to another, there needs to

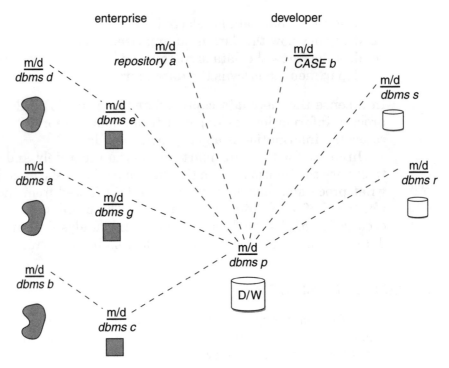

Figure 5.23 One of the technological challenges of managing distributed metadata is that the metadata will reside in a wide variety of technologies.

be compatibility between the metadata infrastructure at the workstation and the underlying technology that resides at the workstation, as shown in Figure 5.25. There is no real purpose for having metadata at any part of the architected environment if the metadata cannot be an active part of development or analysis.

THE ROLE OF THE METADATA MANAGER

Throughout the definition and development of the metadata infrastructure there is the metadata manager (mm). The role of the metadata manager is central to the success that will be enjoyed in the using the metadata infrastructure. The kinds of activities the metadata manager will be engaged in are outlined in Figure 5.26.

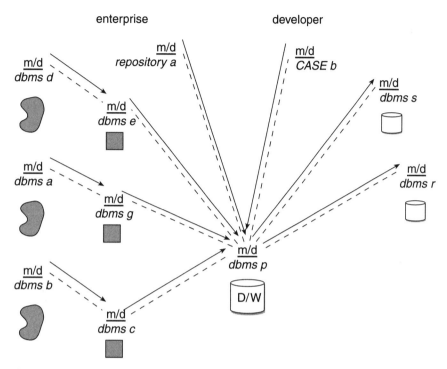

Figure 5.24 The transport of metadata from one technology to another and from one platform to another is another significant technological challenge.

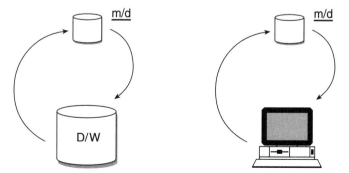

Figure 5.25 Whatever technology the metadata is stored in needs to be compatible with the data warehouse and/or the workstation technology.

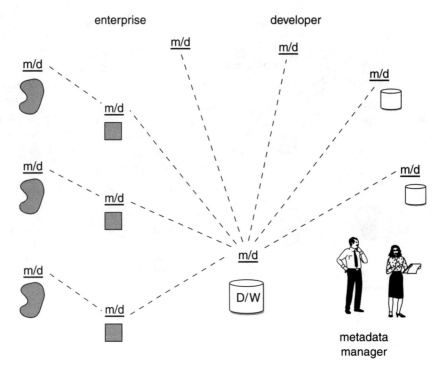

Gathering metadata
Transforming metadata into a useful state
Archiving metadata
Versioning metadata
Coordinating movement of metadata
Resolving technological discrepancies in metadata among the different places
    metadata must be managed
Defining the metadata architecture
Keeping metadata up-to-date

Figure 5.26 The role of the metadata manager for managing metadata.

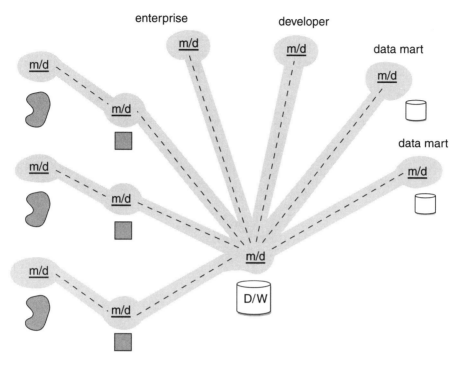

Figure 5.27 Distributed metadata is a cohesive, integrated infrastructure that allows metadata to be shared across the many places it is needed.

DISTRIBUTED METADATA

The net result of the definition and acceptance of the metadata infrastructure is what can be called a *distributed metadata* architecture, as seen in Figure 5.27. The distributed metadata architecture is one in which there is, at the same time,

■ distribution of sharable components, and
■ autonomy and control of unshared, local components.

The distributed metadata architecture meets the specifications as set out in the early parts of this chapter. Figure 5.28 shows that for all the sharing that is an integral part of the dis-

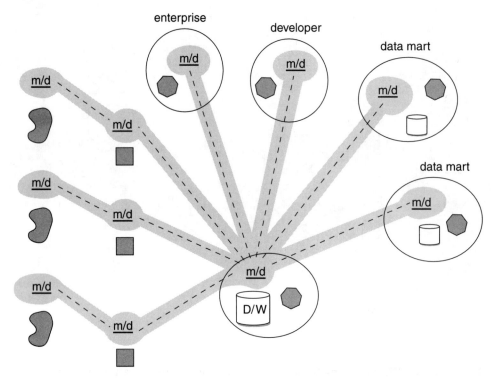

Figure 5.28 At the same time as the needs for sharing and distribution are being met, the needs for private use of metadata and autonomous control of data at the local level are being met

tributed metadata architecture, there is local autonomy and control where needed.

SUMMARY

The world of metadata is complex. Metadata is the nerve center of a larger architecture. It is through metadata that there is uniformity and cohesion between the different components of the architected environment.

The metadata infrastructure is one that must satisfy contradictory goals:

- Allow parts of the metadata architecture to be shared.
- Allow parts of the metadata architecture to be controlled locally, in an autonomous fashion.

The distributed metadata architecture meets the goals and objectives of all the communities that need to use metadata.

The User-Centric Data Warehouse

In the early 1900s telephone calls were made through a series of point-to-point connections implemented manually through chains of telephone operators. The technology of switchboards did not allow individuals to initiate calls without assistance. In order to communicate using the new technology, the user had to work through an operator and ask to be connected to a specific individual at a specific location. Operators at switchboards along the chain did whatever lookups were required and moved physical pins and connectors to complete a circuit. They required specialized training and provided a valuable service. Yet the phone company was worried. Based on projections of increases in phone traffic, an astronomical number of operators would be needed to support the growth in demand, eventually requiring more operators than the population could provide.

The solution the phone companies invented was instantiated by the rotary dial phone which fundamentally altered the landscape of telephony. In effect, all users were asked to become operators; they had to master technology and work with it directly, rather than through an intermediary. Today, rather than calling an operator and asking to speak with John Smith on Main Street in Smalltown, you dial the phone number directly. If you don't remember the number, you simply look it up in a phone book or your directory, or you call for assistance.

While this routine may be comfortable today, it was extremely controversial and a huge gamble when it was first implemented. Operators feared they would lose their jobs. Everyone "knew" that end users would have problems: People would get the wrong number, they would make mistakes, and so forth.

The truth is that by making users into operators the technology has empowered several generations of people who now believe it is their right to place calls from anywhere to anywhere at anytime. Generations of technologists, inventors, and engineers are employed in exciting and challenging careers. Think of the technical innovations that have developed from the need to provide capacity and solve problems related to users on their own telephones. What would the world look like today had telephone technology not evolved when it did?

The introduction of modern data warehouses, front-ended by end-user access tools for decision support, will change the world of corporate information delivery as profoundly as the rotary dial changed electronic voice communications. This technology and system-wide architecture will enable people to do what they have always wanted to do—it may finally, truly empower users.

This chapter will explore a new paradigm. Although it is widely accepted that warehouses solve a persistent problem that plagues data-dependent organizations, what is not as well understood is how to make warehouses successful. Sadly, it is easy to forget that until business users are actually creating their own reports, asking and answering their own questions, and exploring data on their own, the best warehouse will only be an academic exercise. The truth is that user-centric data warehousing is a new paradigm for both systems managers and end users alike just as direct-dial telephones created a new concept of communication.

The user-centric data warehouse offers opportunities for success and failure. There are no well-trodden paths and few signposts along the way to direct the DWA to the optimal outcome. So where do you start? The simple answer is to start out by knowing where you want to end up, then bear that in mind throughout the journey.

This chapter will help you explore the basic geography of the data warehouse. The basic proposition is that if you understand the geology and geography , equip yourself with a good compass, and have a clear idea of your eventual destination, then it is possible to navigate from here to there through the unfamiliar landscape of data warehousing. Through an investigation of the climate of the data warehouse, its terrain and primary features, the DWA can be appropriately equipped before beginning this journey through the unknown. Along the way you will discover the fundamental assertions of data warehousing that differentiate it from previous methods of information delivery and see that data warehouse systems fundamentally alter the relationship between the DWA and the users.

Four questions provide the framework for this exploration:

■ How do data warehouse-based information delivery systems fundamentally differ from those that preceded them?
■ What are the hallmarks of a successful data warehouse project?
■ What are the unique user needs in the data warehouse environment?
■ What results can be expected?

HOW DO DATA WAREHOUSES DIFFER FROM OTHER SYSTEMS?

It is somewhat controversial to claim that data warehouse systems are fundamentally different information delivery systems from those that preceded them. What is the truth that lies behind that statement? The answer derives from a comparison of traditional user interactions with information from those using a data warehouse. Today, in many companies there is a struggle between IS and the end users over information delivery. Sometimes the conflict is cold, highly political, and under the table or, less frequently, it is hot, angry, and out in the open. It is a dispute caused by misunderstandings, lack of knowledge, and incorrect assumptions. Regardless of the cause and the nature of the conflict, both sides typically agree on two things:

- The organization has lots of data.
- IS resources are not effective at turning that data into information on behalf of the end users.

Users commonly feel that IS is slow and unresponsive to their requests for information. On the other hand, IS believes that it doesn't have enough resources to do the job the users request, partly because the user's requests change all the time. IS bottlenecks in report distribution and data analysis are legendary, but sadly, as with many legends, are grounded in a fragment of truth. The average corporate decision maker gets trapped in the IS bottleneck every time he or she needs new information. Delays of weeks are common and multiple months can elapse between users' requests and delivered results when report requests compete for resources with new application development.

Historical Information Access Process—An Illustration

Consider for a moment a common user experience. A business analyst encounters an industry statistic and is curious to see how the company compares to that level of performance. A report which comes each week provides a clue, but at the wrong levels of detail; the existing report might be on a company-wide basis for a week at a time. The analyst needs to see geographic breakdowns comparing the past two years. To the analyst, this seems like a reasonable request. Clearly the company has the data; to see it at different aggregation levels should be straightforward.

Thus far, the elapsed time for this scenario is perhaps 15 minutes—time for the analyst to ask a question, look at an existing report, and imagine how that report could be modified. Now what happens? The data that was used to create the report is not under the user's control—it is not in a local database—and even if it were, the analyst is not a programmer. So the next step is for the user to ask IS to produce a variant on the existing report.

Assuming that the report request is not rejected outright, it goes into a programmer's "in basket." When it comes to the top of the stack, it will either be easy to fulfill because the data does exist or it will require data that is not easily accessible. In the worst case, the basic OLTP systems do not collect data according to the geographic breakdowns requested by the analyst. The programmer may have to make assumptions and create complex decomposition or allocation algorithms to transform the data into its requested form. Eventually the program will be written, run as part of a batch job so as not to interfere with production or on-line updates, and the results will be delivered to the analyst who requested them. In some IS organizations, this modified report may now be added to a standard production run and delivered to everyone who receives the first report.

Typically, the time delay from request to delivery is measured in weeks or months. But this is not the end of the story. If all goes well, when the data arrives at the user's desk in the form of a pile of paper, the analyst will still be curious to discover the answer to the original question. Often, so much time has passed since the original request that the question and the answer are irrelevant—or perhaps the analyst has found another way to get the answer (Figure 6.1). If the analyst is still interested, however, a coherent, interactive analysis may be impossible because the format of the delivered report does not exactly match the analyst's expectations.

The usual elapsed time to this point is four weeks—one hour of analyst time, a few days of programmer time, three weeks of waiting—and the analyst is still not finished. After entering the

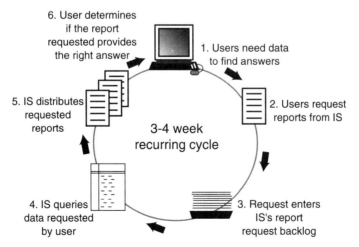

Figure 6.1 Users experience long delays in getting the information they need.

company data and comparing years of history, the analyst sees that the company is doing much better in one of the six regions of the country. What does the analyst do now? To request another report and wait for the answer could take another four to six weeks. Some may give up, but others may choose to start the whole process again with another report request.

It is obvious to even the most casual observer that this process of data analysis is very slow and interrupted by long delays. It does not support interactions; it is completely inflexible, requires lots of effort behind the scenes, and allows lots of opportunity for error. Worse yet, it does not really satisfy the true needs of the user.

Users React and Adapt

In the following example, the user is unusual. Not willing to give up and unwilling to wait, this analyst has an idea for how to "beat the system." Instead of requesting one report at a time, the analyst decides to go for broke. The analysts' request is not single purpose, but rather includes *all* levels, attributes, sums, and comparisons at the same time. The analyst reasons that it can't take that much more time to add a few extra fields, and a few more aggregations and calculations. "If the last report took four weeks, maybe this next one will take five. That is a lot better than asking for 3 smaller reports and waiting 12 weeks to finish the process."

However, the extra items take extra research, the fields don't match and maybe they are in different databases. But the industrious programmer now looks on this request as a challenge, so results do, in fact, return to the user in five or six weeks. The final report in this example is an NxN cross-tab, subtotaled and cross-footed every which way for two years by month and by state; it takes 50 pages in tiny print. When the analyst receives the report it takes several days to locate the useful information, rekey it into a spreadsheet, and draw a few meaningful conclusions.

But is this progress? If all users adapt as in the example, do IS backlogs ever decrease? Will users actually get answers more quickly by attempting to outsmart IS? The answer is "No." As illustrated in Figure 6.2, this adaptive behavior by users makes

Discovery Process	Request A	Request B
User Thought	15 minutes	30 minutes
Time in Queue	3 weeks	3 weeks
Programmer Time	<1 week	3 weeks +
Time to Analyze		
Delivered Result	3 pages: <1 day	50 pages: 1 week
Total Time	<4 weeks	8 weeks

Figure 6.2 A comparison between Requests A and B shows that the organization spends four times more effort producing and analyzing B than A, even though the elapsed time is only twice as long. Users end up in pattern B because, from their perspective, the wait of slightly more than twice the time for eight times more information is worth it.

the situation worse. It takes significantly more work for IS to create ever-more complicated reports. And it is more work for end users to plow through the overwhelming quantity of the results.

Unfortunately, this cycle repeats itself continuously. Corporate information systems are created, managed, and maintained by dedicated, highly trained IS professionals. This IS staff includes designers, system architects, application programmers, and program managers. They are concerned with capturing essential business data and processing it into the systems of record of the organization. IS must produce the paper and electronic records of the transactions of the company. Their focus has been on data integrity, performance, and reliability.

Giving Users What They Request Is Rarely Enough

Only occasionally is IS asked to think about how the data might be used for business analysis. This comes in the form of user requests for reports or decision support systems. Report requests, in writing, via e-mail, in a hallway conversation, or in an executive meeting, frequently take the form of a *design* for a report. Such a report specification includes rows and columns, totals, and calculations. At one time, report requests were even submitted on graph paper that allowed the user to specify the exact column position on the page in which each value was to be placed.

Such a report request does not tell the IS professional tasked with producing it anything at all about the motivation behind the request. Nor can the programmer infer what questions the recipient of the report will answer based solely on the requested report layout. Can IS find out what is really needed and try to find a better outcome? From the IS staff's perspective, they are doing exactly what users want because they are giving users what they ask for.

IS knows those users who are never content, those who request special, custom reports constantly, and those who won't take no for an answer. Moreover, IS resources are being cut, and the staff is being asked to do more with less. So the staff has been led to the wrong conclusion. IS believes that users really need extremely fat, elaborate reports and that end users can't build their own reports because the reports are so complicated and need so much specialized data knowledge. So IS spends extra time adding more reports and more data. More and more complicated tools are acquired which move users farther away from the data and require even larger investments in learning and maintenance.

This never-ending report cycle is a fallacy, caused by incomplete information. Systems designed completely from one perspective or the other will produce entirely suboptimal systems that do not solve the problem. The fallacy at the heart of traditional information delivery systems is the belief on both sides that they understand the other side and can *outwit* them. The opportunity to solve this fundamental problem of data processing and free IS and end users from this state of conflict is the mission of data warehousing. Data warehousing is motivated by the desire to break and establish a common ground and a single solution. It is propelled by the desire to provide a better environment for end-user data analysis and decision support.

The Ideal Environment for End-User Data Analysis and Decision Support

As we have seen, to observe how people use systems today is misleading, because current systems have produced suboptimal and erroneous behavior. Rather, it will be instructive to engage in a hypothetical investigation of a composite "average" user, working with an *ideal* system.

Users who are investigating data when they do not know the answer they expect to find, or are unclear of the parameters they wish to investigate before they start, engage in what is described as *random, directed walk* behavior. Its characteristics are the following:

■ There is an external trigger. A nugget of information catches the user's attention and causes a momentary pause. This nugget may be contained in a standard report, a journal, on the nightly news, in a question posed by a colleague, or in the actions of a competitor.

■ The user starts with a deceptively simple question and follows it with many others, such as, "How much?" "What are we doing?" "Where?" When the user sees the answer to the first question, typically it engenders another. The questions are not predictable in advance, because it is the answer to the first that raises the second. Even in the case when users start with a complicated idea in mind, they frequently are more comfortable deconstructing the idea into a sequence of simple questions.

■ The user needs to conduct the equivalent of a "live interview with the data," not read the results of a fixed questionnaire. Given the unstructured and self-propagating nature of the investigation, it is just plain easier to work interactively than it is to anticipate everything that the user might want to know in advance and ask for it all at once. Since humans are lazy, this is a pattern that will be preferred if available.

■ The process should allow the user to work in *real-time*. Everyone has experienced the frustrations of working through time-delayed, asynchronous communications. An ideal investigatory environment would allow instantaneous response to questions because delays break the train of thought and may place conclusions at risk. Traditional systems that place weeks or months between the idea and the result do not support interactive investigation of data.

When you add these characteristics together and design the ideal system, you will create a fluid, interactive environment that is 100 percent user-driven and is very, very responsive.

Some of the most successful decision support systems built during the early 1990s were constructed under this principle and are testaments to its effectiveness. Such environments enabled users to do what they do best—ask a question and get an immediate answer. Since most people are more effective when they can analyze the answer, then respond, the most natural form of user interaction with databases is on a short-cycle, ask-answer-ask-again pattern.

Anyone who has ever done any form of research knows that you don't know what you really want until you see something. Once the initial observation is taken, or the first reference checked, then you can see what is wrong or right and set a new direction for investigation. When interacting with data, the user's natural process is one of successive refinement. Typical questions start at a high level and are successively refined and focused as new attributes are explored within smaller and smaller areas of focus.

This process of discovery may appear illogical because it reflects individual creativity, but it is highly effective. Unfortunately, this process is almost never observed in the analysis of traditional corporate information systems. But it may be the ideal that data warehouse systems can achieve.

WHAT ARE THE HALLMARKS OF A SUCCESSFUL DATA WAREHOUSE SYSTEM?

What can be done to create a modern data analysis environment in which users can embark upon this random, directed walk? The four key objectives you need to satisfy are shown in Figure 6.3.

The system that meets those objectives is a modern decision support system. What shape would such a system take if you could remove some of the limitations that restrict current systems design? What if

- ad hoc queries could be executed any time, day or night, without impacting performance of OLTP systems;
- turnaround time for most questions (Turnaround time is the total time required to formulate the question and get the response in a useful form) was just a minute or two;

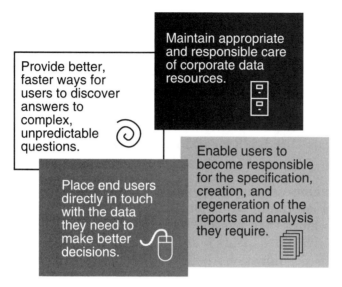

Figure 6.3 The four key objectives your data warehouse should satisfy.

- the system did not have to support constant, high-speed transaction processing, but rather could be designed to optimize aggregating queries;
- data in decision support databases was rationalized, precomputed, and logically and internally consistent;
- database schemas made sense to users, so they would not need programmers to locate and interpret data;
- users had tools they could use on their own to ask and answer their own questions?

For the first time in IS history, it is now feasible to create systems that come close to this ideal. Modern decision support systems, based on well-designed data warehouses, enable nontechnical business professionals to find answers in data by themselves. These systems give full control to those users who master the new technology. There may be hidden complexity—servers, middleware, metadata—but to the user it must all be seamless, painless, and simple. All of that complexity can be hidden beneath simple, powerful desktop data access tools. Properly executed decision support data warehouse projects can increase revenue, simplify data management tasks, and extract value out of legacy data, but only if users are able to access the data on their own, ask and answer their own questions, and share their knowledge with others. When the entire system is comprehensible, responsive, accurate, reliable and fronted by attractive end-user tools, then you have an effective solution.

WHAT ARE THE UNIQUE USER NEEDS IN THE DATA WAREHOUSE?

Data warehouse systems are different from prior information systems because the environment has been turned upside down. Users are more than passive recipients of canned reports; they become active participants in the total data analysis process. Traditional IS organizations believe their data-using community needs reports. If you asked the average IS organization to draw a curve, representing the distribution of its data users versus its need for fixed format reports, you would probably get the graph illustrated in Figure 6.4.

IS managers who have not yet experienced a successful warehouse expect the vast majority of users to need fixed format reports, delivered on a regular basis. Very few users request ad hoc access to data; they ask for reports. "The systems are too hard, the data is too hard to understand, the rules are too complex",

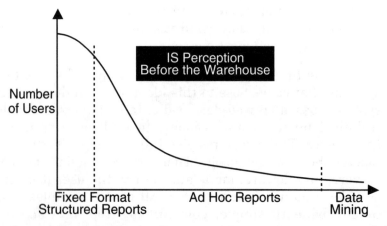

Figure 6.4 An analysis of historical usage patterns suggests that the bulk of users prefer fixed format reports.

are some common explanations for lack of user requests for free-form access to data. From this perspective, it is no surprise that many data warehouse projects start with the requirement that the tools and database design selected be able to regenerate the same 500 reports that are currently coming from the transaction processing system.

But, this model does not match reality. Experience with good data warehouse-based decision support systems shows that in such systems, the true usage model is more like the curve shown in Figure 6.5.

Although there are some users who only use fixed format reports and some users who may need true data mining, or complex statistical or modeling capabilities, most users will start with a few standard reports as templates or models from which they start their own customizations. Users of an ideal data warehouse interact with data differently than users of OLTP systems. The best solution for end users of a data warehouse is a multi-purpose tool that allows them maximum flexibility and simplicity.

A Transportation Analogy

The adoption of data warehouse as an information delivery system represents as fundamental a change for users as the intro-

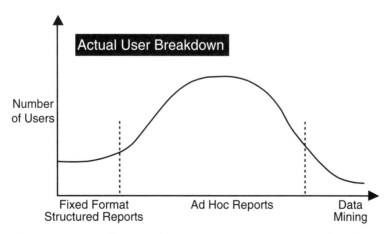

Figure 6.5 In a data warehouse, more users will work with ad hoc query and analysis tools than with any other type of product.

duction of private automobiles made to cities. Prior to the proliferation of private automobiles, people in cities had three methods of transportation: walk; take a bus, trolley, or train; or hire a cab. Few people who did not make a living transporting others knew how to drive. People were delivered *close* to where they wanted to be, then walked the rest of the way. The professionals knew secrets: They could read maps, talk to each other in code, and establish unwritten traffic protocols; they had made an investment and mastered some form of technology.

Enter the private car. All of a sudden, some users have the means to become drivers. Initially, there is chaos on the streets. New drivers don't know the rules or the technology: All they know is where they wish to go. Traffic laws are written; drivers are trained and licensed. A new system is born.

Users of data in OLTP systems are in a similar situation with regard to their need for information. They are given reports that are created by someone else. The reports may be *close* to what the user wants, but the user has to fill in the pieces. Few users know how to "drive" (i.e., how to program), extract data, or create new reports. The lucky ones can ask someone to make custom changes, but most just take what is given and make of it what they can.

For the IS organization, equipping end users with tools that allow them direct access to the data warehouse is the equivalent of the arrival of the private automobile in the city. Buses and trolleys are the standard reports that have always been available, but gradually become less prevalent as the mix of traffic shifts to more individualized transportation methods. Users who use their own tools do have to assume responsibility. IS typically equips users with a car, (the query tool), and always maintains the roads, but the users determine where they want to go and when they will get there. In the data warehouse environment IS has to design and construct the roads, create directional signs so users know where to go and traffic signals so they don't bump into one another, train drivers, and enforce the laws.

Unlike traditional OLTP systems environments in which IS must guarantee the performance of every transaction, it is impossible for IS to test every route, every access path, every possible data warehouse user's query in advance. IS can't police every intersection, or ensure that users get where they thought they wanted to go. Instead, IS has the obligation to create and maintain the infrastructure, create and maintain the data, and finally educate, audit, and observe users, and educate some more.

WHAT IS THE RESULT?

Data warehouse-based information systems establish a new paradigm—a new way of thinking about users and their interactions with data. Perhaps an illustration may make this easier to understand. Assume for the moment that you have created a data warehouse for a good-sized college to support the admissions department. How does the data warehouse help or hinder an analyst's performance?

The issue that has caught the hypothetical business analyst's attention is the question of how best to choose from the pool of student applicants the ones to accept. This is a fairly unstructured area with no easy answer. But the business analyst has to start somewhere, so the first question is: "How many applications have been received year-to-date?" This question results in a single-value response and is quite easy to formulate.

The business analyst might next choose to investigate the trend over time to predict how many more applications will arrive before admissions close. The next step is to show the count of applications by month, for this year and the last two years, so the business analyst can compare years and look for a trend. This produces 36 rows of data. From a quick chart the business analyst observes that December is usually when 50 percent of applications arrive, based on this December's count-to-date, it can be expected that applications will be up 17 percent versus last year.

Perhaps the business analyst is curious about the quality of the applicants and returns to the database with the objective of learning about grade point average, SAT scores, age, and class rank of the applicants for this year and last year. This small query shows that average quality has improved as well which means the college will either have to raise standards or increase the size of the freshman class.

In the days before the data warehouse, this process of discovery might never even have happened. Perhaps the analyst might have asked someone in the IS department to produce a report showing applications by month for the past three years with average SAT, and so forth. That is a difficult report to build because the user needs to see both annual averages and monthly trends. It might have taken a long time to create or the programmer might have produced the wrong data. And it surely would have taken more than 30 minutes.

In this data warehouse-based example the analyst requested three ad hoc queries, none of which produced more than 50 rows of data. Each is likely to have returned results very quickly and might be presented in a variety of ways. With access to a good data warehouse and equipped with a good desktop query tool, this process should take less than 30 minutes.

The user has gained an insight that may well lead to actions or to further investigation. This is the essence of ad hoc access interaction. Users need ad hoc access because the data shows them what they did not already know and leads them in paths they could not predict. It is just this support of ad hoc interaction that differentiates the data warehouse from its predecessor systems.

Everyone has a role to play in data warehouse systems; it is just that some of the roles are new and everyone involved has to learn to think in new ways. People who are reluctant to embrace change or who fail to complete the paradigm shift may have trouble in the new world.

Successful projects have successful users. Data warehouse projects succeed when users are more independent. Successful data warehouses place the users at the center of the project. When everyone recognizes that, a new attitude and approach is the most successful ingredient in the mix. Organizations that understand these fundamental factors that are driving the paradigm shift will succeed in establishing successful data warehouses.

Selecting End-User Access Tools

The objective of this chapter is to provide the DWA with a practical guide to the selection of end-user access tools for the data warehouse. The selection process is based on common sense but, as with almost every aspect of data warehousing, it requires the application of common sense in a new environment. When you are working to change the paradigm of information access in your organization, standard processes may no longer be appropriate. When so much is unknown, it is prudent to get advice. But where do you turn for advice about this new environment? Who are the experts?

The best sources of information are DWAs who have faced the challenges, lived through the paradigm shift, and can, with hindsight, share their opinions and advice. In short, the best sources are DWAs of successful data warehouses.

This chapter presents information drawn from interviews with 15 data warehouse project leaders who have completed the selection of end-user access tools. It is based on the real experiences of people who have built data warehouses, DWAs who have taken the initiative to select tools for their users and deployed those products to the user community. Their experiences and their recommendations are distilled into an aggregate, "best practices" process. Just as there is no "typical household" that lives in the geographic center of the country with 1.95 children and 2.3 cars, it is unlikely that any specific tool selection process will reproduce each of the "perfect" steps outlined in this chapter. But for the DWA who is looking to leverage the experience of other successful projects, these lessons should prove valuable. The chapter is organized into five sections:

1. Including end-user access products
2. How to get started
3. Four representative examples
4. A Framework for "Best Practices Tool Selection"
5. Final Observations

INCLUDING END-USER ACCESS PRODUCTS

The purpose of a data warehouse is to deliver information to end users. This is an unorthodox description, yet it captures an essential truth. All of the other more frequently quoted objectives of a data warehouse—increased profits, reduced costs, better decisions—spring from the successful achievement of the stated objective. When decision makers are enabled to look at integrated, historical data from which they can do trend analysis or make accurate projections, all of those benefits can accrue to the organization. The ultimate measure of success of the data warehouse is the degree to which the end users receive benefits from the information it contains and pass those benefits on to the organization. No matter how intellectually exciting it is to implement a new architecture, collect new information, and resolve age-old data quality issues, the mission of the DWA is to make a system that works for the users.

Part of the obligation of building a data warehouse is to deliver to the end users a preferred access path into the warehouse. It doesn't have to be the sole supported path, but the DWA must pick one as the standard. The DWA must look at the desktop as an extension of the warehouse and put something on each desktop that will work most of the time for most of the people.

Experience shows that data warehouses don't reduce transaction processing costs or reduce the staff that it takes to maintain and build transaction systems because they will all remain in place. Instead, the returns from a warehouse project come when users do things they were never able to do before—make better decisions, save money, increase revenues, and operate more efficiently. When they are successful and see the benefits of the warehouse, those users will express their gratitude to the DWA and the warehouse team in the form of increased and continuing commitment to the data warehouse.

There has always been a difference between the end user's experience of working with a computer system and the experience of the engineer or the developer who creates it. Few of the difficult technical problems that must be solved in data warehousing are apparent to the users. But it is nowhere more pronounced than in data warehouse projects where there is such a tremendous amount of work that goes on hidden from view. Data warehouse projects represent an extreme examples of the difference in perspective between users and IS professionals. Consider the tasks that must be completed for the data warehouse to exist:

- Identify data
- Locate and extract from legacy system
- Cross-reference and check data quality
- Establish client-server connections
- Performance tune

Overall, building a data warehouse is tough and takes a lot of time to get it right. Some people describe a data warehouse as an iceberg: Everything below the surface represents 90 percent of the effort put in by the data warehouse project team that is invisible to the users. So what do users see of the data warehouse? The most visible aspects of the data warehouse and the ones by which the project will be judged, are the portions that rise above the surface: the schema, metadata, and desktop data-access tools you provide.

Other chapters of this book deal with questions of schema and metadata, but the selection of the tools is equally important and is the responsibility of the DWA. It is an interesting assignment. How do you put the best possible face on your complete data warehouse project when all you have to work with is a 14-

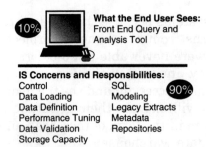

What the End User Sees:
Front End Query and
Analysis Tool

IS Concerns and Responsibilities:

Control	SQL
Data Loading	Modeling
Data Definition	Legacy Extracts
Performance Tuning	Metadata
Data Validation	Repositories
Storage Capacity	

Figure 7.1 The users' perception of the data warehouse is quite different from that of the IS team who is responsible to implement and support it.

inch diagonal computer screen and a mouse? That is the medium through which you have to deliver the entire value of the data warehouse to your end-user community. Also, running on the user's desktop is the access tool you provide. To the users, the tool *is* the warehouse; what they think of the tool will determine what they think of the warehouse. If you equip your end users with tools that they cannot use, don't like, or don't understand, you will be shortchanging your efforts on the entire project. On the other hand, if you give users tools they can use, tools that enable them to view reports and create the analysis they need, then they will say your project is successful.

It is not easy to ensure user success, but one of the easiest steps the DWA can take is to make sure that the tools that users work with are appropriate, enticing, and effective. To that end, the DWA must provide basic tools as part of the total data warehouse solution. User-access tools must not be an afterthought, nor left to the discretion of the user, but part of the solution as it is delivered to the organization. The mission of the DWA is to create and deliver the *whole* solution; desktop data-access tools are a critical component of the system. The methodology outlined in this chapter will enable you to incorporate user preferences into the tool selection process.

Leaving the selection of tools to each individual is a mistake too often made by technologists. Recall the sales history of the PC. There was a time when CPUs were not bundled with keyboards, monitors, hard drives, or with the operating system preinstalled. Each customer had to determine which components met his or her needs at a reasonable cost and had to install the operating system. As a result, few individuals purchased their own computers. Not until complete "systems" were sold in a single box, configured and ready to go, did individuals begin to purchase computers in volume. Your customers need to gain access to the information in the database. You need tools that cooperate with your infrastructure and complement your data warehouse. The DWA is the person who can put those two pieces together and ensure project success.

When end user tools are included in the data warehouse, projects *are* more likely to be successful. In every industry there are examples of complete data warehouse projects that were delivered with data, tools, and training, and resulted in increased value for their organizations.

An academic institution was awarded a sizable grant because of its data warehouse. Admissions and student demographics data had just been loaded into an early prototype data warehouse and the first end users had been trained on the data-access tools, when the deadline for a grant proposal drew near. The grant application required statistics about geographic distribution of students and aid levels. In desperation, the administrator asked an assistant who had just been trained on the data warehouse to see if the warehouse could help. In several hours, the information was located, analyzed, and submitted on time. The grant was awarded and the warehouse proved its value. Had the users not been given tools and training, the grant application would not have been completed on time.

A technology manufacturing company is using their warehouse to study customer purchase profiles. The warehouse system includes data-access tools, standard reports, and common analysis. The company is able to determine, based on analysis of customer purchase activity, which accounts seem to be at risk. The company observed, by studying data in the data warehouse, that customers exhibited a characteristic buying pattern that was a strong predictor of future buying behavior. With the warehouse, the company identified those customers who had fallen off their traditional buying pattern and applied proactive programs to secure their satisfaction and repeat business.

What is interesting about both of these examples is that the data warehouse team did not have any idea when the warehouse was deployed that it was going to be used in these ways with such significant effect. The team would never have included such optimistic scenarios in an attempt to cost-justify the warehouse and, therefore, might have sold the warehouse short. In each case, these were opportunities that the organization simply would not have been able to take advantages of without the data warehouse. The compelling, breakthrough benefits of a data warehouse are frequently of that nature; they occur because end users are given tools and training so they could look into the data warehouse and learn answers to questions they did not know they needed to ask.

HOW TO GET STARTED

If you agree that the DWA should include tools as part of the data warehouse solution, the challenge is to pick the right one. Before you begin to choose access tools, you will probably try to determine what your users are doing today—that would be exactly the wrong thing to do. More first-time DWAs make this mistake than any other.

Here is why this initial approach is a mistake. If the DWA starts by looking at current use, and assumes that those patterns will hold in the data warehouse system, the outcome will not be correct. On average, organizations produce hundreds of reports from transaction processing systems on a regular basis. It is likely that at least 80 percent of the users of online transaction systems are in fact users of canned reports. That represents current usage prior to the introduction and availability of a data warehouse as shown in Figure 7.2. After making such an observation, it is natural to draw the conclusion that the user community wants hundreds of reports.

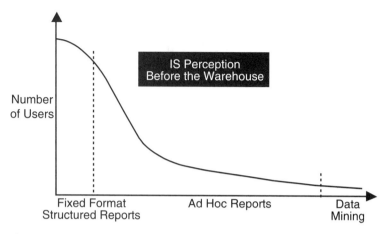

Figure 7.2 Traditional usage patterns predict that more users will work with prefabricated reports than will go off on their own.

The reason users depend upon standard reports is that data in OLTP systems is fundamentally inaccessible to end users. Their only access is by asking a programmer for a report. When asked for a report, most programmers don't write interactive, ad hoc query systems. They produce the report, then get back to their real job. So an analysis of pre-warehouse usage shows 80 percent in the executive information system (EIS) side of the curve trailing to 10 percent in the ad hoc and statistics tools.

But, in a data warehouse, where the system has been designed to make data accessible to end users, the paradigm shifts and the demands shift also. If the DWA gives them a chance, users will change their behavior as they find new ways to meet their fundamental needs within the data warehouse system as shown in Figure 7.3. From the users' perspective, the key benefit of a data warehouse is that they will be allowed to work with information in an ad hoc and interactive fashion. You will not be able to eliminate all of your 500 reports, nor should you try to. But as a starting point, you should plan on delivering only 10 percent of the reports you are building today and let your users do the rest. The choice of which reports you should build initially is a matter of some delicacy: Select those reports that are the most frequently requested, most commonly used, and contain the most useful information.

Some of your users will prefer a fixed-format executive information system "one button" interface that is very rigid and pre-

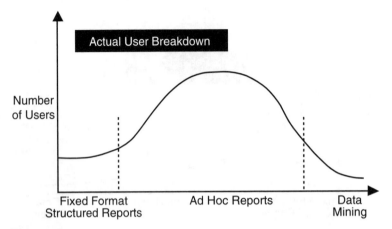

Figure 7.3 Usage of ad hoc tools is the rule not the exception in the successful data warehouse.

programmed. Rich visualization and statistics products are typically used by a very, very small set of users who are willing to invest a significant amount of time in learning products that are highly specialized. You should expect to satisfy the bulk of the users of a data warehouse with general-purpose query, reporting, and analysis tools.

When you plot the number of users of the data warehouse in the mature and well-established system, versus the sophistication and complexity of interface they prefer to work, you get a skewed normal distribution with the bulk of the users working with query or reporting or analysis tools.

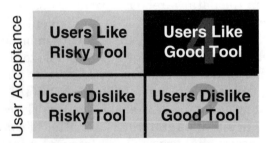

Figure 7.4 Strength of technology versus user acceptance.

The end result of your tool selection process will be one of the four quadrants illustrated in Figure 7.4. Either users will like or dislike the product and the technology will be either a good or bad fit with your systems and infrastructure. It is possible to end up in Quadrant 1 with a product that is technically inadequate and unappealing to the users through a series of compromises, but it is more likely that you will end up in Quadrant 1 if you fail to implement the data warehouse at all. Quadrant 1 is full of out-of-date technology that is hard to maintain and frustrates users. Everyone has some systems with tools in Quadrant 1. Quadrant 2, with "good" technology that is unappealing to users, is the result of decisions in which users have no influence. It is easy to find "good technology" that is robust, stable, and easy to maintain, but that is also user-hostile. For instance, deploying SQL to end users is an example of a Quadrant 2 solution. Quadrant 3 is populated by unstable, expensive, unmaintainable, risky products that are appealing to users because of their interface, graphics, or advertising claims. The objective of the tool selection process is to end up in Quadrant 4. You want to have fundamentally strong, sound, maintainable technology that your end users are actually going to understand and enjoy using.

FOUR REPRESENTATIVE EXAMPLES

Four examples will demonstrate several different approaches to the process of selecting end-user access tools for the data warehouse. Each company employed a slightly different tool selection process and ended up with different results.

Company A

Company A is a manufacturer of computer components that built a data warehouse to help assess the financial performance of various divisions. The team set out to select a standard tool for the data warehouse just three months before the warehouse was scheduled to be released to end users. A 15-person team composed of several data warehouse designers, a few technicians, and a few end-user computing specialists assembled. After a day or two of discussion, the group identified six products that were thought of as the most significant products on the market. These six vendors were to receive a request for information (RFI).

Even though time was short, the team created a lengthy RFI that listed every feature offered by any product in any data-access category that sounded appealing to the team. The team hoped to learn, based on feature availability, which tools were going to be useful for which tasks. One month later the responses were in and evaluated with an elaborate scoring system. Three products were eliminated based on their responses, or lack thereof. Evaluation copies of two of the remaining three products were received and installed by members of the team.

The three finalists were invited on-site to demonstrate their products capabilities. The vendors connected to the company's data warehouse and took questions. They were asked to build reports, answer ad hoc questions, and fit within the data warehouse framework. Next, the team broke into three groups, one for each product. Each group was responsible for learning as much about the product as possible and reporting its strengths and weaknesses to the full team. The team selected the product that would best meet the needs of the organization.

Unfortunately, this story did not have a satisfactory ending. The team had made mistakes. In the RFI, the team had not identified the essential compatibility requirements for all desktop products, nor consulted in advance with the desktop standards committee. As it turned out, the desktop standards committee rejected the selected product because it would not work with the standard desktop configuration. The second mistake was leaving out the incumbent product. They hadn't even considered it at all because it was three years old, and during the discussion of "market-leading" products, it was not even considered. As a third mistake, the team did not clarify who held decision-making authority at the start of the evaluation. Thus, when other constituencies emerged and claimed authority over the decision, the process was called into question and, in fact, was restarted, delaying the entire data warehouse roll-out. Company A's selection process is summarized in Figure 7.5.

	Company A
Team Size	15
How Long	3 Months
# Tools	3
Result	Try Again...

Figure 7.5 A quick project by a large team did not meet its objectives.

Company B

Company B embarked upon its data warehouse to capture manufacturing information for cost control and process improvements.
The data warehouse team established a large subcommittee to select end-user access tools as soon as they had finished the first
database schema design. The more than 20-person team included
representatives from the end users, actual business analysts,
their consulting company, and representatives of a variety of standards committees, and so on. Members of the team were able to
attend a warehouse-focused trade show; many were up-to-date on
the market and they picked 12 products for the RFI. The team included the incumbent product and a product provided by their
database vendor. Six products made it past the RFI assessment,
so, as with Company A, the team broke into subgroups to focus on
each finalist.

Each group acquired an evaluation copy of one of the products, installed it, set it up, and started to build reports against
these preliminary warehouse data. Based on discoveries during
that live testing, three products were eliminated. Representatives from the vendor finalists came on site to demonstrate their
products. The vendors were not allowed to demonstrate against
the company's own data, as it was too proprietary, but they did
take questions live from the team. As a favorite emerged, the
product was installed on the team members' computers so that
everyone would have a chance to use the selected product.

The final stage of the process, winnowing from six to one, was
completed in just seven weeks of elapsed time. Although the
company did not create a test or presentation lab, with perfect
hindsight they would have done so. In retrospect, the effort of in-
stalling and de-installing software, and configuring and con-

	Company B
Team Size	20
How Long	7 Weeks
# Tools	12
Result	Ready to Roll

Figure 7.6 Efficient process selected a well-received product, but it was time-consuming for the team.

necting for demonstrations to the team, was overwhelming and wasted a significant amount of time. The net result of the evaluation, summarized in Figure 7.6, was the selection of a Quadrant 4 product that was acceptable to IS and favorably received by end users.

Company C

Company C planned to use its data warehouse as the reporting system of record and expects to deploy data access to a targeted user community of between 5,000 and 50,000 users over three to four years. Company C's overriding concern was that the vendor of the selected tool has a history of innovation so that over the lifetime of the warehouse the product would probably keep up with technology trends.

Company C appointed a mid-size team of 12 people to the tools selection process. The team was composed of a variety of IS professionals with data warehouse expertise, although no actual end users were included. The incumbent product was an internally developed solution that everyone from the top to the bottom of the organization agreed should be replaced, so it was not included, even in the initial RFI. Company C believed that hands-on assessments were critical to their selection and started very early. They also invested in a 10-computer lab and created a subset of the data warehouse for testing purposes.

Company C put the final three products through rigorous testing, both by representatives of end users and of the IS staff who would be called upon to support the product. The process was elegant. Each product was installed in the lab for three

	Company C
Team Size	12
How Long	6 Months
# Tools 3	
Result	Deployed Successfully

Figure 7.7 Company C involved users and IS staff extensively in a hands-on evaluation lab.

weeks. During that time, IS professionals were invited to learn the product and record their opinions. IS staff built repositories, established metadata, created standard reports, and checked out security and administration features all in a live, hands-on environment. Next, representative end users went through a similar process in which they were required to go through a complete process of building specific reports, answering ad hoc questions, and recording their opinions. It was an extensive and controlled process that exposed 60 users to each of three tools. A single product was selected that was ranked as the best by both end users and IS. As summarized in Figure 7.7, Company C was very careful and took a great deal of time to come to its conclusion.

Company D

This is a widely distributed company with many autonomous offices, none of which has local IS support. The unique challenge of this company's selection process was to identify a highly functional product that users could effectively use on their own with minimal or no IS intervention.

To eliminate tools that were unsuitable because of platform, database, design, or configuration issues, Company D's DWA hired one full-time outside consultant to evaluate the tools and pick two from which the users would choose a single solution. The consultant sorted query tools from application development tools, installed products, built metadata, and learned how to administer the products. Not having any other obligations, the consultant was able to devote full-time to the process of evaluating and learning user tools. The field of potentials was reduced to

	Company D
Team Size	Consultant
How Long	1 Months
# Tools	2 (finalists)
Result	Planning to Deploy

Figure 7.8 Company D is ready to begin deploying end-user access tools to its end users.

two products that appeared to have adequate functionality and would work in the company's environment.

Once two finalists had been selected and approved, the products were subjected to extensive testing in a well-equipped usability lab for blind testing. Users were walked into the lab, handed a manual and a machine that was connected to a subset of the data warehouse, then given three questions to answer. A 10-minute video tape presenting the essentials of the product was shown at the beginning of each user session. No vendor representatives were allowed to speak with end users for fear of contaminating product functionality with the training skills and personality of the vendor representative. Then the Company D team watched and judged usability for each product. From their analysis of what was called the "fumbling factor," the company was able to determine which tool could be learned and used by users without assistance. Ultimately, the ease of use in the environment, as assessed by actual users, was the most important criteria used to choose between the two finalists. Company D's process is summarized in Figure 7.8.

A FRAMEWORK FOR "BEST PRACTICES TOOL SELECTION"

In general terms, the process of tool selection is divided into four stages, driven at each stage by the DWA. Prior to the first stage, though, an evaluation or selection team is chosen by the DWA who is usually its leader. The project team is responsible for the research and decisions at each stage in the process, although the

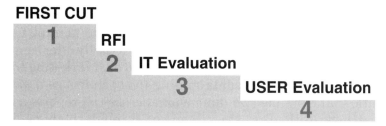

Figure 7.9 The four stages of the end-user tool selection process.

final decision usually is ratified by senior management in the IS organization. Selecting an end-user tool is *not* something the DWA can or should do alone, in isolation. In only one of the 15 evaluations was one person solely responsible and in that instance he was working for a team of five. That team of people can be: only IS, IS and end users, or IS, end users, and consultants. The companies included in this research used all of those combinations. Most teams had at least one user representative, some had more. A few teams had outside consultants working with them as well. The most successful outcomes were produced by teams that included data warehouse technical staff, and had strong participation by end users and their representatives.

The four basic stages shown in Figure 7.9 are: First Cut, Request for Information, IS Evaluation, and User Evaluation. The progression from one stage to the next is essentially the process of winnowing down from the universe of possible choices to the one tool that is chosen to deploy as a standard. Each stage follows a similar process. You start by defining the criteria for the stage. There is a certain amount of work during each stage to determine which products will move on to the next stage and which will be eliminated. Rankings of products from one stage do not carry forward into the next. This ensures that each round is important and initial impressions don't skew the final results.

Stage 1: First Cut

The objective of the first cut is to identify a reasonable selection of 15 or so products to evaluate. As there are so many products competing for attention—many using the same labels but offering different functionality—the biggest challenge of this stage is to sort the apples from the avocados. In the market basket of products, you will need to assess which actually offer comparable functions and which merely claim to do so. Marketing hype can label report writers as data mining tools, charts as data visualization, and simple two-dimensional cross-tab reports as OLAP. Your task in the first stage is to cut through the hype, identify the categories that you want to investigate, and pick a good selection of products.

What are the categories? Are you looking for an EIS solution, a report writer, or data visualization and statistics? Before you begin, you must have a good idea about what kind of usage pattern you will support with this tool. If you believe that access patterns are different in the data warehouse then in OLTP data systems, then you must look for query-report-analysis products that will satisfy the basic needs of the users at the center 80 percent of your data warehouse. It is recommended that you select a different tool for end-user access to the data warehouse than the tool with which users access your OLTP systems.

One of the determining factors during this first cut is the stability of your data warehouse. Is this the first warehouse in your organization? Is it still under development? Is it partially deployed to a few test users? Or do you have a fairly stable warehouse that's been in use for a while? If you have observed that the rate of new tables and new users coming into your warehouse has slowed significantly, then the range of tools you might consider is larger than if you are in development of your first warehouse. A new warehouse, or one that is still under construction, will be changing all the time. New tables will emerge, field and table names will change, tables will merge, fields may be combined or split apart, and the metadata is in turmoil.

When working with a warehouse in flux, avoid any tool that requires significant amounts of set-up or has a cumbersome administration process. Look for a tool that automatically adjusts to the database, and ideally, can work directly with any metadata. Tools that require thick semantic layers or hierarchical definintional overlays are particularly ill-suited to warehouses in flux, since they cannot be used to test the data or see if the tables load correctly.

Other criteria to apply during Stage 1 deal with selecting tools that will work in your operating environment. Specifically, you must determine what systems the products support and what platforms they run on. Be sure to consider how each product will work in your target environment. Some of the existing infrastructure the product will interface with are:

Database System or RDBMS—Oracle, Sybase, Informix, Red Brick, DB/2 and so on.

Desktop Operating System—Windows, Windows 95, Mac OS, UNIX and so on.

Desktop Configuration—RAM, Hard disk, monitor, CPU speed.

Network and Middleware—SQL*NET, OpenClient, ODBC, TCP/IP, SequeLink, and so on.

Metadata models and repositories.

To effectively make these choices, the DWA will have to glean information from a variety of sources, including:

Trade magazines and journals

Conferences, shows, and seminars

Vendor and data warehouse Internet Web sites

Analyst reports

Vendor references

Electronic forums

Systems integrators

Each of these sources has value, but none can be taken as gospel. In a market that is changing rapidly, even the best industry analysts have a hard time keeping up. Published reports that are more than six months old are likely to be out-of-date and an ad hoc request may simply pass on the name of the vendor who presented most recently. Trade media are not perfect either; their "comprehensive" listings of vendors and products in a category are always incomplete and usually mis-categorize 25 percent of the entries. Vendors cause many of the problems. Marketing literature typically makes expansive claims that make it hard for deadline-pressured authors to discern the facts behind the fiction. When one vendor introduces an attractive new feature, competitors jump on the marketing bandwagon by applying the new name to describe one of their existing or planned features that is somewhat related. This practice makes it difficult to tell who has real product and who has only *paperware*.

Trade shows and seminars allow you to see products in action and can be valuable experiences, if you remain skeptical and aware that you are seeing products in a beauty-contest atmosphere. You will see either products demonstrated by experts on carefully crafted databases for maximum "sizzle and speed" or paid performers delivering a message. You can minimize the carnival effects if you make the effort to speak one-on-one with a vendor representative and ask to see a "live," not scripted, demo where you ask the questions.

Vendor recommendations, electronic forums, systems integrators and word-of-mouth are useful sources as well. But be cautious: check the credibility of the source and the experience with projects like yours. Systems integrators rarely give advice for free but, if you have the budget you can hire them to do a needs assessment and tool selection for you. Database vendors who have products of their own to sell are usually strongly motivated to offer you their solution in order to keep competitors out. The fact that a product is sold by your RDBMS vendor, does not make it the best solution for your needs. RDBMS vendors make the majority of their profit from server sales; they have little interest in making the best possible user data-access tools and may not be intimately familiar with the needs of the end user. Word-of-mouth references from other DWAs are great if their projects succeeded within an environment that is similar to yours.

A good rule to follow is always to include the incumbent product in the group that you select for the second round. If there is any sort of data-access product in use at your organization it *must not* be excluded from the initial assessment of potential products. Even though you know it will fail the requirements or come out last in the RFI, it is necessary that it be eliminated by the official process, rather than during Stage 1.

The key selection criteria in Stage 1 are outlined in Figure

Stage 1
Understand product categories
Determine environmental compatibilities
Include incumbent product(s)
Basic research is necessary
Judge external sources by their track records

Figure 7.10 Stage 1 key considerations.

7.10. At this stage, price should not be an issue. Once you are looking at choices from the right category, make an effort to include all options, including some at all price points. In the later stages, the price will become a significant factor, as will the costs of deployment and maintenance. After applying these criteria, you should be able to select not more than 15 vendors to move into Stage 2.

Stage 2: Request for Information

Stage 2 is a technology-based screening based on responses to a request for information. During this stage, eliminate unsuitable candidates and focus on those that you wish to review in depth. The RFI is your opportunity to get the truth about product functionality directly from the vendor. Once responses are returned, the team will assess them to determine which four to six are worth taking to the third stage. Stage 2 should take four to five weeks: one week to prepare the RFI; two weeks to send it out and collect responses; one week to tabulate the results; and one week to resolve inconsistencies.

In preparation for the second stage you will have to create a fairly thorough description of your requirements. This requirements document will turn into the RFI you will send to the vendors. Full team participation is essential, but it need not be a long process. Key elements in the requirements assessment should be:

- System and technology environmental requirements: Don't ask which databases the vendors support. Ask them how well they support the databases you are planning to use.
- Tool administration architecture: Ask how the tool is set up and administered. Determine how much outside assistance or training is required initially and over time.
- Configuration and price: Find out how the product is configured and priced, but don't just ask for a price list. Describe your initial deployment and what you expect to see in six months, and ask for a price for the first and the additional cost to get to the next stage.
- Specific needs: The team may be able to identify six or eight key features or functions that the tool needs to provide, but this may be the least important aspect of the RFI. In competitive markets, vendors play feature and function leap-frog with one another which ensures that most products offer competitive features. In 12 to 18 months, the feature mix will change again as most vendors will offer a new version. Thus, compatibility with your environment and a history of vendor innovation and competitive spirit is more important to assess at this stage than the presence of specific features.

The best RFI should be about five pages, as shown in Figure 7.11. Longer RFIs take more work, but rarely produce more information; they become a survey rather than a means of choosing a product. Too much shorter and you may not be able to find the hidden weaknesses in the products. RFIs should be largely multiple choice or yes-no questions with a few short-answer questions as well. Try not to ask questions that don't produce information that you really need to make a decision. Feature lists that offer three choices—such as, Do you have this feature: "yes, no, or not yet but we have a plan"—do not produce information because 99 percent of vendors will say they have a plan to produce 100 percent of the features that are not already in a shipping product. The 1 percent who don't answer that way are either honest or have terminated development activities on the product.

In a crisp and focused RFI, you should know how you will

System	Admin	Configuration	Features

Figure 7.11 An excellent RFI will ask a focused yet comprehensive set of questions in well-defined areas that are of importance to the data warehouse project team.

value the answer to every question you ask, which are the essential right answers, the nice-to-have's, and the deal breakers. If you have done this sort of thinking ahead of time, when the responses are returned, it should not be too much work to sort them first on the essential and deal-breaker categories, then sort within the possible winners for the top four to six. An easy way to rank answers is with a three-way scale: essential, useful, and extra credit. This works for sorting, not for scoring. You can eliminate any tool that doesn't have 100 percent of the essentials, then sort by the extra credit plus useful ones.

As a matter of policy, assign each RFI to a person on the selection team so that each vendor can be called to confirm the answers to the critical questions on the RFI. When you call, try to talk to a technical person. If you can't get to tech support, call your sales rep and ask to speak with the systems engineer (SE) on your account. During that conversation about the product, you will gain a sense of the vendor's responsiveness, honesty, and reliability.

The conclusion of Stage 2 is to eliminate half the vendors that received RFIs. It is easiest to look for deal breakers and eliminate those who don't have what you need. Deal breakers at this stage are probably configuration issues because it is your obligation to make certain that the product you select will actually work in your environment. After making certain that the products will work, apply secondary factors if you still have too many options. The secondary factors include: your impression of the vendor, references, and word-of-mouth recommendations. If your dealings with the vendor through the RFI process were unsatisfactory, then consider carefully if that vendor should move forward. Questions you might ask of the team are :

Is the vendor responsive?

Did we get straight answers from them?

Is the product going to work on our size and configuration database?

What is the vendor's reputation?

Figure 7.12 summarizes the key considerations for Stage 2. While you are waiting for responses to the RFI, start building your test lab. A test lab may be as little as two computers in a room hooked up to your data warehouse on a network or it can be as elaborate as a full testing center with video cameras, mirrors, and recording equipment. The most successful end-user tool evaluation processes have been ones in which the investment was made to create a testing lab. Key for the test lab is access to a well-defined portion of the data warehouse or access to the whole thing. A lab that can only work with fake or vendor-supplied data will not help you pick which tool will work for you. You can only pick a tool for your end users if you can see how the tool works against your own data.

Stage 2
Use focused RFI to identify weaknesses
Phone interview screening
Set up test lab
Refine configuration requirements
Judge vendor responsiveness and attitude

Figure 7.12   Stage 2 key considerations.

Stage 3: Hands-On Technical Evaluation

Stage 3 is an intensive investigation led by IS to eliminate products that IS cannot or will not support. At the end of Stage 3 only two to four products should be given to end users for their final choice. The key actions in this stage are a hands-on evaluation of the products against your data warehouse. The entire team should participate; vendors can be present as well.

The most important criteria for Stage 3 are product usability, stability, and functionality. In essence, the team must determine if each product really works; if it does, how easy is it to install and how much effort will it require for ongoing training and support. Because you see the product in action, you can determine if it can connect to your warehouse using your chosen network and middleware, operating system, and security.

The initial step in this process is to request an evaluation copy of software from each Stage 3 vendor. The evaluation copy should be a full working version for the administrator; it should be exactly what the DWA will use full-time to support users post-deployment. Areas to check during this initial technical evaluation include:

■ Use of existing metadata versus required creation of other semantic layers.
■ Ease of connection to existing data warehouse schema performance during routine queries.
■ Deployment and administration features.
■ Stability and coexistence with common desktop applications.

After you've installed the software and discovered some issues is the most effective time to bring a vendor to your location to give a demonstration of the product on your own data. This gives you the chance to find out what the product can really do. It can get rough on the vendor representative, but it will certainly help you see where the limitations of the tool are. If the vendor's own presenter is working with your data and can't do the reports you need, one of two things is happening. Either your database design isn't going to support the reports that you need or the tool is missing some fundamental functionality that you will need in your environment. If the vendor can't make it work, it is unlikely that your team can make it work. This will not tell you whether the tool will be easy enough for your end users, but it will identify potential holes.

Information planners will apply their own criteria to the tools you select for end users. They will evaluate tools principally in terms of their support burden. Key for the planner is central deployment for minimal maintenance. In addition, planners will prefer products that allow for changes to the database and the metadata, that are not destructive of the user's work.

At the end of Stage 3, you should be absolutely certain that two or four of the products you brought in for an evaluation will work in your environment. Be certain that you can support the product and that your IS staff feels comfortable with the solution. Since IS professionals are hands-on people, you should encourage everyone to take time to actually use the product. By doing some "role playing" as users, report builders, and database designers, the team can get a pretty good feeling of what it will take to install and support the products. Figure 7.13 shows the major considerations for this stage.

The two to four solutions that you allow to proceed to Stage 4 must be products that you are willing to allow users to pick. You cannot allow a product that you're not going to be able to deploy to slip into the fourth stage. The whole purpose of these first three stages is to find a technology that you're confident in—to preselect options that you will be willing to accept no matter what the users say.

Stage 3
IS does hands-on evaluation
Vendor on-site
Assess functions, stability, design
Does it deliver?
Can you support it?

Figure 7.13 Stage 3 key considerations.

Stage 4: User Evaluation

During the final stage, you will pick a single product to become the standard front-end for your data warehouse. The criteria at this stage are entirely set by your users. The final stage should include both quantitative and qualitative questions about your user's reactions to the products. For example:

- Can the users in my organization make use of this product?
- Will they enjoy it?
- Is it fun to use?
- Is it easy to use?
- Will users accept it enthusiastically?

Stages 1, 2, and 3 are IS-driven; it is largely IS that makes the decisions eliminate tools. But, in Stage 4, IS steps back and allows the users to select their favorite. Of course, IS must be 100 percent confident that all of the tools considered during Stage 4 are the best and meet the "reasonableness" criteria. If you've done your job during Stages 1 through 3, then the work during this last stage is to enable your users to exercise their preference. You have ensured that you are in either Quadrant 2 or 4; now you must allow the users to pick the product that they feel is in Quadrant 4.

Ideally, you will be able to provide a lab for user testing in which you can control, monitor, and observe their reactions. Even if you don't have a lab, you must allow users to interact with the final products directly against their data. Without a lab the process will require more work as you will need to install evaluation copies of the software on selected users' desks, teach users, then collect feedback individually. You should count on allocating at least one full-time person to be the end-user support resource during the user evaluation phase of the project. This person will spend one-on-one time with each new user, to demonstrate, guide, and support. One benefit of having a lab is the ability to teach end users how to use the selected products on their own data with more concentrated staff resources. A lab also helps ensure a comparable experience on each product because you can provide a common instructor, and manage and monitor many people at one time.

In either case, there is just no substitute for having your users do their own work with real data warehouse data. But you cannot allow user evaluation to be an unguided free-for-all. Always assign common projects, tests, and examples that the users can work on for each product. A common evaluation framework allows the users to do apples to apples comparisons, and allows you to document the process and the results for subsequent use. Important questions that can be answered by live user testing are illustrated in Figure 7.14.

Training can be elaborate and extensive and take a day or more, or it can be a simple 15-minute demonstration supported by a carefully sequenced list of tasks to accomplish with the tool. Unusual things can be measured. One company measured "unsupported start-up time." After only a 15-minute demo, the users were given a workstation with the software preinstalled and ready to use. Then the clock started and time was measured until the users received data from their first query. Some users just grabbed the mouse and dove right in, others opened the manual and read from page one, and still others did a combination of both. This company measured the start-up time, then went one step further. At the conclusion of the exercise, they asked the users if it had taken the "right amount" of time to learn the tool answer. So they were able to measure both observed performance and compare that with the user's expectations and satisfaction.

When selecting data-access tools, qualitative measures are as important as the quantitative ones. Observations about user behavior can be recorded: Did the users only do the assignments

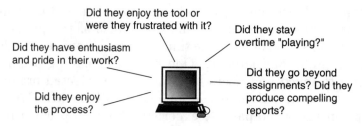

Figure 7.14 You can assess qualitative and quantitative results of user testing by observing and recording carefully.

Stage 4
User acceptance (ease of use, functionality)
Price and license negotiations begin
Team recommendations to management

Figure 7.15 Stage 4 key considerations.

or did they start working on their own questions? Did they bring questions from their desks into the lab to see if the warehouse could help? Could you tell if the users seemed to be enjoying themselves?

While the user evaluation is in progress, solicit best and final bids from the competing vendors. Get two bids: one for the initial users you will support during the first few weeks of the warehouse and the second for the expected number of users after 12 months. Projecting to company-wide deployment to try to drive today's price down, may not help you satisfy the immediate needs of your users in a timely fashion. Figure 7.15 summarizes the key action points for Stage 4.

FINAL OBSERVATIONS

As a second verification of validity of the four-stage process, it is instructive to chart each of the case studies to see how each fits the framework. As shown in Figure 7.16, there are many differences and some striking similarities between the companies studied. One striking similarity that distinguishes successful projects is the fact that they relied upon hands-on experience with the products on actual warehouse data. Five key points summarize the best practices in the evaluation and selection of end-user data-access tools.

1. It is possible to be thorough, efficient, and effective.

It is possible to do a good evaluation that is quick and well-structured. You do not need a 27-page RFI to pick the right tool. RFIs should be used for quick elimination of products that are missing capabilities, incompatible with your system, or vendor

	Company A	Company B	Company C	Company D
Stage 1 Team size How long # Tools	15 (all IS) 1 day 6	**20 (mixed)** **1 month** **8**	Subset of warehouse	Outside Consulting
Stage 2 RFI description How long # Tools	27 pages 2 months 6	**1 page** **6**	2 months	**5 pages**
Stage 3 How long # Tools	**1 month** **2**	Stages 3/4 combined 8	3	**2 months** **2**
Stage 4 Comments	Decision Rejected	Most Efficient Process	**Most** **Thorough**	Fabulous Lab

Figure 7.16 Circled practices are unusual and effective; **Boldface** practices were preferred in hindsight.

nonresponsive. In the examples reviewed, some RFIs were as short as two pages. The advantage of a brief RFI is that it takes less time for each vendor to respond and much less time for the team to read, score, and evaluate the products.

Another way to increase the efficiency and effectiveness of the process is to combine Stages 3 and 4 by running them concurrently. If the preliminary stages were thorough and reduced the number of products to four or fewer, it is possible to evaluate tools from both the IS and end-user perspective. Company B broke its large team into product subgroups with both end users and IS professionals on each subgroup. Each group member individually assessed the product, discussed it with the other group members, then the group made a presentation to the whole team. This process made virtual product *advocates* out of each group until they all saw the product presentations of the other groups. Eventually, it was a unanimous decision, although strong opinions developed around the final two products.

A great inhibitor of efficiency are inadequate resources. Ensuring that adequate resources are dedicated to the evaluation is a constant challenge for IS as other projects drain time and energy from the members of the evaluation team. Outside consultants helped Company D. By hiring a full-time resource from the outside, the warehouse tools evaluation team made certain that the lead evaluator would have enough time to become an expert in the candidate products.

2. The DWA must drive the project from inception to selection.

IS must be in control of the selection of end-user access tools. In a data warehouse environment the end-user tool is a key component of the entire systems and must therefore be provided to end users by IS. Just because IS selects and purchases software, does not mean that they should do so in a knowledge vacuum. Far from it. Of course, IS must take into consideration the needs of the end users, but IS must also ensure that the selected product is technically sound, easily maintainable, and rapidly deployable. The DWA will usually be the head of the selection team and will define the process, manage the process, and ultimately make the final decision.

Most successful evaluations include end users, and their opinions must be respected. Therefore the wise DWA will make sure that every finalist tool will work in your environment. If you don't make sure that you can support the product from a resource, installation, and maintenance perspective, your users might pick something that's easy for them but is infeasible for you. It is the job of the DWA to frame the questions, set the criteria, and gain concurrence of users, IS, and management.

3. There is no substitute for actual use of products against your own warehouse database.

If you can assemble a testing lab with dedicated equipment, it is likely to be worth the investment. But, even without a lab, you must assemble a sample of your data, in the current schema and in the selected database management system, as the basis of your end-user tools selection process. A selection is better than going against the full database, as it is possible that end-user testing might interfere with data design and loading processes that are running concurrently. You must challenge the tools and the vendor to work with your data, not theirs. If the product is missing something, you will not see it during the vendor's own demo, but you might see it when you point the tool at your own warehouse. If a common analysis is difficult, either the schema or the tool is deficient; it is better to discover that before you deploy to end users.

4. Start with the most general-purpose, versatile product as the basic access tool for your data warehouse.

If you are not considering ad hoc query and reporting tools as the first tool for the data warehouse, think again. With the rich functionality and rapid evolution of the query tool class of products, you can be confident that even an average query tool will satisfy most of your users most of the time. (Figure 7.17)

Ad hoc query tools are versatile, flexible, and powerful enough to be used frequently in production reporting systems, EIS systems, or as the access and analysis portion of data mining systems. The reverse is not the case: You can't use an EIS tool or a data mining system to do ad hoc queries. Typically, query tools are easier to maintain, easier to use, and require less training than any other type of data-access tool. The advice of the companies in this study is to pick as your initial product from the category that gives you 80 percent of what you need. Pick a query tool as your standard data warehouse access product because it will give you more of what you need with less effort. Over time you can always add to the warehouse access tool kit with other solutions, as your users and warehouse mature.

5. End users must be involved at the proper time.

If you're going to give a tool to end users, they must be involved in the process. If they're involved in the process and if they express a preference, you have to abide by their decision. The best way to make this work is to have users on the evaluation team from the beginning.

If you involve users in the process, they will be more supportive of your decisions all the way through the process and into deployment. If they have a tool that they like , but the warehouse design isn't perfect, they'll still use it. Even if the data isn't 100 percent perfect the first time, they will be enthusiastic. They

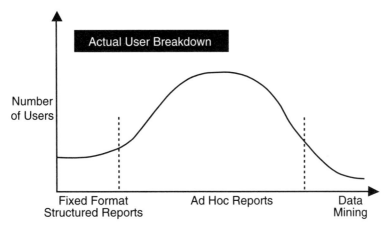

Figure 7.17 Most users of a data warehouse will have the majority of their needs met by a good query tool.

will be more patient. Is that a contradiction? How is it possible that users doing ad hoc queries against a database will be patient when they see how the process could be improved? When users start doing queries against the data warehouse they will see its imperfections and they will let you know about them. But, if they have a product they enjoy using, they will give you the time to make the changes because the product is effective anyway. All the while, with the data that is there, they'll be able to do things they've never been able to do before.

Having users on the team is good for a number of reasons. If they are part of the evaluation process, they will be able to explain the decision process, logic, and rationale when the product is being introduced to the wider user community. Those users who agree to serve on the team will be the front line of defense for those users who have other preferences or who are concerned that their needs are not being addressed.

The net result of allowing users to pick the access tool they prefer is that your users will like the warehouse. If they think well of the warehouse, they may use it more effectively and uncover those unexpected, unpredictable benefits that are the pot of gold beneath every warehouse.

Managing the Integration and Transformation Interface

Sitting between the operational environment, the data warehouse, and the ODS is the integration and transformation interface. This interface is the place where the unintegrated legacy data is integrated and sent to the data warehouse. It does not contain data; instead, it is made up of programs that process data as the data moves through the interface.

The programs that make up the integration and transformation interface are simple in concept. They read data in the legacy environment and place data in either the data warehouse or the ODS, or both. Unfortunately, the integration and transformation interface is deceptively complex, to the point that it requires its own management techniques. Much of the work life of the DWA's staff is dedicated to the management of the integration and transformation interface.

SATISFYING PARAMETERS

The integration and transformation interface must satisfy the following parameters:

- The interface must move data from one location to another.

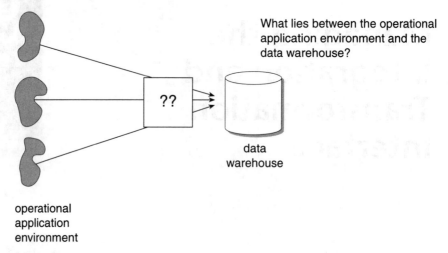

What lies between the operational application environment and the data warehouse?

??

data warehouse

operational application environment

Figure 8.1   Location of the integration and transformation interface.

- The interface must achieve integration.
- The interface must execute efficiently.
- The interface must be able to be created efficiently.
- The interface must be able to be changed easily.
- The interface must be documented in metadata.

The integration and transformation interface is one of the largest aspects of the life of the DWA and must be proactively managed. Figure 8.1 shows exactly where the integration and transformation interface lies.

LEGACY DBMS TECHNOLOGIES

The most obvious issue concerning the integration and transformation interface is dealing with the technologies found in the legacy environment (sometimes called the *source* environment). Figure 8.2 identifies the typical technologies that must be taken into consideration by the integration and transformation interface for the reading of the legacy environment.

In Figure 8.2, the technologies are, for the most part,

- older,
- transaction-oriented,

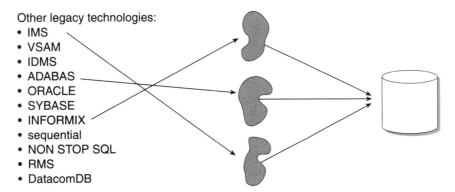

Other legacy technologies:
- IMS
- VSAM
- IDMS
- ADABAS
- ORACLE
- SYBASE
- INFORMIX
- sequential
- NON STOP SQL
- RMS
- DatacomDB

Figure 8.2 The data found in the legacy environment is wrapped up in older transaction-oriented technology.

- complex, and
- intimately tied to the applications that operate on the DBMS technology.

The DBMS technologies that house the older legacy applications usually require that the data be accessed a record at a time. This approach entails program logic that is familiar with the way the data is stored. In many cases, the data from many different subject areas is tied together by the applications. Finally, in order to execute the programs that will retrieve data from the legacy applications, it is necessary to have the legacy DBMS up and running. Finding a window of opportunity for the execution of the integration and transformation interface program becomes a problem in the face of large amounts of data that typically are found in the legacy application environment.

THE DATA WAREHOUSE DBMS TECHNOLOGIES

The source environment is large and complex. But the DBMS technologies found in the source environment are only one parameter the DWA must consider. The next consideration is the technological environment of the data warehouse (sometimes called the *target* environment), as shown in Figure 8.3. These

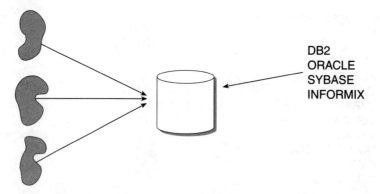

DB2
ORACLE
SYBASE
INFORMIX

Figure 8.3 The data warehouse is housed in more modern technology suited to informational processing.

technologies have the capability of

■ handling a lot of data;
■ allowing the data to be managed in parallel;
■ allowing DSS analysis to be done against the data; and
■ operating in a scalable mode.

Efficient Access of Legacy Data

The legacy data must be able to be accessed efficiently, as well. Figure 8.4 shows that it is necessary to accommodate the data structures of the legacy systems environment.

The legacy environment is made up of many different types of data structures. There are hierarchical structures, network structures, flat-file structures, and so on. Each unique structuring of data has its own efficient ways of access. The integration and transformation interface is not adequate in merely creating the syntax for efficient access of the data. Instead, the interface requires that the syntax that accesses the different legacy technologies be efficient.

Data Conversions

Although accessing the source environment and putting the results in a target environment are important, another considera-

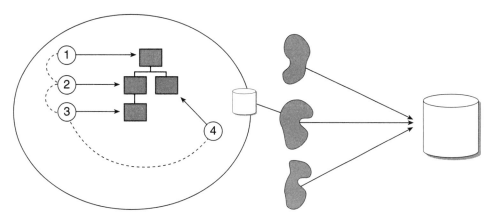

Figure 8.4   The old legacy DBMS must be accessed efficiently.

tion is the ability of the integration and transformation interface to convert from one type of data representation to another. Figure 8.5 shows an EBCDIC to ASCII conversion.

Operating System Conversions

Data type conversion is only the start of the conversion process. Another major type of conversion consideration is that of the operating system. Figure 8.6 shows a typical operating system con-

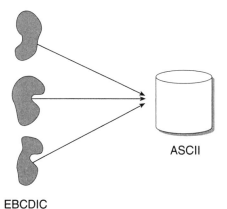

ASCII

EBCDIC

Figure 8.5   An EBCDIC to ASCII conversion is a normal proposition.

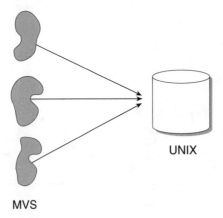

MVS

Figure 8.6 An MVS to UNIX conversion is normal in many cases.

version. The Figure 8.6 shows a conversion being made as data flows from the legacy MVS environment to the data warehouse UNIX environment.

Hardware Architecture Conversions

While the conversion shown in Figure 8.6 is very common, it is hardly the only type of conversion made. There are many other operating systems that can be a source or a target.

But a change in operating systems may be only a superficial change that signals something deeper. Often, when a change in operating systems occurs, the change really is in terms of going from one architecture to another, as shown in Figure 8.7

In Figure 8.7 the shift is made from a mainframe environment to a parallel environment. It is true that the integration and transformation interface must undergo a change in operating systems, but the change in underlying architectures is more profound. This change has major implications for:

■ The structure of data.
■ The structure of programs that run against the data.
■ The computer operations needed for each environment.
■ The software that will be available to make the environment run, and so forth.

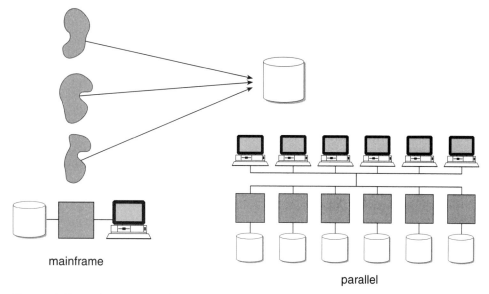

Figure 8.7   A change in hardware architectures is not unusual.

Converting Internal Structures

Not only do the data structures for the legacy environment need to be altered in order to best fit into a data warehouse environment, but the integration and transformation interface must also concern itself with internal structural changes of data. Figure 8.8 depicts an internal structural change of data as data passes from the legacy environment to the data warehouse environment.

In Figure 8.8 data elements are rearranged, deleted, and added. The internal structure of the data in the data warehouse is only vaguely reminiscent of the internal structure of the data as it existed in the legacy application environment.

Resequencing Data

Another common transformation found in the integration and transformation interface is that of resequencing data, illustrated in Figure 8.9. Resequencing often requires many resources, only where there is a small amount of data will resequencing not be a

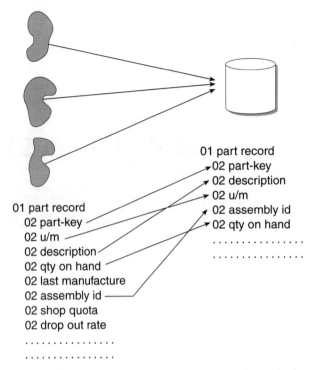

Figure 8.8 Data is reformatted as it passes from the legacy environment to the data warehouse environment.

large issue. In most cases, there is a significant amount of data passing from the legacy environment into the data warehouse environment. Therefore, the DWA must carefully plan how the resequencing will be accomplished.

Application Conversions

The most common activity that occurs in the integration and transformation interface is that of converting data. Figure 8.10 shows a simple case of conversion. Here, the legacy application designers have thought of many ways to represent something as simple as gender. One application represents gender as "m" and "f." Another application designer represents gender as "1" and "0." Yet, another application designer represents gender as "x"

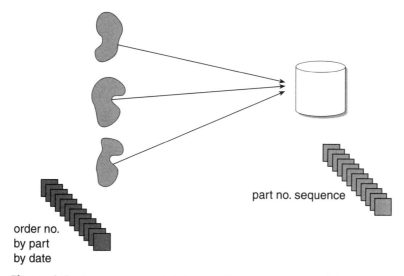

Figure 8.9 Resequencing data is sometimes necessary as data moves from the legacy environment to the data warehouse environment.

and "y," and so forth. In order to achieve uniformity at the data warehouse, there needs to be a single representation of gender. In the example shown, "m" and "f" have been chosen to represent gender. In order to achieve this state of uniformity, a conversion must be done.

The conversion shown in Figure 8.10 is a very simple one. In reality most conversions found in the integration and transformation interface are much more complex.

Choosing from Multiple Sources

Another aspect the DWA must resolve in the integration and transformation interface is deciding which source of multiple sources of data for a single field in the data warehouse is the best. The DWA needs to add logic to the data movement found in the integration and transformation interface in order to select the best source of data. Figure 8.11 shows the selection of one field from many.

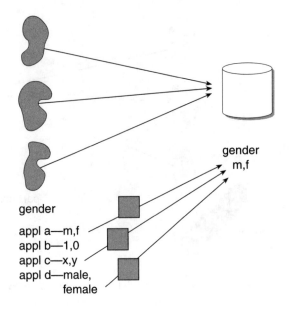

gender
m,f

gender

appl a—m,f
appl b—1,0
appl c—x,y
appl d—male,
     female

appl b

```
.........................
if source.gender = "1" then target.gender = "m"
if source.gender = "0" then target.gender = "f"
.........................
```

appl c

```
.........................
if source.gender = "x" then target.gender = "m"
if source.gender = "y" then target.gender = "f"
.........................
```

appl d

```
.........................
if source.gender = "male" then target.gender = "m"
if source.gender = "female" then target.gender = "f"
.........................
```

Figure 8.10 Conversion is a normal activity.

Supplying Default Values

The DWA also needs to supply default values when there is no source of data, as shown in Figure 8.12. The case for default values almost always occurs for a field within a record. All of the other fields have a source value except for one. The default value that is supplied can be a constant, a calculated value, or a NULL or BLANK value.

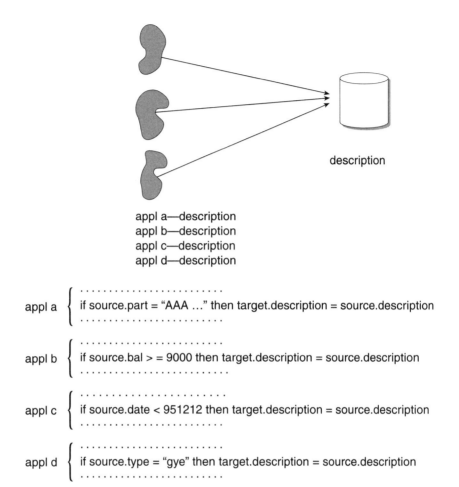

description

appl a—description
appl b—description
appl c—description
appl d—description

appl a { ....
if source.part = "AAA ..." then target.description = source.description
.... }

appl b { ....
if source.bal > = 9000 then target.description = source.description
.... }

appl c { ....
if source.date < 951212 then target.description = source.description
.... }

appl d { ....
if source.type = "gye" then target.description = source.description
.... }

Figure 8.11   In many cases, logic is needed to determine which source of data among many is the best for the data warehouse.

Selecting Data Efficiently

The DWA needs to specify selection criteria as part of the integration and transformation interface. Figure 8.13 shows that the DWA has designated certain legacy data as a candidate for supplying data for the data warehouse.

The DWA needs to be very careful of the program logic that is used to read the data in the legacy environment. If the DWA is not careful, there is a tendency to read far too many records dur-

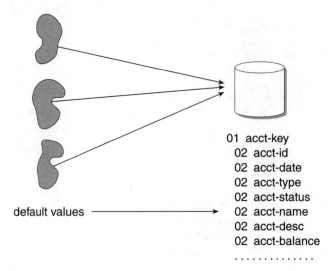

01 acct-key
  02 acct-id
  02 acct-date
  02 acct-type
  02 acct-status
  02 acct-name
  02 acct-desc
  02 acct-balance

default values

Figure 8.12 Default values need to be specified when there are no originating values.

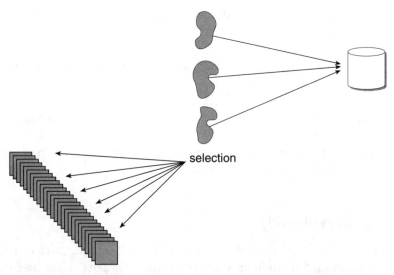

selection

Figure 8.13 Selection of records in the legacy environment must be done because not all records need to go into the data warehouse.

ing the execution of the integration and transformation interface. The selection criteria must be created so that only the legacy records that need to contribute to the data warehouse are read. The criteria also needs to be very sensitive to indexes and the physical ordering of the data in the legacy environment.

Summarizing and Aggregating Data

One of the most useful things the DWA can do to legacy data as it passes from the legacy environment to the data warehouse environment during the integration and transformation interface execution is to summarize or otherwise aggregate data, as shown in Figure 8.14. This figure is an example of the changing of the granularity of data. There is the potential for a great amount of compaction of data using this technique.

Adding an Element of Time

The integration and transformation interface is where an element of time is often added, as seen in Figure 8.15. The data

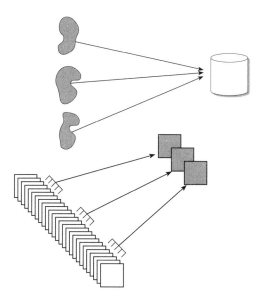

Figure 8.14 Summarization of records as they pass from the legacy environment to the data warehouse environment is a common occurrence.

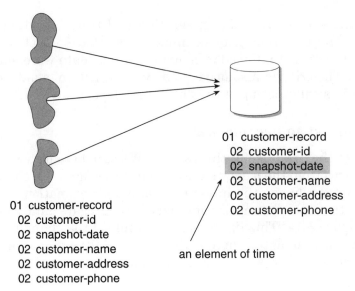

01 customer-record
  02 customer-id
  02 snapshot-date
  02 customer-name
  02 customer-address
  02 customer-phone

01 customer-record
  02 customer-id
  02 snapshot-date
  02 customer-name
  02 customer-address
  02 customer-phone

an element of time

Figure 8.15 For many kinds of data an element of time is added to the data warehouse record as the data passes from the operational environment to the data warehouse environment.

being read on the legacy side of the integration and transformation interface does not have an element of time. As the data passes into the data warehouse, the integration and transformation interface adds an element of time—in this case, "snapshot-date." Each occurrence of a record of data in the data warehouse will have an element of time associated with it. Some data naturally has an element of time, such as transaction data. But other data does not have an element of time that is naturally associated with it in the legacy environment, so it is necessary to add an appropriate element of time.

The DWA makes the specification within the integration and transformation interface. The DWA has many choices—current date, transaction date, derived date, and so forth—and specifies a date that makes business sense.

Reformatting Date Fields

As a simple example of a common conversion that occurs in the integration and transformation interface, the format of date is often

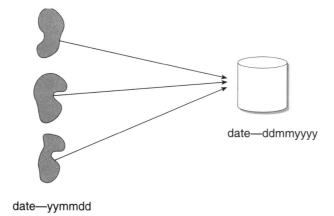

date—yymmdd

Figure 8.16 In many cases, the data needs to be restructured as it passes from one environment to another.

rearranged, as shown in Figure 8.16. The need for date conversion is particularly exacerbated by the advent of the year 2000.

CAPTURING METADATA INTERACTIVELY

The preceding has been a description of some of the major activities that will transpire during the execution of the integration and transformation interface. There are other types of activities that need to be done as well. However, throughout the entire integration and transformation process, metadata needs to be gathered, as shown in Figure 8.17.

The metadata that is gathered during the integration and transformation process is one of the most important aspects of the metadata infrastructure. Taking the gathering of the metadata for granted or assigning the metadata the role of documentation (that never gets done) is a strategic mistake.

BUILDING THE INTERFACE MANUALLY OR BY AUTOMATION

One of the most important decisions the DWA makes is whether to build the integration and transformation interface by hand or

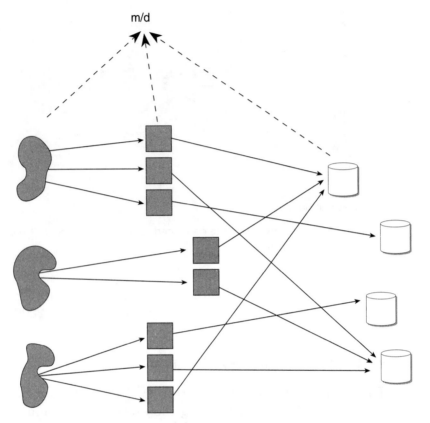

Figure 8.17 With all of the other functions that need to be performed, capturing metadata needs to be done as well.

using a tool of automation. Figure 8.18 illustrates this very important decision.

There are definite advantages and disadvantages to using a tool of automation for this purpose:

Advantages of no tool

- You can start immediately.
- You can use programmers that might otherwise be idle.
- The programmers can program around any set of logic.

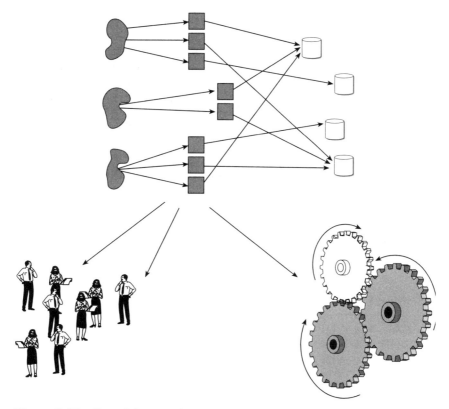

Figure 8.18 One of the most important decisions to be made is whether to create the legacy and data warehouse interface manually or in an automated manner.

Disadvantages of no tool

- There are many programs that have to be built; the logic that a programmer employs becomes intellectually boring after the first four or five programs.
- No metadata is gathered automatically.
- The programs require a lot of time to build.
- The programs are constantly changing and maintenance becomes a burden.
- The cost of building the infrastructure is prohibitive.

Advantages of a tool

- The programs can be built quickly.
- The programs can be maintained quickly and easily.
- Metadata is produced automatically.
- It is easy to change target DBMS or target operating systems.
- The costs are driven down significantly.

Disadvantages of a tool

- There is a learning curve required to use the tool.
- Some logic and some technologies are not easily handled by the tool.

The considerations of the DWA are both technological and economic when addressing the issue of using a tool of automation.

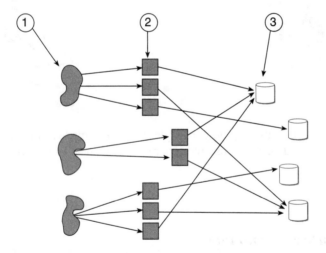

Changes to the data warehouse infrastructure:

1. The operational environment changes.
2. The logic of transformation changes.
3. The data warehouse changes.

Figure 8.19 Because of the iterative nature of DSS processing and the constantly changing legacy environment, the data warehouse infrastructure constantly has to be maintained.

Creating the integration and transformation layer is only one aspect of managing the interface. The longer more important side of managing the integration and transformation interface involves managing change to the interface. The integration and transformation interface is especially subject to change because of several factors.

First, development in the data warehouse environment is iterative. It is the very nature of system-building in a DSS environment that they are built iteratively, in small, fast spurts. Because of the iterative nature of development, the integration and transformation interface changes often, much more so than a similar system in the operational environment.

Second, the underlying operational environment is constantly changing. Every time the operational environment changes, the integration and transformation interface also must be changed.

Figure 8.19 shows the integration and transformation infrastructure and the places where changes are effected. The first place the interface changes is in the operational environment. The second place is in the logic of the interface itself, and the third place is in the data warehouse itself.

THE INTEGRATION AND TRANSFORMATION INTERFACE AND THE DWA

Administering the integration and transformation interface is a big task, perhaps on an ongoing basis, the largest task of the DWA. Figure 8.20 outlines some of the major considerations of the DWA. The DWA must do the following:

- Ensure that there is proper alignment of the integration and transformation interface with the definition of the system of record.
- Design the data warehouse properly.
- Create the integration and transformation interface so that the programs that are created will execute efficiently.
- Schedule the integration and transformation interface for execution.

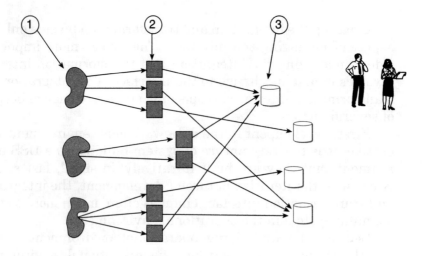

- proper definition of the system of record
- proper design of the data warehouse
- efficiency of execution of the programs
- scheduling for execution
- transport of data from the legacy environment to the data warehouse environment
- periodic maintenance of the interface
- constant addition to the interface
- meeting the technological challenge

Figure 8.20 Administering the integration and transformation layer.

■ Ensure that the legacy data, once selected and transformed, is sent to the proper place and that once sent, arrives there.
■ Periodically maintain the interface.
■ Constantly add to the interface as new iterations of development occur.
■ Use the proper technology for the execution of the interface.

SUMMARY

The integration and transformation interface is one of the most important and tedious aspects of the professional life of the

DWA. The interface is complicated by its many aspects. The integration and transformation interface must take into account:

- Older legacy DBMS technology.
- Newer data warehouse technology.
- Efficient access of legacy data.
- Conversion to or from ASCII to EBCDIC.
- Conversion from one operating system to another.
- Conversion from one hardware architecture to another.
- Reformatting of internal data structures.
- Resequencing of data.
- Application conversions.
- Supplying default values where there is no source.
- Selecting from multiple sources of data.
- Selecting data for refreshment efficiently.
- Summarizing and aggregating data.
- Adding an element of time.
- Restructuring date values, and so forth.

One of the most important decisions the DWA will make is whether to try to build the interface by hand or by tools of automation.

OLAP and the Data Warehouse Environment

Online analytical processing (OLAP) is an important method in the data warehouse architecture by which data can be turned into information. As such, OLAP is typically implemented at either the departmental or individual levels of the data warehouse, as depicted in Figure 9.1. As data warehouse users' understanding of the capabilities of DSS processing increases and as the volume of data grows, the need for more sophisticated techniques to facilitate the use of the data warehouse environment increases.

DEFINITION OF OLAP

The OLAP Council defines online analytical processing (OLAP) as "a category of software technology that enables analysts, managers, and executives to gain insight into data through fast, consistent, interactive access to a wide variety of possible views of information that has been transformed from raw data to reflect the real dimensionality of the enterprise as understood by the user." More succinctly, OLAP is a set of functionality that attempts to facilitate multidimensional analysis. Multidimensional analysis (MDA) is the ability to manipulate data that has been aggregated into various categories or "dimensions." Accord-

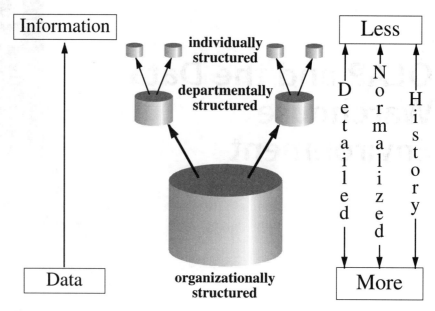

Figure 9.1 The data warehouse architecture.

ing to the OLAP Council, the purpose of multidimensional analysis is to "[help] the user synthesize enterprise information through comparative, personalized viewing, as well as through analysis of historical and projected data."

OLAP is a natural extension of the data warehouse. Indeed, the departmentally structured level of the data warehouse, from the earliest descriptions of the data warehouse architecture, is ideal for addressing OLAP processing. This level of data is also called the OLAP or "data mart" level of DSS processing. Figure 9.2 shows the different names for the departmental level of the data warehouse architecture.

Architecture-Based OLAP Rules

A set of rules of OLAP have evolved from a variety of sources. Many of these so-called rules are really guidelines for vendors of analysis tools and other products, often referred to as OLAP servers, and are not data-specific. Those rules that can be applied to a data architecture as provided by the data warehouse are listed in Figure 9.3.

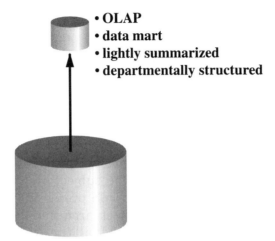

• **OLAP**
• **data mart**
• **lightly summarized**
• **departmentally structured**

**organizationally structured atomic
detailed data warehouse data**

Figure 9.2   Different names of the departmental level of the data warehouse.

• Multidimensional conceptual view
• Transparency
• Accessibility
• Constant reporting performance
• Client-Server architecture
• Generic dimensionality
• Unrestricted cross-dimensional operation
• Intuitive data manipulation
• Flexible reporting
• Unlimited dimension and aggregation levels
• Detail (row-level) drill down
• Incremental database refresh
• Multiple arrays
• Subset selection
• Local data support

Figure 9.3   Architecture-based OLAP rules.

How does the data warehouse architecture support these rules of OLAP? The following sections address each of the specified rules in the context of the data warehouse, and not from the perspective of how a technology or tool should behave.

Multidimensional Conceptual View

The atomic level (current level of detail or organizationally structured level) of the data warehouse provides for the capture of all of the attributes of any given subject area that are appropriate and necessary to support DSS processing for the organization. Any attribute of a subject area can be considered a dimension for the data it describes. If all the attributes needed to support DSS processing have been modeled and the data captured, then any conceptual combination of dimensions can be facilitated in the data warehouse environment.

Transparency

Access to any level of the data warehouse, including metadata, should be transparent to the user. Also, access to and use of any available attribute of data in the data warehouse as a dimension should be transparent to the user as well. From those standpoints, the needs for transparency are met. However, the intent of transparency should not be to provide access to operational data for informational purposes. The data warehouse architecture is necessary to physically separate informational data and processing from operational data and processing, based on the different business purposes that they serve.

Accessibility

If you cannot access the data, then you are not able to turn it into information. The data warehouse supports accessibility of data by physically separating it from the operational environment, structuring it to meet the breadth and depth of the organization's requirements for information through the different levels of the architecture, and providing essential metadata to describe it.

Consistent Reporting Performance

An architected data warehouse with time-variant data and properly maintained metadata will provide consistent results through time. The issue here can be one of the definition of *consistency*. The nonvolatile nature of the data warehouse provides for maintaining the historical accuracy of data; that is, the data in the warehouse is the same today as when it was extracted from its system of record. However, definitions, business rules for data acquisition, and reference data may, and will, change over time. Metadata provides the historical link from the present to the past, and the effective use of metadata will ensure consistent reporting results.

However, if the intent of the term "consistent reporting performance" is that the run time, response time, or machine utilization for any given query be consistent every time it is run, regardless of environmental or other circumstances (such as network traffic, database locking, processor load, badly fragmented local disk, etc.), then this is not only a technology issue, but an unrealistic one as well.

Client/Server Architecture

The data warehouse is an architecture and not a technology. As such, it is platform-independent. A client/server physical architecture helps separate the data acquisition, data access, and data manipulation processing functions, as well as the processing requirements of different levels of the data warehouse architecture. The data warehouse can take advantage of the current state-of-the-art of technology, but the design of the data warehouse to meet the informational requirements of the organization should not be constrained by any technology.

Generic Dimensionality

From a data modeling standpoint, all of the attributes of a given entity should be able to be grouped logically and be available for access and analysis in the form of dimensions. However, other than time, attributes, and therefore dimensions, are usually specific to a given subject. There may be shared or common definitions, but dimensions, by definition, describe the data for which they are a characteristic.

Within the data warehouse architecture, any attribute that is needed as a dimension by a target user should be available to that user as a dimension. In this regard, all dimensions, and the attributes or groups of attributes that they represent, are "generic."

Unrestricted Cross-Dimensional Operations

The data warehouse does support unrestricted cross-dimensional operations. This is usually referred to as *drill-across*. The only limitation will be the design of the database. If the atomic data is designed to capture all of the (appropriate based on business requirements) dimensions of an entity, then departmental levels can be constructed to support any cross-dimensional operation.

Intuitive Data Manipulation

"Intuitive" is a subjective term. What may be obvious to one person may be meaningless to another. This is where metadata is essential because it provides definitions of the data in a business context for all users, so that "intuitive" perceptions of a data element or business rule can be verified and used with greater understanding and certainty. No tool can take the place of education, and an understanding of how data and the resulting information can and should be used to support the business objectives of the organization.

Flexible Reporting

At this point, the rules seem to be getting a bit redundant. If data can be accessed in a multidimensional conceptual manner with unrestricted cross-dimensional operations and can be manipulated intuitively, that would seem to be pretty flexible already. However, it still falls back to how the atomic and departmental levels of the data warehouse have been structured. If the atomic level is at the appropriate level of detail with the necessary attributes and robust historical integrity, and the departmental level or data mart is designed to meet the focused informational requirements of the target users, then there should be adequate flexibility to meet those users' needs. If the data mart does not meet their needs, then it can be rebuilt or replaced by another data mart sourced from the atomic level of the data warehouse. If the atomic level does not contain the necessary data, then it can be enhanced to include, and the necessary data acquisition programs modified or constructed to capture that data.

Unlimited Dimension and Aggregation Levels

Again, this functionality would depend on how the atomic level of the data warehouse is designed. The data warehouse architecture supports the ability to do this. The architecture should also be flexible enough, as mentioned in the preceding section, to be modified to meet the organization's evolving requirements for data and information.

Detail (Row-Level) Drill-Down

The architected data warehouse will support some drill-down capabilities at both the individual and departmental levels, with the ultimate ability to drill down to the atomic level, provided that the level has been designed properly. Understanding how to utilize a given level of the data warehouse and which level contains which degree of data granularity can be determined from appropriately maintained metadata.

Incremental Database Refresh

The time-variant nature of the data warehouse requires that data be periodically added, appended, inserted, or updated, depending on the characteristics of the data, how it behaves in the system of record and the organization's informational requirements for it. The data warehouse architecture is designed to facilitate this capability, as are relational database management systems. Unfortunately the multidimensional database management systems available today do not support incremental refreshing of data; the entire database must be reloaded with the current and the new data in order to reflect incremental changes. For this reason, multidimensional databases are not yet at the stage technologically where they can adequately support the atomic level of a data warehouse. However, they can be very effective tools for implementing a data mart at the departmental level of the data warehouse, if the volume of data needing to be refreshed and the frequency of the refresh are manageable.

Multiple Arrays

This is one of the techniques used to facilitate managed redundancy, and is especially effective at populating the departmental and individual levels of the data warehouse. The data warehouse can and should support the appropriate number and kinds of arrays to meet the informational requirements of the different target users. However, the ability to manipulate multiple arrays simultaneously is a function of the end users' data access knowledge and skill, and the tools being used.

Subset Selections

Selecting subsets from the atomic level of the data warehouse is one of the techniques used to populate the departmental and individual levels. Also, it is a form of managed redundancy at the atomic level, where a subset of the atomic data may be summarized for general consumption by the end-user community as a whole. The data warehouse architecture, with the existence of metadata to effectively describe the data so that a subset can be selected properly, supports this feature of OLAP.

Local Data Support

The data warehouse architecture supports physically locating the data as close to the end user as appropriate. A decentralized implementation of the data warehouse architecture, especially at the departmental and individual levels, is one of its most powerful features. As mentioned in the chapter on managing metadata, special care should be given to providing the appropriate metadata to each local instance of data.

THE SOURCE OF OLAP DATA

The OLAP level of data originates from the organizationally structured level (current level of detail) of data in the data warehouse. This detailed, historical data is the heart of the data warehouse and forms a perfect foundation for the OLAP level of data. The organizationally structured level of data is fed by the operational environment and, in turn, feeds the OLAP level. Figure 9.4 shows the relationship between the organizationally structured level of data in the data warehouse and the OLAP level of data.

Some of the characteristics of the OLAP level of data are:

- **Smallness.** Compared to the organizationally structured level of data, there is far less data that resides in OLAP. As a rule, there are two to three orders of magnitude less data in an OLAP environment than in an organizationally structured (current level of detail) environment.
- **Flexibility.** OLAP processing is much more flexible than that which occurs at the organizationally structured level of data warehouse processing. OLAP is flexible because there is much less data to contend with and the software found at the

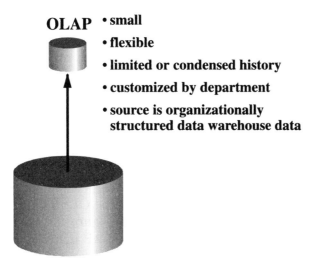

OLAP
- small
- flexible
- limited or condensed history
- customized by department
- source is organizationally structured data warehouse data

Figure 9.4 Characteristics of the departmental level of the data warehouse.

OLAP level is designed for flexibility. In contrast, the software found managing the organizationally structured level is designed to manage large amounts of data.

■ **Limited History.** The OLAP environment rarely contains as much history at the same level of detail as maintained in the organizationally structured level of the data warehouse. The organizationally structured level typically contains from 5 to 10 years worth of detailed data, while the departmentally structured OLAP data will either contain a similar time span of much more condensed data or a much smaller time span of similar detail.

■ **Customized.** The OLAP environment is customized by department to suit the particular needs of the business function that owns and manages it. The detailed data in the data warehouse is truly organizational (or corporate) in nature.

■ **Pre-Categorized.** Departmentally structured data in the OLAP environment is usually organized into predefined categories to facilitate the informational requirements of a specific department, while organizationally structured data maintains all of the categories required for the entire corporate structure.

■ **Source.** The source of data for OLAP is the detailed data found in the organizationally structured level. The source of data for the organizationally structured level is the operational environment.

DIFFERENCES BETWEEN OLAP AND ORGANIZATIONALLY STRUCTURED DATA WAREHOUSE DATA

There are many significant differences between the departmentally structured (OLAP) and the organizationally structured levels of the data warehouse. One of the most important aspects of the OLAP environment is its departmental customization. Figure 9.5 shows that different instances of the OLAP environment can exist for different departments. In Figure 9.5 there is an OLAP instance for finance, a separate OLAP instance for sales and yet another instance for marketing, all originating from the organizationally structured level of the data warehouse.

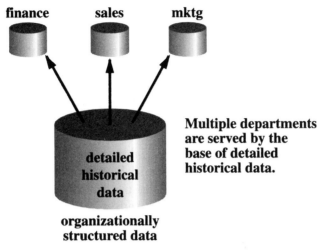

Figure 9.5   Multiple departmental instances.

Figure 9.6 shows the methods by which the customization for a department from data in the organizationally structured level of the data warehouse to the OLAP level can be achieved. The customization for a department can take many forms, such as:

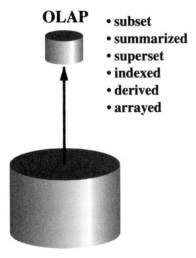

OLAP
- subset
- summarized
- superset
- indexed
- derived
- arrayed

Figure 9.6   Techniques for creating departmental data.

- **Subsets.** Finance will select some detailed data while marketing will select other detailed data.
- **Aggregations.** Accounting will summarize its data one way, while finance will summarize its another way. These different approaches may apply to different data being summarized, to different ways in which the aggregated results are calculated, or to different sets of categories by which the aggregated data is organized.
- **Supersets.** One department will denormalize its OLAP data by joining data from tables A and B, while another department will join data from tables B and C.
- **Indexing.** One department will index its data on keys ABC and BCD, while another department will index the same data on keys CDE and DEF, and so forth, to provide more optimal search paths that meet their different departmental requirements for informational processing.
- **Derivations.** A department may want a particular metric precomputed and the results stored in its OLAP environment. A similar metric may be stored at the organizationally structured level, but the department wants to compare its department-specific calculation to the organization-standard one.
- **Arrays.** In order to make the data in its OLAP more useful, a department may opt to create an array of data to assist it in its informational goals. For example, data that is stored one record per month in the organizationally structured detail may be required as an array of 13 months to represent a contiguous year *and* facilitate current-year-previous-month analysis.

There are as many ways to customize the data for a department as there are departments. Indeed, a department is not limited to a single OLAP instance, but may require several OLAP environments to meet all of the department's business requirements for information.

The data that feeds the OLAP environment is the detailed data of the organizationally structured level of the data warehouse. Because this data is organizational in nature, it is not optimized to suit the needs of any given department.

One of the issues that naturally arises in the customization

organizationally structured data

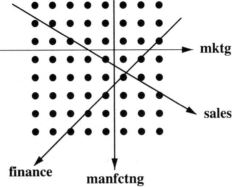

Different departments look at the same detailed data in different ways. Without the detailed, organizationally structured data as a foundation, there is no reconcilability of data.

Figure 9.7 Organizationally structured data.

of OLAP environments is that of data reconcilability. With each department taking its own perspective of the corporate data found in the data warehouse, isn't there a problem with a loss of data reconcilability? The answer is "no." Figure 9.7 illustrates why. It shows that the same detailed data is looked at in many different ways by different departments. Because all departments are operating from the same foundation of detailed data, there is always reconcilability of data; however, the departmental data is customized. In this way, detailed data provides a very satisfactory foundation for OLAP processing.

Another way in which organizationally structured data forms a very good foundation for departmental OLAP processing is that the price of creating this detailed foundation must be paid for only once. Suppose an OLAP environment is to be created for the financial planning department. It is no small task to create the proper detailed foundation. But once the detailed foundation is created for the financial planning OLAP effort, then the very same foundation can be used for the sales OLAP effort, for the accounting OLAP effort, and so forth. Once the organizationally structured environment is created, there is no further incremental cost to the use of the detailed data found therein. As many OLAP environments as desired can take advantage of the organizationally structured data once built.

OLAP WITH NO ORGANIZATIONALLY STRUCTURED DATA

The designer who is building the OLAP environment may be tempted not to build the organizationally structured level of the data warehouse, and just build OLAP immediately on top of the operational environment. After all, the organizationally structured level of the data warehouse is

■ expensive,
■ complex, and
■ not easy to build.

Figure 9.8 depicts the problems associated with skipping the organizationally structured level of the data warehouse in support of OLAP environments. These can take one of two forms: the direct end-user access (the *virtual* data warehouse) and unarchitected OLAP data marts.

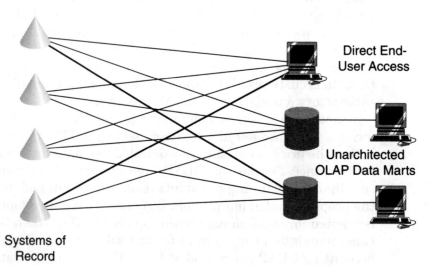

Figure 9.8 Direct access to operational data for informational purposes.

Building OLAP directly on top of the operational environment is a grave mistake for a variety of reasons:

■ The operational environment is not designed to support integrated processing, but the OLAP environment *assumes* that data integration has been done somewhere prior to it.
■ The operational environment contains only a limited amount of historical data. The OLAP environment *requires* historical data.
■ Each OLAP instance must build its own customized interface to the operational environment. The development effort to do this is not trivial.
■ Each OLAP instance puts an additive drag on the performance of the operational environment. The collective drag of many OLAP environments is very significant.

For these reasons (and many more!), building the OLAP environment directly from the operational environment is a very poor idea, indeed. Note the number of times that the systems of record must be accessed in order to provide data for access or populate unarchitected data marts. Each extract "line" represents a cost to the organization in terms of processing time and resources, and provides an opportunity for the resultant data in the target environments to be inconsistent. Figure 9.9 represents the architected data warehouse environment, where the departmental level of the data warehouse supplies an OLAP environment for those users who require it.

EXPLORERS, FARMERS, AND TOURISTS

Because of the differences in the volume of data found in the two environments and the difference in direct end-user interfaces, there is a difference in the communities of users who access the data warehouse. As a rule, the organizationally structured data serves the explorer community while the OLAP environment serves the farmer and tourist communities. Figure 9.10 depicts these differences.

The detailed data serves the explorer community because it is organizationally oriented (corporate), supports random access,

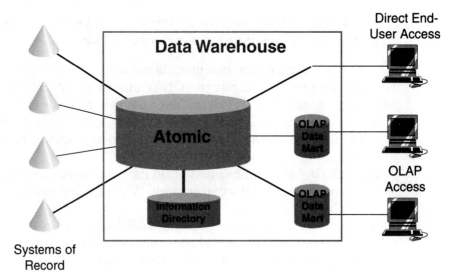

Figure 9.9 The data warehouse architected solution for OLAP.

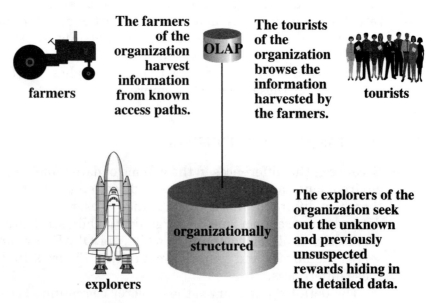

Figure 9.10 Farmers, explorers, and tourists.

and is complete and historical. The OLAP environment supports the farmer community because the data is customized before it is sent to the OLAP environment. In order to customize the data, it is necessary to know how the data is to be used; the farmers of the world can foretell this. The farmers are make these decisions based on how the tourists consume their products. In other words, supply and demand applies to the data warehouse architecture in determining what needs to be populated in the OLAP environment.

There are some exceptions to this rule of the different communities of users. Because of the limited amount of data found there, the large number of indexes, and the elegance of the interface, some exploration can be done in the OLAP environment. But OLAP-level exploration is cursory, looking at the broad picture, not the detailed one. For the most part, the OLAP environment exists for and is optimal for the farmer and tourist communities, not the explorer community.

OLAP AND THE WORKLOAD

One of the interesting benefits of building an OLAP environment is the redistribution of workload from data access (queries) only against the organizationally structured data, to a combination of data acquisition from the organizationally structured environment to the OLAP environment, and data access against both. Figure 9.11 depicts these differences before and after the OLAP environment is built.

When there is no OLAP environment, all queries *must* be run in the organizationally structured environment. There simply is no other choice. Running all queries in the organizationally structured environment may be no problem as long as there is not much data there or as long as not much processing is occurring there.

But, the instant that there is much data in the organizationally structured environment or considerable processing against that environment to facilitate data access, then the need for the OLAP environment becomes apparent. Some of the factors that accelerate the need for an OLAP environment to fa-

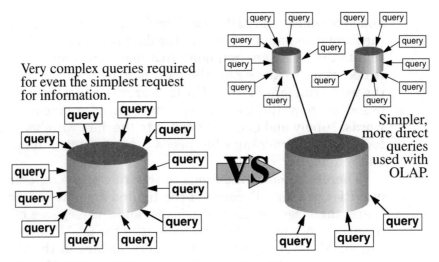

Figure 9.11 OLAP shifts the workload profoundly!

cilitate more efficient data access in the quest to turn data into information include:

■ Preaggregating data for better performance.
■ Precategorizing data for enhanced understanding and usability by end users.
■ Standardizing calculation, metrics, and other derived data to ensure accuracy throughout the organization.
■ One access point (organizationally structured data) vs. many (OLAP data).
■ And so forth.

Once the OLAP environment is created, the bulk of the queries are executed away from the organizationally structured environment. Note that not all queries are shifted to the OLAP environment. Even in the most mature DSS environment, there are always a number of queries that simply cannot be done outside the organizationally structured environment of the data warehouse. Corporate data explorers must certainly have access to this detailed data. The level of detail or type of data that is needed is such that *only* queries at the organizationally structured level will suffice.

The shift of query processing from the organizationally structured level of the data warehouse to an OLAP environment has much to be said about it:

- It is economical.
- It is highly flexible.
- It allows customization of data to occur for a given department.
- It takes advantage of different software to meet different requirements, residing on the OLAP platform.
- It allows significant portions of data to be isolated.
- It allows subsets of data to be isolated.
- And so forth.

MYSTERIES OF THE HYPERCUBE REVEALED

The problem with providing drill-down, drill-across and slice-and-dice capabilities has been that data has historically been stored in two-dimensional formats. Flat-files and relational database management systems (RDBMSs) are, by definition, two-dimensional. An RDBMS maintains tables that are made up of columns that describe rows of data; a flat-file can easily have a tabular definition applied to it as well. Analyzing data by only two dimensions is limiting; most information users need to look at data in a variety of ways. Sales results by distribution channel and by product would be a two-dimensional view of an organization's sales data. Add the ability to view data over time, and there are now three dimensions by which the user wants to manipulate the data. Figure 9.12 illustrates this simple three-dimensional model of data.

In order to manipulate data in multiple dimensions, a metaphor known as a *hypercube* is used to visually represent multidimensional data. Figure 9.13 illustrates how the hypercube can be used to visualize the "slicing and dicing" of the sales data in the three selected dimensions.

However, since the data warehouse is time-variant by definition, using the z-axis of the hypercube to represent time does not accomplish true multidimensional analysis. Time is a component of every entity in the data warehouse; therefore, time

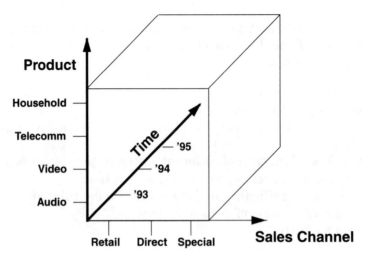

Figure 9.12 A supposed three-dimensional view of sales data.

must be a component of every analysis, whether one or many time periods are being analyzed. If instead of time you used another "by" category for the z-axis of the hypercube, such as customer location, then the three dimensions would be more accurately described for a single time period, as seen in Figure

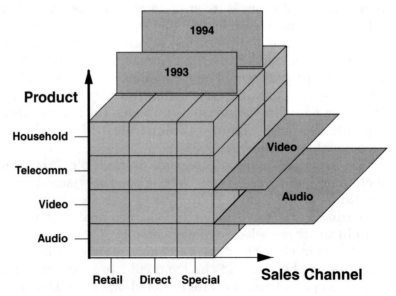

Figure 9.13 "Slicing and dicing" the data.

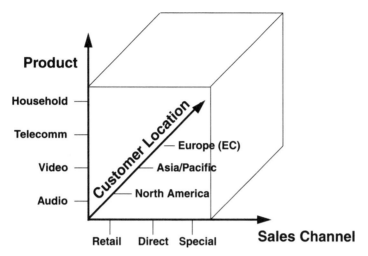

Figure 9.14   A "true" three dimensional view of data.

9.14. Figure 9.15 illustrates the "slicing and dicing" with these new dimensions.

Since the data warehouse is time-variant, *cubes* of data can be constructed for multiple time periods and the data analyzed

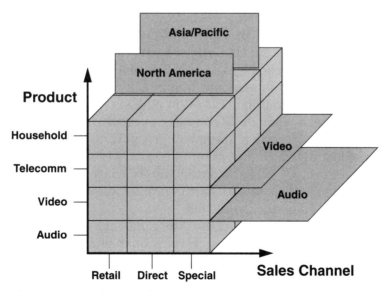

Figure 9.15   "Slicing and dicing" the "True" three-dimensional data.

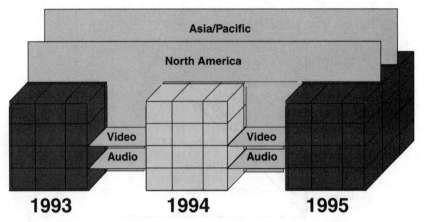

Figure 9.16 "Slicing and dicing" across multiple time periods.

across these time periods, as depicted in Figure 9.16. Four dimensions are effectively being used to analyze the sales data, but this is a more accurate representation of the role that time plays in multidimensional analysis in the data warehouse environment.

Providing the ability to analyze the data in this manner can be accomplished with a relational database without too much difficulty. However, in order to do so, the data being analyzed must usually be queried and returned in a more granular format, then organized by the analysis tool so that it can be examined in a multidimensional manner. A mistake that users and data warehouse supporters often make is in trying to access the data through a single SQL query to return it in a multidimensional manner. Such a query will probably be overly complex and cause the RDBMS's query optimizer to "choke." A more realistic approach is to return the data in appropriate sets or subsets and allow the analysis tool to manipulate the data in order to provide multidimensional capabilities.

The hypercube is a useful metaphor for describing multidimensional data. However, three dimensions (excluding time) are often insufficient for a user's analysis purposes; representing more than three dimensions with a cube is difficult. If, for example, in addition to sales channel, product, and customer lo-

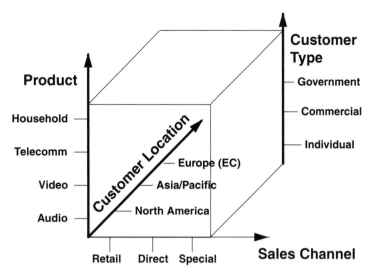

Figure 9.17 Four-dimensional view of data.

cation, a user wanted to analyze the sales data by customer type, the number of dimensions would be four, as illustrated in Figure 9.17.

Add the reality that time is a dimension for processing purposes and the total number of dimensions is now five. It is at this point that multidimensional analysis begins to pose a problem for relational and "flat" data.

DRILL-DOWN PROCESSING

If, in the hypothetical sales analysis, the user wanted to manipulate the data by supplier or selling location in addition to sales channel, product, and customer geography, these categories would not add additional dimensions. Supplier is probably an attribute of product; selling location is probably a level within the hierarchy that makes up each sales channel. The aggregation of data to some level of a hierarchy is not an essential component of multidimensional analysis, but represents the ability to *drill down* through levels of detail. For example, Figure 9.18 shows what the hierarchy of sales channel might be.

Higher Level
of Aggregation

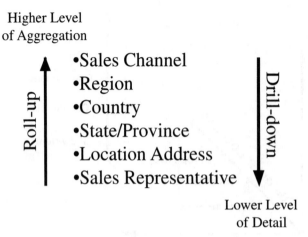

Lower Level
of Detail

Figure 9.18 Example sales channel hierarchy.

Sales Channel represents the highest level of aggregation and Sales Rep, the lowest level of detail. Geographic location is a *roll-up* of the detail to either Region, Country, State or Province, or Store Address, depending on the business requirements of the user. Likewise, the user may want to *begin* his analysis at a higher level of aggregation, then drill down through the different levels to a lower level of detail to get a different perspective of what made up the amounts at the higher level. Rolling up and drilling down are useful *features* of the OLAP environment while performing multidimensional analysis, but different levels of a hierarchy are not different dimensions in and of themselves; therefore, they are not considered a *requirement* for providing multidimensional capabilities.

Figure 9.19 shows the OLAP support of drill-down processing. There are two types of drill-down processing that are relevant: inter-OLAP drill-down processing and OLAP-to-organizationally structured data drill-down processing. Inter-OLAP drill-down processing is used to show the relationships of summarization between the different instances of data within the OLAP environment. This is also known as *drill-across*. More detailed data exists at the organizationally structured level of the data warehouse, which supports a further level of drill-down beyond the design of each departmental OLAP instance.

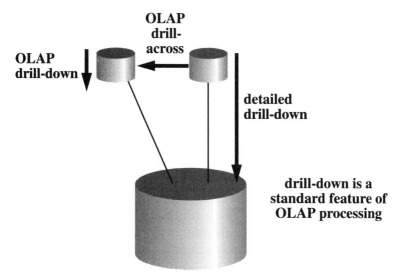

Figure 9.19   OLAP drill-down and drill-across.

SUMMARY

Online analytical processing, or OLAP, has been defined by a set of rules, most of which can be addressed by the data warehouse architecture. Some of these rules are directed at specific technologies, such as database management systems or end-user access tools, and are therefore not pertinent when discussing an architected solution for meeting an organization's informational requirements. However, for those rules that are architectural in nature, the data warehouse facilitates them easily.

As with data marts, there is a temptation to create an OLAP environment that is stand-alone, independent of an architected data warehouse environment. While this may meet an immediate need for information for one group—or even several groups—within the organization, this unarchitected approach will quickly lead to a collection of stand-alone informational environments that are difficult to manage and do not provide consistent data that can be trusted throughout the organization. OLAP capabilities should be incorporated as part of an overall informational architecture, populated with data from the atomic (current detail) level of the data warehouse and fulfilling a departmental level set of business requirements for information. In this way, the OLAP environment is part of a total information architecture and enjoys such benefits from membership in such an architecture as metadata, integrated data based on organizational standards, and a high degree of data integrity.

In summary, OLAP can be accomplished by using the data warehouse as the *architected foundation* for the organization's informational processing requirements, either in an enterprise-wide or distributed manner. Use the appropriate *design techniques* to ensure that the data required for informational processing is at the appropriate degree of granularity to support the entire organization's requirement (atomic data), and at the appropriate degree of summarization, selection, denormalization, or other technique (such as a star schema) at the departmental level. Then, use the appropriate tools to either *access* relational data in a multidimensional manner, or *manage* multidimensional data directly.

Managing OLAP in the Data Warehouse Environment

As the data warehouse users' understanding of the capabilities of informational or decision support processing increases, there is a corresponding increase in the need for more sophisticated techniques to facilitate the use of the data warehouse environment. Online analytical processing (OLAP) can be a useful technology. But, as with all technologies aimed at turning data into information, the easier it is for the end users to understand and access that information, the more work is required to support and maintain those capabilities.

DATA MODELING FOR OLAP

The OLAP environment may or may not have a data model built for it, as shown in Figure 10.1. The use of a data model in the environment is questionable because the environment is subject to change at a moment's notice. The high degree of flexibility of the OLAP environment is such that some types of data and results are created and destroyed faster than they can be modeled. On the other hand, some of the data in the OLAP environment is very stable and, in fact, *should* be modeled. Whether a model is applicable depends on the kind of data being considered. There

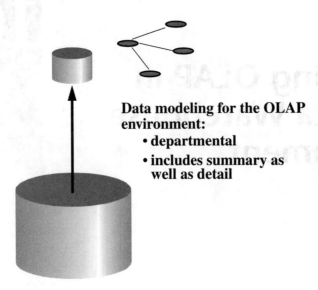

Data modeling for the OLAP environment:
- departmental
- includes summary as well as detail

Figure 10.1 Data modeling for the OLAP environment.

are several important kinds of data found in the OLAP environment:

- Permanent detailed data
- Nonpermanent detailed data
- Static summary data
- Dynamic summary data

Figure 10.2 shows the different types of data found in the OLAP environment.

Permanent detailed data comes from the organizationally structured (Atomic) level and is regularly needed in OLAP processing. It is detailed from the standpoint of the department that owns the OLAP platform. In actuality, the OLAP permanent detailed data may well be summarized as it passes from the organizationally structured level of the data warehouse into the OLAP environment. In that respect, what is detailed in any one instance of the OLAP environment may be summarized from the perspective of the corporate DSS analyst. Referring back to Figure 10.1, the data warehouse architecture supports maintaining

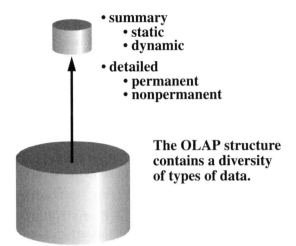

• **summary**
  • **static**
  • **dynamic**

• **detailed**
  • **permanent**
  • **nonpermanent**

**The OLAP structure
contains a diversity
of types of data.**

Figure 10.2   Data modeling for the OLAP structure.

the appropriate level of detail and summarization to support the informational requirements of the entire organization, as well as the different functional requirements of different departments within the organization.

The second kind of data found in the OLAP environment is nonpermanent detailed data. This data is brought into the OLAP environment on a one-time only or temporary basis. Nonpermanent data is used for special reports and analyses. The data model for the OLAP environment applies to permanent detailed data but not to nonpermanent detailed data.

Static summary data can be recalculated repeatedly with the same result, regardless of when the calculation is made. Nearly all of the data that is summarized in the OLAP environment is static. As such, a data model should be created that identifies the static summary data belonging in the OLAP environment. The farmers that constitute the OLAP community will tell the data modeler what summarized data is needed. The database administrator (DBA), or whoever is responsible for monitoring the activity against the data warehouse, will also be able to provide input to the data modeler as to what detailed data should be summarized and how, based on patterns of use.

Normally, some small amount of dynamic summary data is found in the OLAP environment. Three of the most common occurrences that affect whether dynamic data will be found in the OLAP environment are:

1. Changes in how the department wishes to manipulate OLAP data.
2. Corrections to detailed data in the organizationally structured environment.
3. Changes in how the different levels of aggregation of a complex categorization are organized.

One of the characteristics of the OLAP environment is its flexibility. Some departments, especially those engaged in "what if" types of analyses such as marketing, have extremely dynamic requirements for information. The OLAP environment, representing the departmentally structured level of the data warehouse architecture, can react and respond to these frequently and often, radically changing requirements without requiring a change to the underlying organizationally structured level of the data warehouse.

While the data in the data warehouse is defined as "non-volatile," there are circumstances where, for whatever reason, organizationally structured data must be corrected. The most common cause of these corrections is business processing rules that fall outside of the business rules used to trigger data acquisition for the data warehouse. While these situations usually do not have a significant impact on the data customized in the OLAP environment, there may be exceptions.

The other, more common reason for summary data to be considered dynamic is changes to the structure of complex categories. A department (or even the entire organization) may have a business requirement to analyze historical data based on the new method of organizing a category, such as sales or product hierarchies. If the data stored in the organizationally structured level of the data warehouse is at the appropriate level of detail, then re-summarizing this data will not present a problem. The actual *processing* of this re-summarization may be considerable, but the *ability* to meet this requirement of turning data into information will exist.

PROVIDING OLAP CAPABILITIES IN THE DATA WAREHOUSE

There are primarily three approaches to providing *complex* multidimensional analysis capabilities within the data warehouse architecture:

1. Managing the data in a star schema at the departmental level.
2. Using a "true" OLAP tool that can access normalized relational data.
3. Using a multidimensional database at the departmental level.

Much has been written and said regarding *two-tiered* and *three-tiered* hardware architectures. While the data warehouse architecture should be independent of the technology on which it resides, these two hardware architectures provide a useful backdrop for discussing the three approaches to providing OLAP capabilities.

Figure 10.3 depicts a two-tiered hardware architecture. Each tier handles a distinct set of processing functions and data management responsibilities. In this case, the enterprise server supports all data acquisition functions and manages the organizational and departmental data. In the latter capacity, the database maintenance system running on the server would facilitate the query engine in support of end-user access. The client, typically a workstation or other personal computing platform, maintains the data access, analysis, and manipulation software, as well as any personal or individual level data. Both atomic and departmental data can be accessed by the client and metadata is also maintained by the server.

Any OLAP processing that takes place in this configuration is usually known as relational OLAP, or "ROLAP," where a multidimensional analysis (MDA) tool on the client accesses a relational database on the server. Some MDA tools have the ability to access an appropriately normalized relational database. Other MDA tools, however, require a star schema (discussed later) to facilitate multidimensional processing. The star schema preprocesses data into a central *fact* table with related *dimension* tables. The

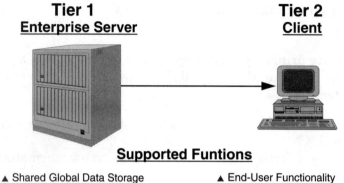

Supported Funtions

▲ Shared Global Data Storage
▲ Shared Application Logic

▲ End-User Functionality
▲ Data Display
▲ Personal Data Storage
▲ Personal Application Logic

Data Warehousing Application

▲ Atomic Data Acquisition
▲ Organizational Level Data
▲ Secondary Data Acquisition
▲ Departmental Level Data

▲ Data Access Processing
▲ Individual Level Data
▲ Data Manipulation

Data Warehousing Architecture

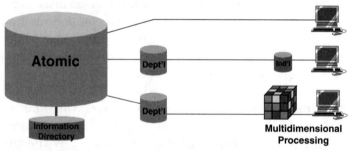

Figure 10.3 Two-tiered architecture and data warehousing.

unique keys of each dimension table make up a compound key in the fact table. The benefits of this approach are that the data in the star schema is preprocessed into known dimensions and pre-categorized based on a specific set of business requirements for information, making access by the MDA tool on the client more efficient. The downside is that the data warehouse database administrator must maintain star schemas for each group of informational business requirements; aside from the fact that more database objects translate into more work overall for the database administrator, star schemas in particular can be very processing-intensive to load, update, and maintain.

In Figure 10.4 the three-tiered architecture introduces a de-

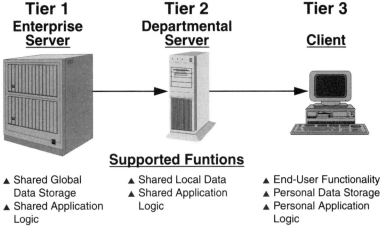

Tier 1
Enterprise Server

Tier 2
Departmental Server

Tier 3
Client

Supported Funtions

▲ Shared Global Data Storage	▲ Shared Local Data	▲ End-User Functionality
▲ Shared Application Logic	▲ Shared Application Logic	▲ Personal Data Storage
		▲ Personal Application Logic

Data Warehousing Relational OLAP Application

▲ Atomic Data Acquisition	▲ Secondary Data Acquisition	▲ Data Access Processing
▲ Organizational Level Data	▲ Departmental Level Data ("Star" or other)	▲ Individual Level Data
		▲ Multidimensional Data Manipulation

Data Warehousing Relational OLAP Architecture

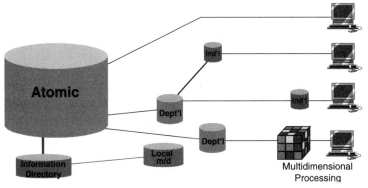

Figure 10.4   Three-tiered architecture and ROLAP data warehousing.

partmental server between the enterprise server and the client. This departmental server can be used for a number of purposes. The most common is to support and maintain a departmental instance of the data warehouse. Organizations will often define a "departmental" requirement on a geographic basis. Regional or other field offices may need access to a subset of integrated, corporate data. A regional server that is periodically updated from the organizational data cuts down on network traffic overall and physically locates the data closer to the users, furthering their informational self-sufficiency.

Another use of a *middle-tier* server is to maintain individual data, where that data meets an individual business function as opposed to meeting the business requirements of an individual person. This might be a set of highly focused data supporting an EIS used by a small (but significant) group of executives.

With either the departmental or individual instances, the middle-tier server can take on some of the data acquisition functions for populating the departmental data. This permits the enterprise server to be configured to meet a smaller, more focused set of data processing and storage criteria, as well as detailed access. The middle-tier server should also maintain a subset of metadata appropriate to support the departmental and individual users who will access the warehouse data there. Any individual level data acquisition should be managed by this tier, too.

In this configuration, where the departmental server is supporting departmental and possibly individual levels of the data warehouse, OLAP processing, as in the two-tiered example, takes place on the client. The departmental data may be structured in a star schema, but the multidimensional processing capabilities reside with the application running on the client.

Figure 10.5 depicts a *true* OLAP architecture. In this case, a multidimensional application is running on the departmental server, requiring less complex processing and, correspondingly, less expensive hardware at the client tier. The multidimensional capabilities of the departmental server are being met by either a set of specifically designed and actively managed star schemas, by software specifically designed to reside on and support a three-tiered architecture, or by a multidimensional database management system (MDDBS). These systems differ from rela-

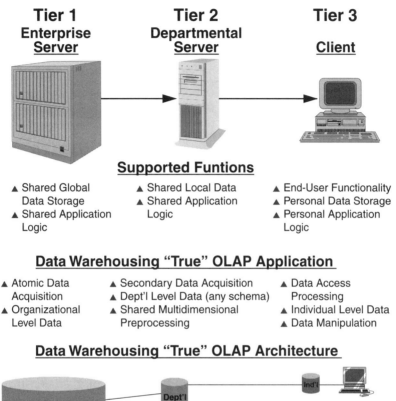

Figure 10.5   Three-tiered architecture and "true" OLAP data warehousing.

tional database management systems in that they are currently highly proprietary in nature, typically do not directly support SQL, and can support significantly less volume of data than even an "average" RDBMS. However, it has taken relational database management systems nearly two decades to reach the level of functionality that they enjoy today, so there is every reason to believe that the functionality and capabilities of multidimensional database management systems will also improve with age, and

The star schema structure is especially applicable to the OLAP environment.

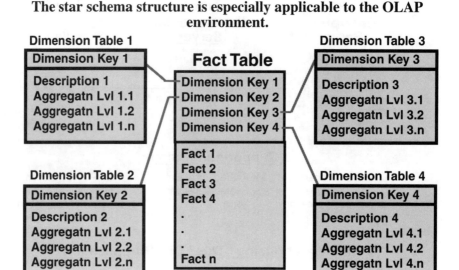

Figure 10.6 A description of a star schema.

probably more rapidly than did RDBMS. For now most multidimensional needs can probably be met through a combination of departmental database design and client application functionality. However, a multidimensional database management system may be an excellent option for a departmental instance if the functionality it provides is what the business requirements of the target users demand.

In every architectural option previously described, the key factor is that more work must be done on either or both of the servers in order for processing on the client to be made easier to understand or require a less complex access tool. The challenge is to find the appropriate balance between work done by the client and work done by the server(s), where the criteria for "appropriate" includes the end users' ability to turn data into information and IS's ability to support the data warehouse in a cost-effective manner. The data warehouse architecture should drive the selection of technology options; if a "favorite" technology constrains how the data warehouse can be architected, then users will ultimately suffer from a lack of necessary information appropriately structured. Also, a single tool or product may not meet all of an organization's information requirements or skill levels. Too often companies look for a single product, a "silver bullet," to meet all of their informational processing needs. Just as a mechanic has many tools at his command, so, too, should an organization look beyond a single solution to meet all of its end-user access or other informational needs.

The Star Schema and ROLAP

The data model that is created for the OLAP database design leads to a physical design. The basis of a ROLAP physical design is typically a combination of properly normalized data and one or more star schema. For those entities of data that do not occur frequently, the data model and normalization serve as the basis for physical design. For those entities that have one or more of the following characteristics, the star schema serves as a basis for physical design:

- Data instances are frequently occurring and additive.
- Contain a number of data elements that need to serve as "by" categories in analyses.
- One or more categories are hierarchical.

Figure 10.6 is a description of a star schema.

Figure 10.7 is an example of a star schema and, as described in Figure 10.6, has several components. At the center of the star schema is the fact table which represents quantities of data that can be aggregated without losing their meaning and need to be described by more than two dimensions (plus time). The purpose of the fact table is to streamline the informational processing that must make use of the numerous occurrences of data found in the fact table: See Figure 10.8. The data in the fact table is made up of data elements from the organizationally structured level that are additive in nature; that is, the values in these data elements can be summed in a variety of ways without jeopardizing the integrity of the data.

Surrounding the fact table are the dimension tables, which are described in Figure 10.9. The dimension tables are descrip-

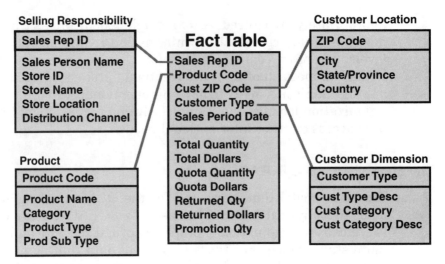

Figure 10.7 An example of a star schema.

tive in nature, not additive; dimension tables describe or "categorize" the data in the related fact table. There is a pre-joined foreign key relationship relating the fact table to the dimension tables. The key of the fact table is a compound key made up of the keys of all of the dimension tables. The result is that there will be a row in the fact table for every unique combination of the domains of all of the keys of all of the dimension tables. Conse-

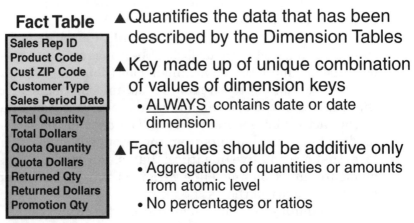

Figure 10.8 The fact table of a star schema.

Selling Responsibility

Sales Rep ID
Sales Person Name
Store ID
Store Name
Store Location
Distribution Channel

Customer Dimension

Customer Type
Cust Type Desc
Cust Category
Cust Catgry Desc

▲ Describes the data that has been organized in the Fact Table

▲ Key must be a unique value

▲ Key should be most detailed aggregation level *required*, if possible (e.g., ZIP Code)

▲ Manageable number of aggregation levels

▲ Dimension does not have to be a hierarchy; can be a combination of attributes

Figure 10.9 Dimension tables of a star schema.

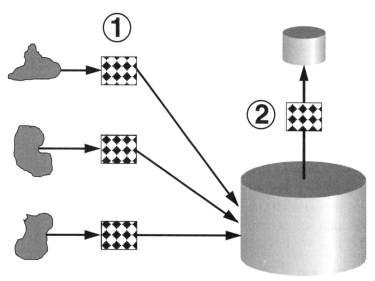

Figure 10.10 The order in which the data warehouse architecture is built.

quently, the key of the dimension tables should be at the lowest level of detail necessary to support the business purpose for which the star schema was created. This may be different for multiple star schemas that contain similar data but in different combinations. For example, one star schema may have geographic location defined as zip code, while another star schema only needs to support city as the lowest level of detail.

THE ORDER OF BUILDING THE COMPONENTS

There is a predictable order in which the various components of the data warehouse architecture are built, as shown in Figure 10.10. The organizationally structured level of the data warehouse is the first component of the architecture that is built and populated. The organizationally structured data begins its journey in the operational environment. From the operational environment, the data is transformed and integrated. The organizationally structured portion of the data warehouse is then populated. After a serious amount of detailed data has been accumulated, the OLAP environment (departmentally structured) is begun. Only after a significant amount of organizationally structured data has been gathered does it make sense to start building the departmentally structured environment.

Data Acquisition for OLAP

Moving data into the OLAP environment from the organizationally structured level of the data warehouse is a nontrivial task. Figure 10.11 shows the positioning of the program required for the data acquisition of data into the OLAP environment. Several functions are accomplished in this movement of data. These functions are not necessarily mutually exclusive and include:

- Selection of a subset of detailed data.
- Summarization of detailed data.
- Customization of the detailed data into departmental format.
- Pre-categorization of detailed data to meet departmental requirements.

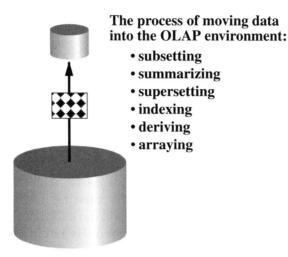

The process of moving data into the OLAP environment:

- **subsetting**
- **summarizing**
- **supersetting**
- **indexing**
- **deriving**
- **arraying**

Figure 10.11 Data acquisition for OLAP.

- Creation of supersets by merging and joining detailed data.
- Creation or update of arrays of detailed data, and so forth.

Some of the issues that must be resolved in the creation and execution of the program that feeds the OLAP environment from the detailed data warehouse environment are

- frequency of refreshment;
- efficiency with which the detailed data is read (acquired);
- amount of detailed data to be acquired;
- platform for sorting, joining, merging, and so forth;
- ability to know what data already resides in the OLAP environment so that the same record is not (unintentionally) created twice;
- that unnecessary records will not be created; and
- whether data once processed is to be appended or updated into the OLAP environment, and so forth.

One of the interesting aspects of the data acquisition programs that load the OLAP environment from the organizationally structured environment is their mutability. The organizationally structured-OLAP interface is an unstable interface because the OLAP environment supports informational processing that inherently implies instability because of the exploratory nature of its use. For this reason, the interface needs to be as flexible as possible, because maintenance of the interface will be an everyday occurrence.

Another aspect of the program that loads the OLAP environment from the organizationally structured environment is the efficiency of operation. The simple access of organizationally structured data is the first issue of efficiency. Assuming indexes are used wisely, the next issue is that of *combining* acquisition programs. If the same detailed data is going to be acquired by more than one OLAP environment, there must be a single program acquiring organizationally structured data that feeds all of the OLAP instances that must be supported. By having a single pass done against the organizationally structured environment, very efficient OLAP data acquisition processing can be accomplished. The OLAP environment is populated by the internal data of the organization, as well as external data sources, as seen in Figure 10.12.

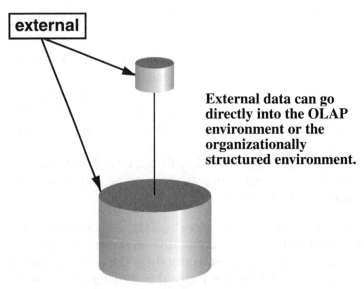

external

External data can go directly into the OLAP environment or the organizationally structured environment.

Figure 10.12 Data acquisition of external data.

External Data and OLAP

External data can come from any number of sources. It may be fed directly into the OLAP environment or into the organizationally structured environment where it can then be passed along to the OLAP environment. When external data is fed directly into the OLAP environment, the implication is that there is no other corporate use of it outside of the department that controls that OLAP instance, as shown in Figure 10.13.

When there is a corporate need for that external data, then the data is fed into the organizationally structured portion of the data warehouse where it is available to any instance in the OLAP environment, as shown in Figure 10.14. This design may be the result of an up-front decision or may evolve over time from the previous example of just populating an OLAP instance with external data. External data may undergo some amount of refinement before being placed in the OLAP environment, such as:

- editing fields,
- removing selected records,
- joining records to other data,
- summarizing the external data, and so forth.

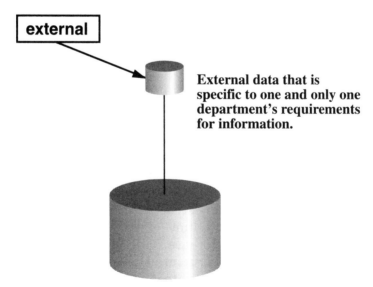

Figure 10.13 External data loaded directly into departmental (OLAP) level.

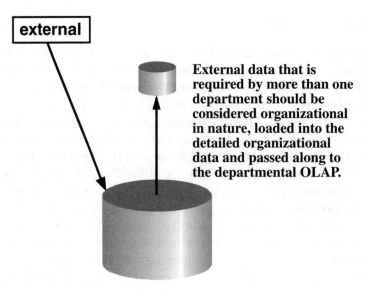

external

External data that is
required by more than one
department should be
considered organizational
in nature, loaded into the
detailed organizational
data and passed along to
the departmental OLAP.

Figure 10.14 External data loaded into organizational level.

Indexing OLAP in the Data Warehouse Environment

One of the substantive differences between the OLAP and the detailed data warehouse environment is that of indexing. Figure 10.15 shows that the OLAP environment can be highly and generously indexed while the detailed environment should be sparsely indexed.

As many as 30 or 40 indexes are in the OLAP environment while as few as two or three indexes are in the detailed environment. There are several reasons for this disparity in indexing. The first involves the volume of data found in the two environments. Where there is a modest amount of data, such as in the OLAP environment, the luxury of having many indexes can be enjoyed. Where this is an immodest amount of data, such as that found in the organizationally structured environment, there can be only a few indexes. But volume of data is not the only consideration in the indexing difference.

With organizationally structured data, consider the need for control and integrity of the data being integrated and transformed from the various production sources. Any performance

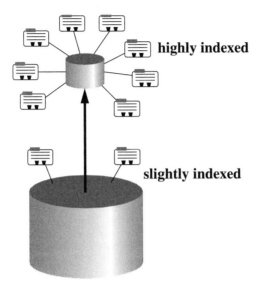

Figure 10.15   Comparison of indexing between atomic and OLAP levels.

requirements on this atomic level of data must be directed towards the population of the data warehouse from production sources of data. The departmentally structured level of the data warehouse is where improved end-user performance can be addressed. Indeed, in order to realize the goal of turning data into information end-user performance *must* be addressed and delivered at a level that is acceptable to those accessing the data.

There is much direct end-user access that occurs in the OLAP environment, while, relatively speaking, there is little direct end-user access that occurs on detailed data (once the organizationally structured environment is mature). Because of the disparity in direct end-user access, there is a very real difference in the need for indexing in the different environments.

One of the important distinctions made between the two environments is the end-user interface found at each level. Figure 10.16 depicts the different interfaces. It shows that the OLAP interface is optimal for DSS access and analysis of information. There is a direct end-user interface to organizationally structured data, but it is often a much cruder and simpler interface. Much of the activity that occurs in the organizationally struc-

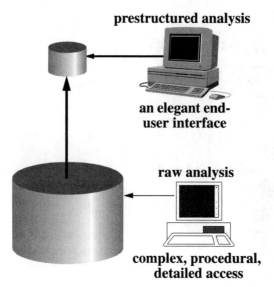

prestructured analysis

an elegant end-user interface

raw analysis

complex, procedural, detailed access

Figure 10.16 Different uses of atomic and OLAP levels.

tured environment is the selection and gathering of data. Very few analysts conduct detailed, heuristic analysis of data there. Those who do are the corporate explorers; they typically have more powerful and, correspondingly, difficult-to-use access tools. These analysts are typically very knowledgeable about the organization's data. Not only are they comfortable using procedural tools to interface with the organizationally structured data, but they also discover things in this vast amount of detailed data that were previously unknown or unsuspected.

METADATA FOR THE OLAP ENVIRONMENT

Metadata is one of the more important aspects of the OLAP environment because it keeps track of what is in the OLAP environment, where it came from, and how it got there. Since all of the business rules involved in populating the organizational and OLAP levels of the data warehouse can and will change over time, metadata is an essential part of using data in the multidimensional OLAP environment. Without metadata it would be impossible to recognize and understand changes in the data across the different time periods due to changes in the business rules that were the basis for data acquisition at those points in time. When doing an analysis or a new report, the end user in the OLAP environment first turns to metadata in order to determine what data is available as a basis for the analysis. Figure 10.17 shows metadata in the OLAP environment.

The components of OLAP metadata are very similar to those found in the organizationally structured level of the data warehouse; they include:

    I. Descriptive information about what is in the OLAP environment
      A. content,
      B. structure,
      C. definition, etc.
   II. The source of the data (the organizationally structured data or external data)
  III. The business name and technical name of the data
  IV. A description of the summarization, subset, superset, and/or denormalization processes that describe the data's journey from the organizationally structured level into the OLAP environment

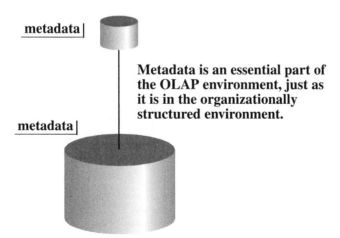

Metadata is an essential part of the OLAP environment, just as it is in the organizationally structured environment.

Figure 10.17 Metadata for the OLAP level.

V. Metrics that describe how much data of what types is found in the OLAP environment

VI. Refreshment scheduling information, describing when OLAP data has been populated

VII. Modeling information, describing how the data in the OLAP environment relates to the corporate data model and to the OLAP data model (if one exists)

Metadata in the OLAP environment is somewhat more complex than metadata found elsewhere in the data warehouse because there is a need for a specialized kind of metadata to support the OLAP environment. Figure 10.18 illustrates the need for a unique kind of metadata in the OLAP environment.

There is a need for both local and global metadata in the OLAP environment. Local OLAP metadata relates immediately to the department that the OLAP instance serves. There might be financial planning OLAP metadata, sales OLAP metadata, and marketing OLAP metadata. At the same time, there is a need for OLAP metadata that is global to the entire OLAP environment. Global OLAP metadata might include descriptions of

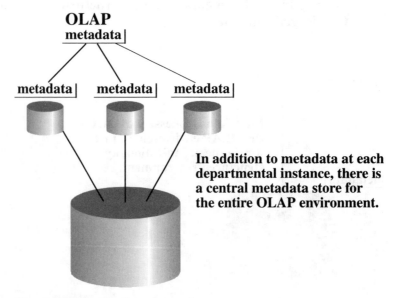

In addition to metadata at each departmental instance, there is a central metadata store for the entire OLAP environment.

Figure 10.18 Distributed metadata.

how different departments relate to each other, how sources of data differ, how data might flow from one OLAP environment to another, and so forth. As with metadata for any and all aspects of the entire data warehouse architecture, OLAP metadata needs to be supported as an interactive part of the process of the OLAP environment.

One of the important uses of metadata in the OLAP environment is that it can (indeed, should) be used interactively in the query process. Once the end user has examined the OLAP metadata to determine what the possibilities are, the end user can then use the metadata interactively in the query process.

PLATFORMS AND OLAP

Two-tiered and three-tiered platforms were previously discussed, with respect to the different ways in which OLAP capabilities can be provided within the context of the data warehouse architecture. One of the important aspects of the data warehouse organizationally structured-OLAP relationship is that there may be significant functional differences between the two environments. If there are very stark differences, the two environments are best placed on different platforms, as seen in Figure 10.19.

The figure shows that there could be more differences than just platform between the two environments: which DBMS best supports each, budget, and the type and number of end users. As a rule, the expenditures for the creation and management of organizationally structured data warehouse data is placed in the corporate IS budget, while the OLAP expenditures should be placed in each of the departmental budgets that have a need for a departmentally structured environment. Organizationally structured data users, for the most part, are the corporate explorers who need to get at raw corporate data. The users of the OLAP environment are the departmental analysts who have a parochial interest and perspective of the data found in their OLAP instances. There are mostly farmers at the OLAP level.

When the organizationally structured level of the data warehouse is small, it is probably most cost-effective to combine the organizationally structured data of the data warehouse and the

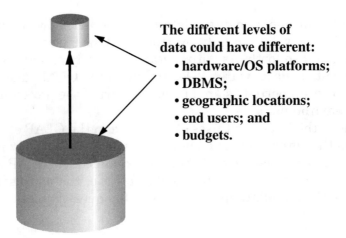

The different levels of
data could have different:
 • hardware/OS platforms;
 • DBMS;
 • geographic locations;
 • end users; and
 • budgets.

Figure 10.19 Comparison of platform components between atomic and OLAP levels.

OLAP environment together onto a single platform. Once the organizationally structured data blossoms to significant volumes, there is no real possibility that the two environments can be subsumed into the same physical environment.

In most cases, separating the organizationally structured and OLAP environments onto separate platforms is an evolutionary process. An organization will begin with a single physical implementation of its data warehouse environment, including the organizationally structured and OLAP levels. Then, over time, the existence of various factors at various degrees of completeness will force the necessity of separating the two environments onto different physical platforms. Sometimes these factors can be predicted during the design of the data warehouse; consequently, the overall design takes into consideration a certain degree of physical separation between organizationally structured and OLAP data and processing. Whether the initial implementation of the data warehouse does or does not include OLAP processing and whether it is initially separated or sharing a single platform, eventually most data warehouses evolve to the point of requiring that the organizationally structured and departmentally structured levels have their own, dedicated platforms. Some of the factors that affect the decision to separate or not to separate include:

- **Size.** The size of the organizationally structured level of the data warehouse, whether initially or through the natural growth process of a data warehouse (addition of and changes to subject areas, mushrooming end-user requirements for OLAP capabilities, etc.), may require all of the resources of a given hardware platform. Likewise, there may be real physical limitations to the RDBMS of choice to maintain the organizationally structured level, requiring that any OLAP instances be housed elsewhere.
- **Performance.** The primary responsibility of the organizationally structured level of the data warehouse is to maintain integrated data from a variety of sources in a manner that facilitates informational processing for the entire organization. Fulfilling this requirement may be threatened by end-user access to the OLAP environment or vice versa.
- **Number of Departments.** The sheer number of departments requiring OLAP capabilities may be mathematically impossible to support on a single platform.
- **Volatility.** The kinds of changes to the underlying data structure of an organizationally structured level necessary to support the informational requirements of the organization may be too disruptive to the OLAP environments, affecting their stability and performance.
- **Geographic Location.** For a distributed or decentralized organization, it may be more efficient to physically locate an OLAP environment at geographically diverse locations. These could be across the street, state, nation, or world from the organizationally structured level, or any combination thereof.
- **User Autonomy.** It is not uncommon for end users to complain about sharing resources with other departments, claiming that it negatively impacts their performance. True or not, perception is reality; in order for the users to feel that they can turn their data into information, they may require a physically separate environment to call their own. There may also be security or other confidentiality issues requiring that some OLAP data be physically separated from the rest

of the data warehouse environment. Whatever the reason, budgetary independence plays a significant role in whether a separate OLAP environment can be made available to these departments.

■ **Platform Considerations.** Some applications of OLAP processing capabilities may need to take advantage of unique or physically diverse platforms. A multidimensional database and/or server may be the appropriate configuration for a given group, rather than a multidimensional tool accessing a relational database, requiring separation.

For these reasons and because of the differences in budget and control of the different environments, there usually is no problem with having separate platforms for the different environments. Figure 10.20 represents a platform shared by both an organizationally structured environment and an OLAP environment, while Figure 10.21 shows them separated. Note that not all instances of an OLAP environment within an organization's data warehouse will warrant a separate physical environment. In some cases, one or more OLAP instances must or should be physically separated, while one or more others can continue to

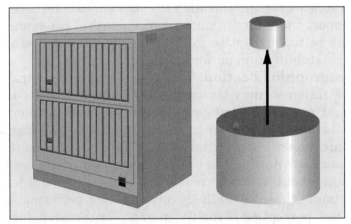

**Single physical platform supporting both
organizationally structured and
departmentally structured environments.**

Figure 10.20 Single platform for both atomic and OLAP levels.

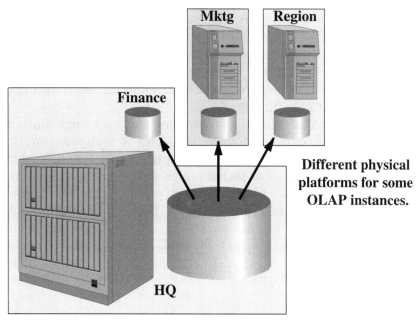

Figure 10.21   Distributed platforms for atomic and OLAP levels.

function on the same physical platform as the organizationally structured level of the data warehouse.

SUMMARY

In its most general form, OLAP is a means of facilitating multidimensional analysis. Since an RDBMS or a flat-file system are two-dimensional in nature, other methods must be explored for providing MDA. One method is to employ certain data design techniques, such as a star schema, to simulate a multidimensional structure in a two-dimensional environment. Another is to utilize an end-user tool that can access relational data, then provide MDA capabilities within the tool. And finally, a multidimensional database management system can be used to directly store the desired data multidimensionally.

Any of these options are acceptable and should be driven by the business requirements to access the data in an OLAP environment and the nature of the data itself. In all cases, the OLAP environment is best suited at the departmental level of the data warehouse architecture, so that the informational requirements of one group can be specifically met without jeopardizing or constraining the requirements and capabilities of other groups within the organization.

As with all aspects of managing the data warehouse, managing OLAP capabilities in the data warehouse environment should be driven by business requirements for information, not by any one or set of technologies. A technology-based approach will constrain the ability to effectively meet the informational requirements of the OLAP users as their requirements evolve over time. The corollary to this, however, is that one approach to providing OLAP may need to be replaced by another at some point in the future; with this change may come different tools, products, or technologies.

Managed Redundancy in the Data Warehouse Environment

Managed redundancy is one of the distinct characteristics of the data warehouse. It helps support informational processing in that it is a means of turning data into information by providing the appropriate subset of data to targeted end users based on the end users' business requirements for information.

The concept of managed redundancy is introduced by the very existence of the data warehouse; data is physically separated from the operational environment due to distinct differences in data design and processing requirements between the informational and operational environments. The concept of managed redundancy is extended further between the atomic, the departmental, and the individual levels of the data warehouse architecture, as shown in Figure 11.1.

TYPES OF MANAGED REDUNDANCY

But managed redundancy does not stop there. Several different ways exist for the same data to be stored redundantly in the data warehouse, including:

- Same data existing at the different levels of the data warehouse architecture.
- Denormalized data occurring redundantly.

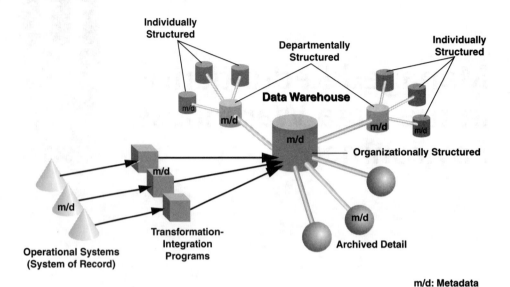

Figure 11.1 A mature data warehouse architecture.

- Artifacted data occurring redundantly.
- Same data structured at different degrees of granularity in the same level.
- Same data captured differently based on different time-variant criteria.

Redundancy between the Different Levels of the Data Warehouse Architecture

The concept of managed redundancy is introduced by the very existence of the data warehouse and is extended further in that the atomic, departmental, and individual levels of the data warehouse architecture themselves represent redundant data. But this redundancy is not merely replication; each level of the data warehouse is architected to meet different informational requirements within an organization. To that end, the data in each instance of each level of the data warehouse architecture is designed with a specific set of functionality in mind.

Figure 11.2 illustrates some of the general differences between the levels of the data warehouse architecture. The different levels of the data warehouse architecture are:

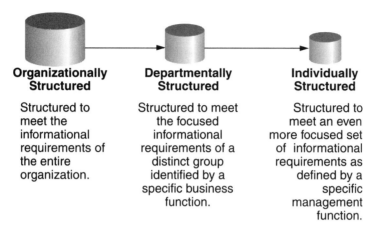

Organizationally Structured	Departmentally Structured	Individually Structured
Structured to meet the informational requirements of the entire organization.	Structured to meet the focused informational requirements of a distinct group identified by a specific business function.	Structured to meet an even more focused set of informational requirements as defined by a specific management function.

Figure 11.2   Levels of the data warehouse architecture.

- **Organizationally Structured.** Also known as *atomic, corporate,* or *current detail* data, this level—the heart of the data warehouse—is structured to meet the informational requirements of the entire organization. Data which has been archived (*archived detail*) also belongs to this level.
- **Departmentally Structured.** The data at this level of the data warehouse architecture is structured to meet the focused informational requirements of a distinct group identified by a specific business function. The data at this level has also been referred to as *lightly summarized* or *departmental* data.
- **Individually Structured.** The data at this level is structured to meet an even more focused set of informational requirements as defined by a specific management function. The data at this level has also been referred to as *highly summarized* or *individual* data.

Figure 11.3 depicts the characteristics of the different levels of the data warehouse architecture and the role of each in turning data into information. Note that the atomic level data is not tuned for performance, but for storage, control, and integrity of the data in the data warehouse. It is the function of this level of the data warehouse to preserve the *historical integrity* of the informational data in the data warehouse, just as it is the function of the operational system to ensure *referential integrity* of operational data.

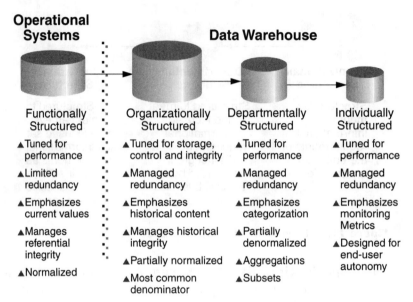

Figure 11.3 Characteristics of the levels of the data warehouse architecture.

Note also that each level of the data warehouse architecture manages redundant data. In some cases, the data is aggregated from one level to another, but not necessarily; the informational requirements of a departmental or individual level of data may require a subset of the atomic level data, not summarized data. It may require that the more normalized data at the atomic level be denormalized (or "flattened") in order to make it more understandable and usable to the target end user. Turning data into information by focusing on specific departmental or individual informational requirements may also require that specific business rules be applied to the data as part of populating the appropriate level. So, *informationalizing* data by populating a "higher" level from a "lower" level in the managed redundancy of the data warehouse architecture may require:

■ Summarization of data to categorize it into dimensions.
■ A subset of data based on the informational requirements, by selecting either:
  ■ specific rows that meet the appropriate criteria, or
  ■ only those columns of data required, or
  ■ a combination of the two.

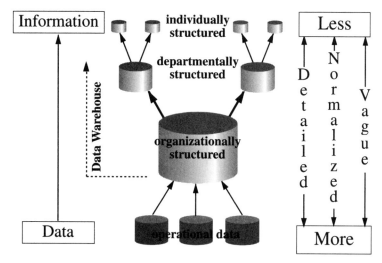

Figure 11.4 Relative degrees of characteristics from data to information.

- Denormalizing data into a fewer number of rows to make it "flatter" and therefore easier to comprehend.
- Applying business rules to derive data that meets the specific departmental or individual requirements for information, or
- A combination of any of the above.

As data becomes information by moving from its operational sources through the data warehouse architecture, the degree of normalization, detail, and functional precision is not based on a set criteria but varies based on the evolving organizational, departmental, and individual requirements for information, as shown in Figure 11.4

Redundancy Due to Denormalized Data

One of the simplest forms of redundant data in the data warehouse is denormalized data. Denormalizing data is a technique that can take two primary approaches: storing definitions of reference codes along with the codes themselves and storing repeating occurrences of the same data element in multiple columns or *buckets* in a single row. Figure 11.5 represents a fully normalized physical data model. Figure 11.6 demonstrates how denormalizing reference data can create redundancy in the data warehouse.

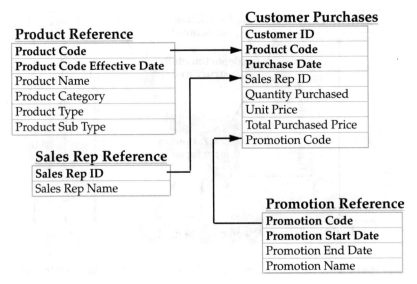

Figure 11.5 Normalized data model with reference data.

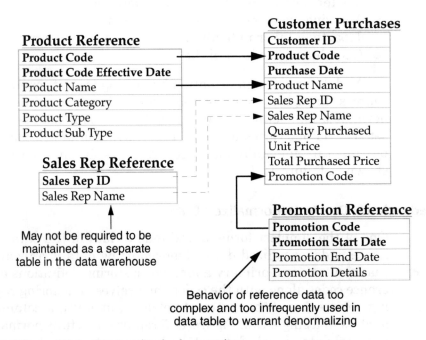

Figure 11.6 Denormalized reference data.

There are several reasons to denormalize data in this way. One is that reference definitions may change over time; therefore, by storing the applicable definition along with the reference code or other information, the accuracy of that relationship is guaranteed throughout the historical context of the data warehouse. A new or different definition can always be applied to the data, since the reference code has been stored; however, in a significant majority of the uses, the definition at the time the data was captured and stored in the data warehouse is the one that is desired by end users.

The second reason to generate redundant data by denormalizing reference definitions is to make the data easier to use by end users. Since the ultimate goal of informational processing is to turn data into information, denormalizing reference definitions assists in meeting this goal by not requiring end users to constantly join data tables with reference tables in order to render natural-language definitions of archaic or confusing codes. This permits, in a single simple SQL statement, the user to *qualify* the query by the codes (the most efficient method) and *display* the translated definitions (the most informative method), without requiring a join. It eliminates unnecessary joins and results in more efficient queries, since the only joins necessary are between data tables to qualify sets of records, not between data tables and reference tables to merely return descriptive values.

Note that the reference description for promotions is not denormalized from the Promotion Reference table into the Customer Purchases table. This illustrates that, while denormalizing reference data may be helpful for the reasons previously stated, it is not always a useful technique. In this hypothetical situation, the analysis of the source system's data determined that promotions only account for 15 percent or less of all purchases, and promotion codes by themselves are not unique, because they are reused with sufficient frequency and must be used in conjunction with their start (and sometimes end) dates. Therefore, it is more efficient (at least at the atomic level) to require a join between the Customer Purchases table and the Promotions Reference table on those occasions when promotion code was populated and the reference data required, rather than to account for all of the promotions data in each Customer Purchase record, when it would only be populated 15 percent of the time or less.

Some reference entities may still be valuable to the data warehouse since, as demonstrated by the Product Reference table in Figure 11.6, there may be a referential hierarchy that provides for different ways to aggregate and categorize the detailed data for different purposes. Other reference tables, such as the Promotions Reference table in Figure 11.6, may need to have changes recorded historically in order to provide valuable time-variant reference data. (This criteria often applies to hierarchical reference data, as well.) Simple reference tables, however, such as the Sales Rep Reference table in Figure 12.6, that do not represent a hierarchy and for which changes do not need to be maintained for historical purposes, should probably be eliminated and their descriptions stored in the appropriate "data" table along with (or in place of) the encoded value they represent.

When denormalizing data by creating arrays or *bucketing* the data, values from the same data element found in related normalized rows are stored in a set number of sequenced columns in a single row. The sequenced columns replace a distinguishing key character and its corresponding values in the normalized rows. Figure 11.7 illustrates this "bucketing" approach which results in a flatter, denormalized view of the data.

This technique is often used when populating a departmental or individual level of the data warehouse, where the data is stored in a more normalized fashion in the atomic level in order to preserve the accuracy and integrity of the data. However, if there is a general organizational requirement to access this data, then capturing and storing it in a more normalized manner will facilitate accuracy over time; storing it redundantly in denormalized arrays or *buckets* at the atomic level will facilitate ease of use and understanding to the organization at large.

Redundancy Due to Data Artifacting

Artifacting data is a technique used to preserve relationships between data elements when one or more of the elements in question are dynamic in nature. That is, if the value of one data element changes, it may be desirable to capture the value of another, related data element, even though the second data element's value did not change. In this way, it is not necessary to try to find the appropriate records from several different tables in order to *reconstruct* an historical point in time.

How is this different from simply taking a snapshot of a record when something on it changes in the source system? Some data is dynamic in nature, while other data is static. Capturing all of the static data when any dynamic data changes will result in too much redundancy (*un*managed redundancy). Also, some data elements do not have a significant relationship to one another. For example, a change in a customer's address may have little or no bearing on a change in his status or what discount plan he belongs to; it merely reflects a change in his demographics and not his account profile. Likewise, data elements, while somewhat static, may have a significant relationship to other data elements and vice-versa. For example, a sales director

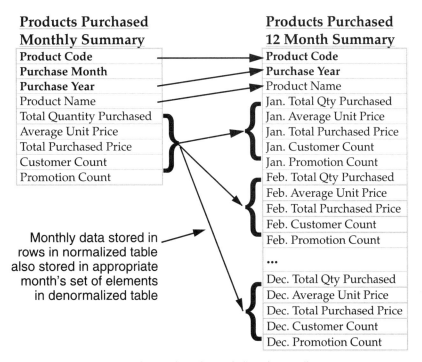

Figure 11.7 Denormalizing data through "Bucketing."

may want to know which of his account managers has customers that are constantly changing their status, reflecting account instability and a potential lack of properly qualifying customers, leading to greater customer retention costs. Conversely, if an account manager takes over the responsibility for another account manager's accounts, then the new account manager should now be receiving residual commissions for that existing account.

Figure 11.8 is an example of artifacted data between two tables, one that maintains complete current customer information and another that preserves historical context of changes between related data elements. Note that the time component of the two tables is different; the Customer Information table is keyed on the last effective status date for the customer, while Customer Information History is keyed on changes to either status, discount plan, or account manager information for the customer. Also, the Customer Information record contains an artifacted data element as well: "Customer since" records the date the customer first became "active."

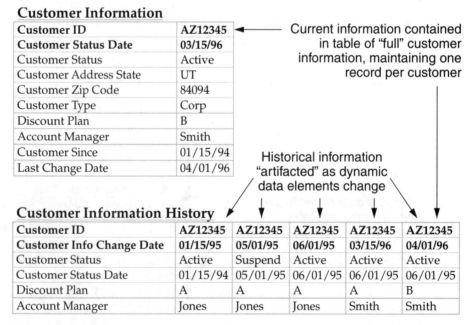

Customer Information

Customer ID	AZ12345
Customer Status Date	03/15/96
Customer Status	Active
Customer Address State	UT
Customer Zip Code	84094
Customer Type	Corp
Discount Plan	B
Account Manager	Smith
Customer Since	01/15/94
Last Change Date	04/01/96

Current information contained in table of "full" customer information, maintaining one record per customer

Historical information "artifacted" as dynamic data elements change

Customer Information History

Customer ID	AZ12345	AZ12345	AZ12345	AZ12345	AZ12345
Customer Info Change Date	01/15/95	05/01/95	06/01/95	03/15/96	04/01/96
Customer Status	Active	Suspend	Active	Active	Active
Customer Status Date	01/15/94	05/01/95	06/01/95	06/01/95	06/01/95
Discount Plan	A	A	A	A	B
Account Manager	Jones	Jones	Jones	Smith	Smith

Figure 11.8 Redundancy due to data artifacting.

Redundancy Due to Different Granularity of the Same Data in the Same Level

Since the organizationally structured level of data is designed to meet the informational requirements of the entire organization, it is very typical to find data in this level that is somewhat granular and detailed, as well as summarized versions of the exact same data. This is due to the fact that the detailed, granular data is required to support the drill-down capabilities of the data warehouse and to provide for a wide range of uses and means of categorizing that data throughout the organization. At the same time, a significant section of the organization may need access on a regular basis to the same data pre-aggregated to a certain level higher than that of the detailed data. Since it is more efficient to process the data once and store it for simple access, as well as ensuring the historical integrity of the business rules used to process the summarized data, the existence of both the granular, detailed data and a summarized version of the same data at the atomic level to support organizational requirements is an effective use of the data warehouse architecture. Figure 11.9 illustrates how the organizationally structured level of the data warehouse can contain both detailed and summarized versions of the same data and Figure 11.10 depicts an example of tables containing both the detailed and summarized organizationally structured data.

Figure 11.11 illustrates how data that began as departmental in nature can evolve over time to meet broader, organiza-

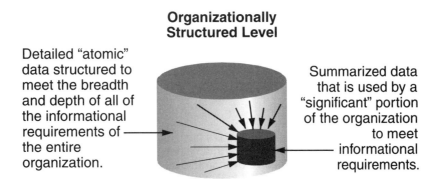

Organizationally Structured Level

Detailed "atomic" data structured to meet the breadth and depth of all of the informational requirements of the entire organization.

Summarized data that is used by a "significant" portion of the organization to meet informational requirements.

Figure 11.9 Redundant data within the organizationally structured level.

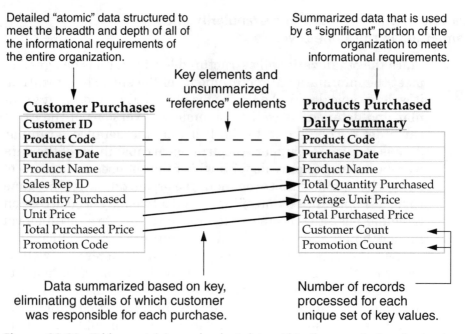

Detailed "atomic" data structured to meet the breadth and depth of all of the informational requirements of the entire organization.

Summarized data that is used by a "significant" portion of the organization to meet informational requirements.

Key elements and unsummarized "reference" elements

Data summarized based on key, eliminating details of which customer was responsible for each purchase.

Number of records processed for each unique set of key values.

Figure 11.10 Tables containing redundant data within the organizationally structured level of the data warehouse.

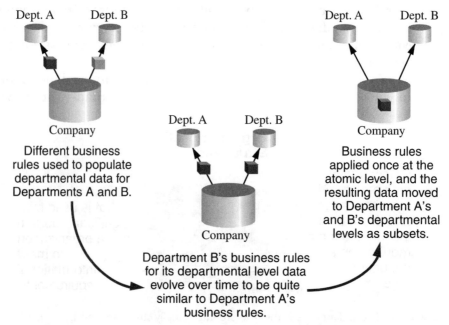

Different business rules used to populate departmental data for Departments A and B.

Business rules applied once at the atomic level, and the resulting data moved to Department A's and B's departmental levels as subsets.

Department B's business rules for its departmental level data evolve over time to be quite similar to Department A's business rules.

Figure 11.11 Departmental data becomes organizational in nature.

tional requirements for information. At first, Department B's requirements for information were different from Department A's requirements. The business rules used by Department A to derive information needed in their departmental instance of the data warehouse were different than the business rules used by Department B for similar information. However, over time Department B decided to adopt one of the key business rules used by Department A. Rather than process the same data the same way twice, the Data Warehouse Administrator chose to derive and store the information at the organizationally structured level, and replicate a subset of the organizationally structured data to the Department A and B instances, based on their selection criteria for the data. The derived data in both A's and B's departmental instances is now identical, regardless of the selection criteria used to determine with which rows each instance should be populated.

Redundancy Due to Differences in Time-Variant Criteria

Not every time interval will meet every business requirement for information. Since the goal of informational processing is to turn data into information, it is necessary to understand what points in time are important to the users of that information. For example, one business requirement may be to record changes in data, regardless of the time period in which the changes occurred or the interval between changes. Another, equally important business requirement may be to do point-in-time comparisons from one time period to the next for the same data. These are different business purposes for the same data. The differences don't stop there, between event-oriented and point-in-time comparisons. There may be a need to trend the same data based on different points in time. Figure 11.12 illustrates these differences.

One business function calls for capturing data at the end of each week so that weekly trends can be monitored. Another business function calls for end-of-month analyses, comparing a snapshot of the same information that is being captured weekly, but on a calendar-month basis. Since most months do not end on the same day as the end of a week, this requirement results in the need to capture the same information redundantly, but based on a different time interval. Other business requirements may re-

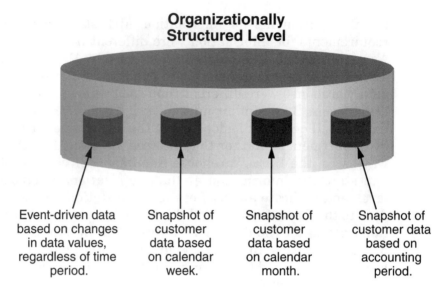

Event-driven data based on changes in data values, regardless of time period.

Snapshot of customer data based on calendar week.

Snapshot of customer data based on calendar month.

Snapshot of customer data based on accounting period.

Figure 11.12 Redundant data due to different time requirements.

sult in similar differences, such as the end of an accounting month, which may vary from month to month based on when the close actually takes place. Another significant business event may be the successful completion of a billing cycle; there may be multiple billing cycles in a month, with each billing cycle taking place on the same day every month, such as the fifth, fifteenth, and twenty-fifth of every month. Each of these business functions requires data to be captured based on a different set of temporal rules, resulting in the need to store and maintain similar if not identical data redundantly. However, since the time periods or events that determine when this "identical" data is captured and stored are different, each distinct time period's data is, by definition, different, and therefore not truly redundant from an informational perspective.

Rather than store these separate time *types* of data, more time-granular (and therefore more detailed and voluminous) data could be captured and maintained at the atomic level. However, this may result in a greater volume of data than the sum of the three time types. Also, if this is not the proper level of time granularity to support the informational requirements of the entire organization, then this more granular and detailed data will always need to be summarized and processed up to a more appropriate and workable level before end users can begin using it. Managed redundancy in the form of multiple occurrences of the appropriate level of detail of data is, therefore, more efficient in meeting the goal of turning data into information than managing a much larger, singular quantity of data at a very fine degree of time granularity. In other words, historical integrity is better served by capturing and storing data in the appropriate manner based on business requirements for information, even if the result is the same data captured at different time intervals.

SUMMARY

Managed redundancy helps support informational processing and is one of the distinct characteristics of the data warehouse. Through managed redundancy, data is turned into information by providing the appropriate subset of data to targeted end users based on the end users' business requirements for information. Without managed redundancy, all users from all levels of skills and with vastly different requirements for information would have to access a single repository of data. That single instance of data would not be structured to meet individual or groups of users' needs, but would, by necessity, be a detailed and complicated set of data that has to meet all the needs of a diverse group of information users.

The concept of managed redundancy is introduced by the very existence of the data warehouse, in that it is an informational data environment that is separate from the operational data environment. The managed redundancy concept is extended further by the existence of physically separate departmental and individual instances of data, populated from the atomic (current detail) level of data that serves as the foundation for all informational processing.

Managed redundancy can be accomplished in many ways for different reasons throughout the data warehouse architecture. Metadata, that key component of any data warehouse, serves as the means of understanding how different instances of the same data are structured to meet different business purposes.

12

Data Warehouse Team Roles and Responsibilities

In every business activity there are roles that must be played and responsibilities that must be fulfilled in order to realize the activity's objectives. The design, development, implementation, and management of a data warehouse require some very specific and unique roles and responsibilities; these are in addition to those roles and responsibilities that are necessary for any project to be successful.

The roles and responsibilities necessary to ensure a successful data warehouse break down into two major categories: Those carried out by **Information Systems (IS)** and those required of the intended *end users* of the data warehouse. This chapter will concentrate on the Information Systems role; Chapter 14 will address end-user roles.

A role is a function or position; a one-to-one relationship between a role and a resource will not necessarily exist. Throughout the iterative lifecycle of a data warehouse, an individual may (and probably will) play several different roles, sometimes simultaneously, but those roles will usually stay within one of the two primary categories—Information Systems or end user. Within Information Systems, there are the following categories of roles:

- Data warehouse management
- Analysis and design of the data warehouse environment
- Development of data warehouse processes
- Supporting roles

There are other roles that must, may, or should exist in the development and management of any data warehouse, depending on the nature and culture of the company or organization engaged in such an undertaking. These are categorized as *involved roles* and include such "standard" roles as IS management, steering or review committee, operations support, system administration, administrative support, and so forth. These roles are not unique to a data warehouse; their existence is dependent upon the size and scope of the data warehouse, as well as the organization's culture and budget.

This chapter will focus on the minimum kinds of specific roles necessary to manage a data warehouse. Additional supervisory, administrative, support, review, and other roles may be required by an organization's culture or overall project management methodology, but are not necessary for a successful administration of a data warehouse. Indeed, more often than not these additional roles add layers of complexity and overhead, requiring communications and tasks that are often unnecessary and which dramatically diminish the ability of the data warehouse team to rapidly and iteratively implement informational capabilities and respond to the organization's swiftly changing requirements for information. In order to provide a foundation for understanding the different roles necessary to develop and manage a data warehouse, Figure 12.1 depicts the data warehouse

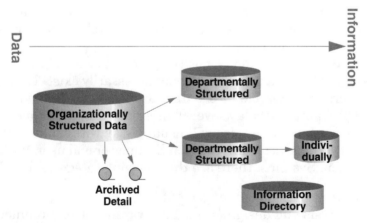

Figure 12.1 Data warehouse environment.

architecture and illustrates the different levels of data that can exist within the architecture to meet the different informational requirements of the organization.

DATA WAREHOUSE MANAGEMENT ROLES

Information Systems bears the primary responsibility for the management of a data warehouse and, subsequently, has the greatest variety of roles. The overall administration of a data warehouse involves four key roles: Data Warehouse Administrator, Data Warehouse Organizational Change Manager, Database Administrator, and Metadata Manager.

Data Warehouse Administrator

In every business activity there is (typically) one individual who is ultimately responsible for managing that activity. The Data Warehouse Administrator (DWA) has ultimate responsibility for the data warehouse, including procuring, scheduling, and coordinating work among human resources, preparing status reports, leading design reviews, ensuring team members and end users are trained effectively, and managing other activities related to the data warehouse as specified by the organization's management. Figure 12.2 depicts the responsibility area of the DWA.

As mentioned, every business activity requires someone who assumes ultimate responsibility for the success of that activity: conducting it in accordance with the organization's goals and objectives, meeting stated deliverables on time and in scope, and doing so within budgetary and other parameters. Figure 12.3 lists the major responsibilities of the DWA.

This role is, obviously, not unique to a data warehouse; there are, however, some specific responsibilities that *are* unique to a DWA. Primarily, the DWA must understand the fundamental concepts and architectural paradigm of a data warehouse and what distinguishes it from a traditional operational application. Secondly, the DWA must understand that the functionality of the data warehouse must be driven by the end users of the organization and their requirements for turning data into informa-

The Data Warehouse Administrator is responsible for all aspects of the development, maintenance, and management of the data warehouse.

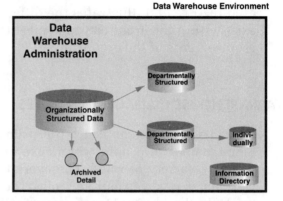

Figure 12.2 Data warehouse administrator's responsibility area.

tion, not just by technology or the data that exists within the organization. This is referred to as a *top-down* approach, as opposed to a *bottom-up* approach, which refers to IS's perception that a data warehouse is something the organization needs and if they build one, the end users will use it and it will, by default, be successful. The perception that a data warehouse will benefit the organization is usually accurate, but if the informational requirements that the data warehouse is attempting to meet are not driven by the end users (and from the higher up within the

Data Warehouse Administrator

• **Overall responsibility for the data warehouse environment**

• **Manage the implementation of each iteration of the data warehouse**

• **Ensure that the data warehouse continues to meet the informational requirements of the organization**

Figure 12.3 Data warehouse administrator's responsibilities.

organization, the better), then the end users' perception of the value of the data warehouse will be minimal and the success of the data warehouse will be extremely difficult to achieve.

Data Warehouse Organizational Change Manager

Figure 12.4 depicts the responsibility area of the data warehouse Change Manager. A Change Manager manages an organization's expectations and perceptions of the data warehouse, and its capabilities, limitations, and impact on all aspects of the organization. ("Change management", in this context, does not refer to managing changes to software components or other traditional technically-oriented activities associated with managing an application environment.)

In most organizations the development and implementation of a data warehouse represents significant change in a number of areas. Those who currently provide reports or other unarchitected methods of providing informational capabilities may feel

The Data Warehouse Organizational Change Manager is responsible for understanding and managing the changes to the organization that are inevitable with the introduction of each iteration of a data warehouse.

Figure 12.4 Data warehouse organizational change manager's responsibility area.

threatened by the data warehouse; their existence within and value to the organization is represented by the reports or extract files they produce. The data warehouse will replace and improve on those capabilities. These people often make excellent subject matter experts (covered later in the chapter). However, they must be approached and handled appropriately so that they do not feel "used" or manipulated, but understand that their inherent knowledge of the organization's informational requirements makes them indispensable members of the data warehouse team. It is the Change Manager's responsibility to ensure that this happens. Figure 12.5 lists the major responsibilities of the Data Warehouse Organizational Change Manager.

The Change Manager is also responsible for the internal marketing of the data warehouse. This is a continuous process, one that is essential in preventing a data warehouse that is architected to provide strategic informational capabilities from digressing into an operational reporting repository. End-user and management expectations and understanding of data warehouse capabilities are managed through this process of internal marketing. This role is especially important during the initial con-

Data Warehouse Organizational Change Manager

- Assess the impact on the organization that the data warehouse will create due to its changing the status quo

- Work with affected individuals and groups to alleviate fears and diffuse conflict

- Help "displaced" information workers find and understand their new roles in the data warehouse environment

- Work with entire organizations and those groups affected by each new iteration

Figure 12.5 Data warehouse organizational change manager's responsibility.

sideration and commitment to develop the data warehouse, as well as just prior to and during implementation of an iteration of the data warehouse. Each iteration of new data warehouse capabilities will require a corresponding internal marketing effort. The Change Manager must be continuously involved in the data warehouse to ensure that it is and continues to be of value to the organization, as perceived by its end users specifically, and management in general.

Database Administrator

It is essential that the organization's data warehouse team has a sufficient number of full-time, dedicated Database Administration resources to support the data warehouse. The nature of the differences between operational and informational systems requires a separation of the Database Administrators who support these two different environments. If a single Database Administration staff is responsible for both the operational systems and the data warehouse, the data warehouse design and data integrity inevitably suffer. Business priorities that require the Database Administration staff to support the operational systems are not the same priorities for informational systems; the latter always "takes a back seat" to the former. Having a separate data warehouse Database Administration staff that is responsible for the care and maintenance of the data warehouse and responsible to the DWA helps ensure that the integrity of the data in the data warehouse will not be compromised by severe or catastrophic production problems with the operational systems. A data warehouse Database Administrator (DBA) will also be able to focus directly on meeting the business requirements of the informational end users and will not need to constantly shift between the significantly different architectural issues that distinguish operational data structures and informational data structures.

The data warehouse DBA is responsible for the physical data storage environments for the organizationally, departmentally, and individually structured levels of the data warehouse, as well as the Information Directory, which houses the business and technical metadata for the data warehouse. Figure 12.6 illustrates this responsibility area.

The Data Warehouse Database Administrator is responsible for all physical data structures of the data warehouse environment, including the Information Directory.

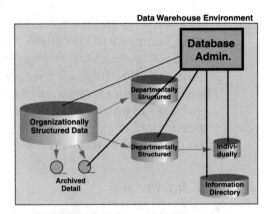

Figure 12.6 Database administrator's responsibility area.

The value and necessity of the appropriate number of skilled Database Administration resources on the data warehouse team cannot be overemphasized. Without adequate Database Administration resources, the health and integrity of the data warehouse will suffer significantly and rapidly, eroding user confidence in their ability to trust the data in the warehouse, or its performance and usability. The lack of adequate DBA time, commitment, and understanding of the data warehouse paradigm is one of the leading factors in the failure of data warehouses. Figure 12.7 lists the major responsibilities of the Data Warehouse DBA.

Data Warehouse Database Administrator

• Maintain the physical data environment of the data warehouse

• Continuously monitor data acquisition and data access activities

• Make necessary adjustments to the ever-evolving data warehouse data structures

Figure 12.7 Data warehouse database administrator's responsibilities.

Metadata Manager

The responsibility for maintaining and providing access to the metadata that describes the data warehouse architecture and content is unique to data warehouse management. Although there are aspects of database administration, data access, and data acquisition in performing the metadata management role, it is sufficiently important in and of itself to warrant a separate responsibility role within the data warehouse team. The Metadata Manager must ensure that the metadata in the Information Directory is synchronized with the production sources, business rules governing data acquisition, and the business rules driving data access, as well as sources of conceptual metadata such as CASE tools and new applications under development. Figure 12.8 illustrates this area of responsibility.

This management team member must ensure that the means of accessing the metadata meet the requirements of the end users so that navigating the metadata, and therefore the data warehouse itself, is clear and comprehensible. The Metadata Manager should also bear the responsibility for training end users (through the train-the-trainer process) in understanding the data available to them through the data warehouse and the business relationships that data has to the production sources and the business functions of the organization. Figure 12.9 lists the major responsibilities of the Metadata Manager.

The Metadata Manager is responsible for all metadata in the data warehouse environment (the *content* of the Information Directory).

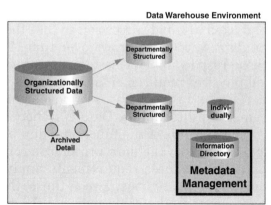

Figure 12.8 Metadata manager's responsibility area.

Meta Data Manager

- Ensure all technical and business metadata is current and accurate
- Ensure users are able to navigate and understand metadata based on their business requirements and perspective
- Work with end users to gather business meta data from queries and other uses of the data warehouse
- Work with IS operational support groups to proactively identify changes to systems of record

Figure 12.9 Metadata manager's responsibilities.

ANALYSIS AND DESIGN OF THE DATA WAREHOUSE ENVIRONMENT

Ideally, a data warehouse should be architected from a high-level, enterprise-wide perspective, while the implementation of a data warehouse should take place iteratively. This means that small, achievable objectives should be outlined and the analysis, design, development, and implementation of these objectives conducted in rapid succession so that the overall functionality of the data warehouse grows over time. There are two key roles whose responsibility it is to analyze and design the functional and physical requirements to meet the objectives of each iteration of the data warehouse's development: Business Requirements Analysts and the Data Warehouse Architect.

The analysis of the functional and physical requirements of any iteration of the data warehouse consists of three groups of activities: business requirements analysis, data analysis, and source system analysis. Two of these, the data analysis and the source system analysis, comprise the *bottom-up* portion of determining the design of the data warehouse to meet the informational requirements for the organization. As previously mentioned, this differs from the *top-down,* informational requirements that are also necessary to ensure that the design of the data warehouse not only includes all of the data available from the appropriate systems of record, but also that the right data is extracted and structured appropriately to meet the informational requirements of the organization. Figure 12.10 illustrates the differences between the *top-down* and the *bottom-up* approaches of these three analyses.

The goal of informational processing is to turn data into information. It is the integration of these three approaches, the top-down business requirements analysis and the bottom-up data analysis and source system analysis, that yields the complete picture of the data content and structure required to design the data warehouse. The Business Requirements Analysts

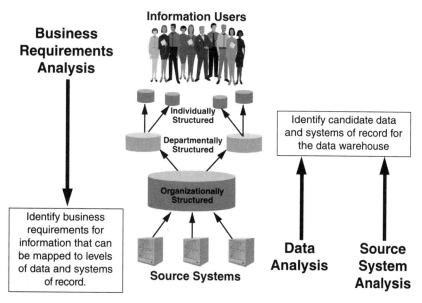

Figure 12.10 Purposes of different analyses.

identify and decompose the organization's requirements for information, then describe how those requirements need to be organized from individual, departmental, and organizational perspectives. The Data Warehouse Architect identifies the data that is available from the organization's (and external) operational systems and constructs an information model that is appropriate to meet the organization's high-level requirements for information. The Data Warehouse Architect also evaluates the functionality of these operational systems and recommends the appropriate system(s) of record for the data warehouse. The findings of these three analyses are then integrated and the results are the functional characteristics, physical data models, and overall architecture of the organizationally, departmentally, and (if necessary) individually structured levels of the data warehouse.

Business Requirements Analysts

Business requirements analysis identifies the informational requirements of the organization, from the documentation and decomposition of key business metrics to the physical requirements for deploying components of the data warehouse. The outputs of this activity include the identification of the subject areas to be populated in the data warehouse, the order in which they should be implemented, and an understanding of the scope of effort required to meet the informational requirements of each iteration. These are essential for the development stages of the data warehouse to be properly executed. For each iteration of the data warehouse, the business requirements analysis involves identifying and defining key business metrics, choosing the triggering events for data snapshots, determining naming conventions, and planning the frequency of data acquisition into the data warehouse.

Full-time Business Requirements Analysts will be needed at the beginning of a data warehouse project to analyze existing sources of data and any existing attempts at providing information to the organization, conduct user interviews, analyze the information gathered from the interviews, and marry the results of these analyses with the information model produced by the Data Warehouse Architect. This work is in preparation for building the map chains and organizing other background information needed by the Data Acquisition Developers (covered later in this chapter) to build the extract, transformation, and load programs, as well as providing the Data Access Developers (covered later in this chapter) with the background information that they will need to develop the methods by which the end users will access the data warehouse. Figure 12.11 depicts the responsibility area of Business Requirements Analysts.

Aside from the DWA, who has ultimate responsibility for the data warehouse, Business Requirements Analysts have some of the most vital and important responsibilities in the iterative process of designing, constructing, implementing, and managing a data warehouse. They are the primary link between those who need to turn data into information (the end users) and those who will be providing the ability to do so (the rest of the data warehouse development and management team). Data warehouse Business Requirements Analysts should be able to identify, interpret, and communicate what end users' requirements for information truly are, as opposed to simply asking "what would you like?" When possible, this ability should be based on the analysts' own practical experience of being a user (possibly

Business Requirements Analysts are responsible for understanding the users' business requirements for information and communicating them to the rest of the data warehouse team.

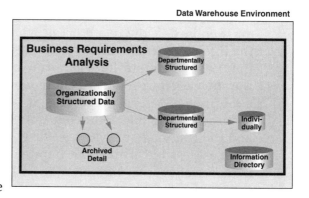

Figure 12.11 Business requirements analysts' responsibility area.

and preferably as a user of the same analysis or reporting systems as that of the end users they are interviewing). Whether Business Requirements Analysts have this direct experience, they should have the interpersonal communications skills and knowledge of the organization's business to

- identify and analyze any current means of attempting to turn data into information;
- formulate questions for interviewing end users in order to determine their requirements for information;
- *listen* to end users state their requirements for information and help them *clarify* the descriptions of those requirements;
- understand those requirements in terms of the organization as a whole and the line(s) of business that the organization participates in; and
- translate and decompose those requirements so that each piece of derived information is understood in its business context.

This chain of analysis lies at the heart of the Business Requirements Analysts' ability to help design and develop a data warehouse that is successful in transforming data into information. Figure 12.12 lists the major responsibilities of the Business Requirements Analysts.

Many organizations are concerned about "yet another round of annoying interviews" that their end users and management must endure. If the results of previous interviews are available, the Business Requirements Analysts and the DWA may feel that these are adequate for an initial implementation of the data warehouse. However, as the management of a data warehouse is a continuously iterative process, it is important that the process of interviewing and following up with senior decision makers and their managers begins as early in the data warehouse lifecycle as possible. This must happen in order to ensure that the data warehouse is now and will continue to meet these end users' informational requirements.

It is often desirable that the original team of Business Requirements Analysts assist in the simultaneous development of the data acquisition and data access processes (covered later in

- Determine scope of each iteration

- Determine business requirements of organization and target users

- Analyze existing informational sources and methods

- Interview target users and management

- Oversee testing and implementation of data access methods and user training

- Continue to work with users after implementation to ensure functional value of the data warehouse to the organization

Business Requirements Analysts

Figure 12.12 Business requirements analysts' responsibilities.

the chapter) in order to provide continuity and leadership based on the knowledge and understanding of the organization's requirements for information that they will have acquired up to that point.

Data Warehouse Architect

The Data Warehouse Architect is responsible for interpreting the organization's informational requirements with regard to the data available to the organization. This is accomplished by analyzing potential source systems to identify candidate subject areas and the data relationships between them, then creating the appropriate data models. A data model serves as the blueprint for organizing the structure and content of data in the warehouse, and is absolutely essential for the design, development, and management of any data warehouse. Figure 12.13 identifies the responsibility area of the Data Warehouse Architect.

The content and structural requirements of a data warehouse are significantly different from those of an operational system. For example, an operational system's data model will strive

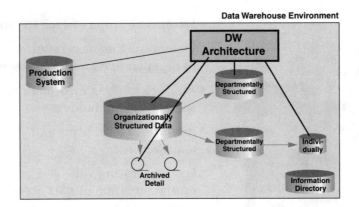

The Data Warehouse Architect is responsible for understanding the systems of record, designing the data acquisition functions, and the data warehouse technical environment.

Figure 12.13 Data warehouse architect's responsibility area.

for as little redundancy as possible in order to preserve data integrity and operational performance. A data warehouse data model, on the other hand, embraces managed redundancy of data in order to ensure that the informational requirements of the entire organization, as well as general and specific functional requirements for information within the organization, are met.

In the best of circumstances, a single conceptual model serves the needs of the organization for both operational and informational data requirements. From the conceptual model, operational and informational models diverge from one another and take different design paths to meet different organizational requirements. Unfortunately, not all organizations have a current, comprehensive conceptual data model from which the Data Warehouse Architect can begin designing the data warehouse. However, data models may exist for some or all of the operational systems that will serve as the sources of data for the data warehouse. The Data Warehouse Architect can take these models and use them as a starting point for designing the data warehouse data model.

If time and resources permit, these operational data models

can be used as the basis for creating an enterprise-wide conceptual data model. However, in the interest of rapidly designing and deploying the data warehouse, this effort may need to be planned for and undertaken after several iterations have been implemented. An alternative would be to purchase or otherwise acquire a generic conceptual data model that is appropriate for the organization's line of business and customize it for the organization. If a data model does not exist for one or all of the operational systems that could serve as the system(s) of record for the data warehouse, the Data Warehouse Architect will need to quickly construct an operational data model from the physical descriptions of the file or database structures of those systems.

The Data Warehouse Architect is also responsible for *maintaining* the logical and physical data models of the data warehouse because of the iterative implementation of new sources, subject areas, and capabilities, as well as the ongoing process of managing the data warehouse to support the organization's changing requirements for information. Data model maintenance is something that few organization's pursue, but it is vital to the health of its informational capabilities.

The second area of responsibility of the Data Warehouse Architect is the identification and analysis of potential source systems in order to determine the appropriate system(s) of record for the data warehouse. This source system analysis focuses on the selection of the appropriate source of data for the atomic level of the data warehouse.

Finally, the Data Warehouse Architect is also responsible for designing and supervising the preparation of the data warehouse technical environment. Most of this work is done for the initial iteration. It includes estimating the size of the data warehouse, at least for the initial and several more iterations; designing the technical environment and recommending the appropriate vendors and products, including end-user and developer workstations; and ensuring that the components of the technical environment are acquired, installed, and available *before* they are required by the developers, the DBA, or the end users. Figure 12.14 lists the major responsibilities of the Data Warehouse Architect.

- Analyze potential sources of data for the data warehouse
- Determine systems of record
- Design data warehouse technical environment
- Design functional attributes of each iteration
- Oversee testing of data acquisition processes and their implementation into production

Data Warehouse Architect

Figure 12.14 Data warehouse architect's responsibilities.

After the initial implementation, the Data Warehouse Architect must be sure that the data warehouse technical environment will continue to support the informational requirements of the organization. This includes conducting a sizing analysis for each iteration to be sure that the existing hardware, software, and other components are capable of supporting the new iteration, as well as reviewing the results of monitoring data acquisition processing and end-user access to the data warehouse.

DEVELOPMENT OF DATA WAREHOUSE PROCESSES

Once the analysis and design of the functional and physical requirements for an iteration are complete, these designs must be turned into programs, processes, and procedures. These will affect either data acquisition, data access, or other maintenance functions for the data warehouse.

Data Acquisition Developers

Data acquisition is the process by which data is acquired from production sources in order to populate the data warehouse in a manner that supports informational processing. Data Acquisition Developers have the responsibility for all tasks that involve extracting data from a system of record, performing any transformations to that extracted data, and populating the target. Primarily, this involves acquiring data from production systems and populating the organizationally structured level of the data warehouse. However, the population of departmentally structured, individually structured, and archived detail levels of the data warehouse also fall within the Data Acquisition Developers' charter.

New production sources of data, changes to existing production sources, and changes in the business rules for acquiring data from production sources are ongoing maintenance tasks that the data acquisition group must constantly address. This requires frequent communication with those responsible for supporting production systems in order to be aware of and prepare for upcoming changes to those sources of data to the data warehouse, as well as with representatives of the end-user community (Subject Matter Experts, covered later) to understand when data that is available from production sources is required in the data warehouse or when changes to business rules need to be implemented. The same kind of tasks are required to support departmental and individual databases; however, the source for these levels will be the organizational and departmental levels, respectively. Figure 12.15 identifies the Data Acquisition Developers' area of responsibilities and Figure 12.16 lists some of those major responsibilities. In those situations where user departments manage their own departmental or individual levels of the data warehouse, the data acquisition group should facilitate training and support for those departments' technical support staff.

Data Access Developers

Data access is the process by which end users access the data in the data warehouse; information analysis refers to the application of business rules to that accessed data in order to begin the process of turning it into information. Executive Information System (EIS) applications are tailored for executive decision-making through detection and analysis of business trends, mon-

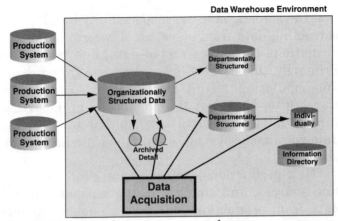

Data Acquisition Developers construct the programs, processes, and procedures to extract, transform, integrate, and load data into the data warehouse, and to populate the departmental and individual levels of the data warehouse from the atomic level

Figure 12.15 Data acquisition developer's responsibility area.

Develop programs, processes, and procedures to:

Data Acquisition Developer

• Extract data from systems of record

• Filter, integrate, transform, standardize, and otherwise process the extracted data

• Populate the atomic level of the data warehouse

• Populate departmental and individual levels of the data warehouse

• Summarize and otherwise "informationalize" data in the data warehouse environment

Figure 12.16 Data acquisition developer's responsibilities.

itoring of problems, measuring and tracking performance, and providing competitive analysis. The data warehouse is the ideal foundation for EIS applications because it provides a framework for integrating and summarizing data in a nonvolatile, historical format.

As depicted in Figure 12.17, Data Access Developers are responsible for ensuring that the end users of the organization are able to use the data in the data warehouse to meet their informational requirements. Primarily, this means developing and maintaining the data access, information analysis, and EIS application(s) (collectively *data access applications*) that enable the end users to take advantage of the capabilities of the data warehouse. The Data Access Developers also carry the responsibility for developing and maintaining data-access application training materials and training end users or representatives of end-user groups who will then train the end users in their group ("train-the-trainers").

Data access applications are inherently different from traditional operational applications and involve special considerations, such as hardware platform use, volume of data, processing patterns, maintenance of information, and updating the information analysis application to accommodate the ever-

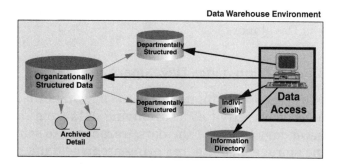

Data Access Developers are responsible for constructing access methods, paths, and predefined applications to enable end users to access the data in the data warehouse environment, including metadata.

Figure 12.17 Data access developer's responsibility area.

Develop programs, processes, and procedures to:

- **Enable unlimited access users ("explorers") to access the data warehouse**

- **Build predefined pathways and other parameters within which limited ad hoc access users (farmers) can utilize the data warehouse**

- **Provide predefined applications for nontechnical information users (tourists) to access the information in the data warehouse**

Data Access Developer

Figure 12.18 Data access developer's responsibilities.

changing needs of the organization. The development of a data access application typically includes determining strategy, formalizing requirements, designing the application, and managing development, testing, and implementation of that application. Figure 12.18 lists the major responsibilities of the Data Access Developers.

Data Warehouse Maintenance Developers

Data warehouse maintenance is a somewhat broad category that includes such activities as archiving data from the atomic level (or secondary levels) of the data warehouse to some form of non-online storage medium, restoring archived data, monitoring the population and access of the data warehouse, monitoring security, and so forth. Data Warehouse Maintenance Developers are responsible for developing these essential utilities, as illustrated in Figure 12.19.

A significant role that the Data Warehouse Maintenance Developers also play is the monitoring of the business uses of the

Data Warehouse
Maintenance Developer

Develop programs, processes, and procedures to:

• Archive atomic level data

• Restore atomic level data

• Perform referential integrity (if necessary)

• Monitor data acquisition and data access activities

• Facilitate data warehouse security

• Any other maintenance activities as required by the organization

Figure 12.19 Data warehouse maintenance developer's responsibilities.

data warehouse (as opposed to the technical monitoring of the database that the DBA performs). By monitoring and understanding how the data in the data warehouse is used, the Data Warehouse Maintenance Developers can help refine the structure and content of the data warehouse to ensure that end users are able to access the data they need in as efficient a manner as possible by feeding this information back to the Data Acquisition Developers or Database Administrator. Likewise, when an ad hoc process is regularly used, the Data Access Developers can integrate that process into the data access application(s), making it available to the entire organization and allowing the end user(s) who developed that ad hoc process to move on to developing new analyses.

SUPPORTING IS ROLES

In addition to these roles and responsibilities of the core data warehouse team, there are several supporting roles necessary for the successful management of a data warehouse. Most of these are made up of existing IS team members, including:

- The executive IS sponsor
- A data quality analyst
- The DBAs and managers of the operational sources of data
- Data center operators
- Clerical support
- Anyone else who may need to contribute to the data warehouse process

Of these support roles, two of them, the executive IS sponsor and the data quality analysts, warrant additional explanation of their unique participation in the management of the data warehouse.

IS Executive Sponsor

Also known as *champions* and vital to the success of any project, Executive Sponsors are especially important to a data warehouse. Two kinds of Executive Sponsors are needed for the data warehouse to be successful: the IS sponsor, and a user sponsor. The IS sponsor should be the CIO, CFO, or whoever the highest ranking IS manager is. It is this person's responsibility to ensure that the entire IS organization understands the objectives and capabilities of the data warehouse, and that appropriate support resources are available to the data warehouse team. Since the IS department itself is often the source of detractions to and criticisms of a data warehouse project, the IS sponsor's role in ensuring an understanding and support of the data warehouse throughout the IS organization is essential. Figure 12.20 illustrates the IS sponsor's role in the development and management of the data warehouse.

Data Quality Analyst

Another function that must be performed in the implementation of the data warehouse is ensuring that the quality of the data acquired from production sources is high enough to meet the organization's requirements for information. If the organization uses a data warehouse management tool to develop the software to

- Ensure support of entire IS organization for the data warehouse

- Interface with high-level management peers to arbitrate or resolve escalated issues

- Provide funding for the data warehouse environment, including iterations not specifically funded by target users

IS Executive Sponsor

Figure 12.20   IS executive sponsor's responsibilities.

extract and load data, the code generated does not require the rigorous testing that manually developed code would, since the tool generating the code will pre-test it in order to ensure that code is logically correct, based on the business rules used to construct it. Therefore, most of the testing required when implementing any of the levels of the data warehouse is focused on ensuring that the data that was *supposed* to be extracted and loaded *was indeed* extracted and loaded, and that it was done properly. This means that all of the mappings and any transformations or other business rules applied to the data were done appropriately. (In this case, "appropriately" is defined as "in accordance with the identified business requirements"; any resulting incorrect data is usually due to incorrect or incomplete entry of those business rules into the development tool.)

However, even if the extracts, mappings, transformations, and loads execute as designed, poor quality data may still enter the data warehouse environment. Since one of the defining characteristics of the data warehouse is that it is nonvolatile, it is inappropriate to manually correct any low quality or incorrect data directly in the data warehouse itself. Rather, the cause of the incorrect data must be determined, that cause and the data affected in the systems of record corrected, and the corrected data allowed to flow into the data warehouse through the appropriate data acquisition process. This correction may result in the incorrect data being replaced (or overwritten) by the data acquisition process; this is not a violation of the "non-volatile" rule, but an example of the proper implementation of this important rule of data warehousing.

As depicted in Figure 12.21, the Data Quality Analyst (DQA) is responsible for identifying any incorrect data or data of questionable quality, identifying the cause of this occurrence, and *recommending* that appropriate actions be taken to ensure that this data is corrected and that future data captured by the data warehouse data acquisition processes continues to be correct. Note, it is not necessarily the DQA's responsibility to correct the data in question. If the data warehouse data acquisition processes are functioning as designed, and that design is correct, then the source of the incorrect data is usually the system of record. In some cases, the cause of data error is an *undocumented feature* of the system of record: a *bug*. If so, it is the responsibility of those managing the operational applications to correct the system of record; until they do so the erroneous data will continue to flow into the data warehouse. In other situa-

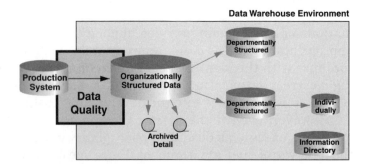

The Data Quality Analyst is responsible for ensuring the data loaded into the data warehouse has been "scrubbed" and is as accurate as appropriate to meet the informational requirements of the organization.

Figure 12.21 Data quality analyst's responsibility area.

tions, the cause of the data error is in the physical data store of the system of record. If so, then the DBA for that system must make the appropriate corrections to the operational data. However, most "bad" data in the data warehouse is a result of an unknown or incorrect business procedure; that is, it is not the source system application that is causing the data errors, but how that system is *used* which results in incorrect or unanticipated data in the data warehouse. Figure 12.22 lists the major responsibilities of the DQA.

In any of these situations, the DQA can only be responsible for identifying the potential cause, recommending a corrective course of action, and incorporating this information into the Information Directory so that the data warehouse end users have access to this diagnostic metadata. The actual correction of such data problems is undertaken by others. The DWA ensures that this takes place or that the appropriate level of management makes the decision that it would be more costly to make this correction than to continue to allow erroneous data to be populated in the data warehouse.

Data Quality Analyst

• Review data loaded into the data warehouse for accuracy

• Recommend maintenance enhancements to data acquisition processes to improve accuracy of data warehouse data

• Make recommendations to operational support for enhancements to systems of record to improve accuracy of operational data

• Review referential integrity of data warehouse data

• Review historical integrity of data warehouse data

Figure 12.22   Data quality analyst's responsibilities.

SUMMARY

There are several key roles necessary to realize the development and on-going management of a data warehouse. Figure 12.23 depicts the data warehouse architecture and the distinct roles involved with developing and managing it. An organization undertaking a data warehouse needs to recognize that these roles should be distinctly separate from existing roles within the organization. The primary responsibility of most existing IS personnel is to ensure that the operational systems perform properly so that the day-to-day functions of the business can be met. This typically divides into an operations group and an application support group. There are other functions as well, such as data administration and end-user support, but these can be classified as either "operations support" or "application support" in nature. The overriding purpose of all of these roles is to facilitate and maintain the organization's operational data environment.

Since informational data and processing is distinctly different from operational data and processing, requiring one staff to

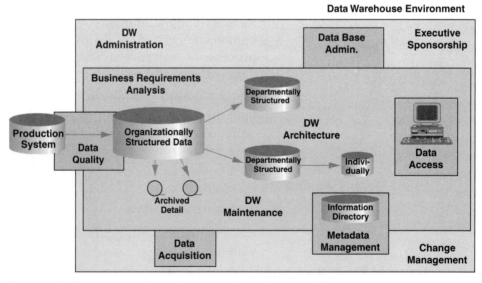

Figure 12.23 Data warehouse IS team roles and responsibility areas.

meet both the informational and operational requirements of the organization does not make sense. A separate data warehouse team, made up of the roles described herein, and working in co-operation with IS's existing operational and application support teams, will ensure that the informational needs of the organization receive the proper functionality and support.

Data Warehouse Staffing Requirements

13

A typical data warehouse will usually grow in scope due to the natural process of iteratively implementing new capabilities and improving existing ones. As a result, an individual resource that may start out fulfilling several different roles will eventually have to focus on one particular role over time and additional resources must be added to assume those responsibilities that must be divested.

INITIAL DEVELOPMENT STAFFING

One of the key success factors in developing a data warehouse is keeping the initial development team relatively small and functionally agile. Organizations that put together large, multitiered and status-report-centric teams rarely realize the benefits that can be derived from the rapid design, development, deployment, and iterative enhancement of a data warehouse.

Table 13.1 gives a brief description of the IS staffing for the initial development of a typical data warehouse, measured in full-time equivalents (FTEs). FTEs do not necessarily need to be "new-hires"; in fact, staffing from within the organization from

Table 13.1 Suggested IS Staffing for Initial Data Warehouse Development

Role	Description	Minimum Initial FTEs
Data Warehouse Administrator	Manages overall project, from inception through initial implementation and on into maintenance and additional iterations.	1
Data Warehouse Organizational Change Manager	Manages organization's expectations and perceptions of data warehouse, its capabilities, limitations, and impact on all aspects of the organization.	Less than 1
Database Administrator	Creates and manages the physical database(s) that make(s) up all levels and aspects of the data warehouse.	1
Metadata Manager	Manages the business and technical metadata, ensuring they are current, accurate, and properly integrated.	Less than 1
Business Requirements Analysts	Identifies and analyzes the organization's business requirements for information and assists in the design of the data warehouse to meet those requirements.	2
Data Warehouse Architect	Creates and maintains the data models for all levels of the data warehouse. Analyzes source systems to determine system(s) of record. Designs data acquisition and technical environment.	1
Data Acquisition Developer	Creates and maintains programs and processes that perform the extracts, transformations, and loads of data from sources to targets.	1 to 3
Data Access Developer	Creates and maintains the programs, processes, and predefined "pathways" that enable end users to access the data in the data warehouse.	1 to 3
Data Warehouse Maintenance Developers	Creates and maintains the programs, processes, and procedures to perform such maintenance tasks as archive, restore, security, monitoring, etc.	1
IS Executive Sponsor	Responsible for supporting the data warehouse project in terms of providing funding, resources, and representation to high-level management peers.	1 (not a full-time role, but crucial for success)
Data Quality Analyst	Monitors and ensures quality of data in data warehouse meets organization's requirements.	Up to 1

existing information workers and key end users is a more effective way of architecting a data warehouse that turns data into information. In some cases, however, new resources will need to be added. These new FTEs can be hired as employees or can be contract or consulting resources if the need for their roles is temporary or transient.

The following is a more detailed description of some of the resources required to fill the roles necessary for the initial design, development, and implementation of a data warehouse. The resulting data warehouse will not be a comprehensive, enterprise-wide endeavor, only the first iteration; it will meet a specific business function and form the foundation for the ongoing, iterative development of the organization's informational capabilities. Figure 13.1 is a representation of the IS data warehouse team.

Data Warehouse Administrator

It is assumed that the Data Warehouse Administrator (DWA) will be involved in all aspects of the project and supervision of project-related activities on a daily basis, in addition to other management activities such as staff meetings, budgeting, re-

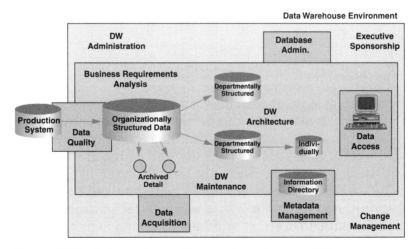

Figure 13.1   Data warehouse IS team roles and responsibility areas.

quired meetings with upper management, and so on. The administrator must be a full-time, dedicated resource and should be empowered to make a significant level of critical decisions in order to rapidly deliver the initial implementation of the data warehouse.

Data Warehouse Organizational Change Manager

During the first iteration of the data warehouse's design, development, and implementation the DWA fulfills the role of Change Manager. Although change management is one of the most significant tasks that the DWA will undertake, it will not be a full-time function during the initial implementation of the data warehouse.

Database Administrator

As stated during the description of this role, it is essential to the success of the data warehouse project that a full-time DBA be assigned to the team from the beginning of the project. The data warehouse DBA can conduct or assist with the data modeling necessary during the analysis phase of the data warehouse project, prior to actually designing and building the physical data warehouse database. The lack of a full-time, dedicated DBA who understands data warehouse design has been the cause of many data warehouse project delays, and sometimes failures.

Metadata Manager

Metadata management does not require a full-time resource during the development of the initial implementation of a data warehouse. This role can be fulfilled by someone fulfilling any of the other roles, but is especially well suited to either the DBA or a Business Requirements Analyst. However, like the Data Warehouse Architect role, growth in metadata and the need to maintain the links between business and technical metadata in the Information Directory will be an ongoing activity, and the need for a Metadata Manager will always evolve from part-time to full-time.

Business Requirements Analysts

The minimum number of Business Requirements Analysts for any data warehouse undertaking is two. Business requirements analysis is one of the most important and time-consuming activities of designing a data warehouse. Having a minimum of two resource people for this important task helps to rapidly identify and understand the business requirements for the first iteration of the data warehouse, and prevents a lone explorer of business requirements from getting lost in the woods of details and possibilities. More than two analysts is an indication that the initial scope of the data warehouse is too broad for a rapid implementation; this is not an incorrect approach, but should be considered by the organization when it is determining its overall goals for beginning the data warehouse process. These same resource personnel can fulfill other roles in the rapid deployment of an initial data warehouse, such as Data Acquisition Developers or Data Access Developers, if the number of human resources available to the project is a constraint.

Data Warehouse Architect

A single Data Warehouse Architect working in parallel with the business requirements analysis activities should be an appropriate balance of resources and time required to complete the initial analysis phase of the data warehouse project. The availability and state of existing data models—or if new models must be developed from an analysis of source systems—will determine whether this is a part-time or full-time role. Since the creation of new data models for future iterations and the maintenance of existing data models to support and reflect enhancements to existing capabilities will be an ongoing activity to support the data warehouse, the need for a Data Warehouse Architect will always evolve from part-time to full-time; the question will be, how rapidly will this evolution take place?

Data Acquisition Developers

If a data warehouse management tool is used for the development of the extract, transformation, and load procedures, then the number of Data Acquisition Developers required for the initial implementation will be relatively small. In general, one full-time resource person should be sufficient for these activities; however, the complexity of integrating data from old, poorly documented or elaborate systems of record may require additional people, possibly as many as two more for a total of three. These resources will not be required, however, until the initial analysis and design of the data warehouse has been completed; therefore, Business Requirements Analysts can fulfill some or all of the resource requirements for Data Acquisition Developers once their analysis and design activities have concluded. This shift in responsibilities from one role to another will keep the total number of resource personnel required to an absolute minimum and will ensure a more rapid continuity of the transfer of information between activities. It will, however, reduce the ability of the data warehouse team to undertake additional analysis and design activities until the initial iteration has been completed.

If a data warehouse management productivity tool is not used for the development of extract, transformation, and load programs and procedures, then the minimum number of data acquisition personnel required is at least five times the number required when using such a tool in order to realize the same capabilities in the same time frame.

Data Access Developers

The number of Data Access Developers required for the initial implementation of a data warehouse is directly dependent on the kind, quantity, and complexity of the end-user access capabilities necessary to ensure a successful first iteration. Since this activity will be the foundation for all future data-access application capabilities, it will require a significant investment of time and resources. At a minimum, one full-time person should be available for this role; however, it may easily require two or three.

Existing application developers from other projects may be an excellent source of Data Access Developers in order to ensure that the data warehouse access applications are consistent with others used throughout the organization, if that is necessary or desirable. Otherwise, depending on the complexity and/or their knowledge of the product being used to develop the access application(s), one or more of the Business Requirements Analysts can be used to fulfill this role, for essentially the same reasons as stated in the description of minimum data acquisition resources.

Data Quality Analysts

The number of resources necessary to ensure that the data in the data warehouse is of the appropriate quality is directly dependent on the quality of the data in the systems of record and the organizational need for data quality. Data quality in informational analyses is not an absolute; some organizations may need to decide between a given level of data quality and other capabilities of the data warehouse, such as difficult integration of data from diverse sources or substantial end-user access capabilities. The initial analysis of the available source systems should provide an indication of the amount and duration of data quality analysis that will be necessary for the initial implementation. Beyond that, the quality of the data loaded into the data warehouse should be continuously monitored; however, the frequency of that monitoring is, again, dependent on the organization's requirements and the health of the operational systems providing the data. Several resource personnel may be required during the early stages of implementation; after implementation that number may dwindle to a minor part-time role, or a single full-time person may need to be retained.

DATA WAREHOUSE MANAGEMENT STAFFING

Growth in the number of resources required to manage the data warehouse while also increasing its capabilities by adding new subject areas, sources of data, and other informational functions, will generally be incremental. Table 13.2 identifies some of the factors that affect growth in the number of full-time equivalents (FTEs). The following is a more detailed description of the impact on staffing some of these roles as the data warehouse increases in functionality, scope, and size.

Table 13.2 Suggested IS Staffing for Ongoing Data Warehouse Management

Role	Additional FTEs per Iteration
Data Warehouse Administrator	0 (Team leaders may be required if the data warehouse functionality grows to sufficient proportion to warrant them.)
Data Warehouse Organizational Change Manager	Possibly up to 1 after several iterations.
Database Administrator	Up to 1 for each 2 or 3 additional iterations for maintenance.
Metadata Manager	Minimum of 1 after first iteration and thereafter.
Business Requirements Analysts	2 additional after initial implementation; Up to 1 for each 2 or 3 iterations thereafter for maintenance.
Data Warehouse Architect	Minimum of 1 after first iteration and thereafter.
Data Acquisition Developer	Up to 1 for each 1 or 2 new iterations and for their maintenance, depending on growth in user demand.
Data Access Developer	Up to 1 for each 1 or 2 new iterations and for their maintenance, depending on growth in user demand.
Data Warehouse Maintenance Developers	0 to 1 after several iterations, depending on complexity of maintenance functions.
IS Executive Sponsor	0 (No additional resource needed.)
Data Quality Analyst	Possibly 1 or more after initial iteration, depending on quality of data from new systems of record and the ongoing quality of existing systems of record.

Data Warehouse Administrator

There should be little or limited increase in the number of staff required to manage new iterations while simultaneously maintaining the existing functionality. However, it may be necessary to establish team leaders for some of the other groups (Business Analysis, Database Administration, etc.) in order to effectively manage the staff necessary to support a growing data warehouse that includes maintenance and new development activities.

Data Warehouse Organizational Change Manager

The need to expand the role of Change Manager to a full-time position is dependent upon the reaction to and acceptance of the data warehouse and its capabilities. If the organization is resistant to change, or if misconceptions about what a data warehouse is and what it is not persist, then a full-time Change Manager should be considered, especially as the data warehouse and the number of users accessing it (and affected by it) grows.

Database Administrators

Each new subject area added to the data warehouse will have a large incremental impact on the staffing requirements for Database Administration. This does not necessarily translate into a one-to-one increase in the number of resources, where each new iteration requires an additional DBA. The steady increase in the number of iterations implemented over time will, however, result in a correspondingly steady increase in the need for more resources to support the growing organizationally structured level of the data warehouse. In addition, each new departmentally structured and individually structured level will add a large incremental need for more Database Administration resources. In some cases, this need can be offset somewhat by having the User Support Technician responsible for individual and even some departmental levels, but there is a corresponding loss of control over data integrity and metadata with such an approach. This approach also merely moves the requirements for new staff to different (non-IS) departments and does not alleviate the need for these resources to increase.

Metadata Manager

As stated previously, the natural growth in the amount of metadata and the need to maintain the links between business and technical metadata in the Information Directory will be an ongoing activity; a Metadata Manager will always evolve from a part-time to a full-time resource. This may not happen until after several iterations; it is directly dependent on the amount and frequency of change to the metadata and the growth in the number and kinds of business requirements as represented by different groups of end users. It should not be necessary to have more than one full-time Metadata Manager, although this may become necessary in certain extreme situations. The use of a metadata management tool will help keep this requirement down to an up-to-one full-time resource level.

Business Requirements Analysts

The number of Business Requirements Analysts required will be a direct function of the scope, deliverables, and project time frame for additional iterations of a data warehouse. After the implementation of the first iteration of the data warehouse, the business requirements analysis activities will need to split into two different directions: management of existing capabilities and the development of new ones. Maintenance includes modifying the existing capabilities in order to continue to meet the (changing) requirements of users, while new development reproduces the steps taken to implement the initial iteration for each additional iteration. Therefore, after the initial implementation of the data warehouse, it is strongly recommended that the number of Business Requirements Analysts at least double to four in order to meet these split responsibilities.

After this initial increase, the number of Business Requirements Analysts should not need to increase significantly. The organization will only be able to absorb a certain amount of new capabilities while mastering the informational functions that have already been provided. These resource personnel should continue to work with the end-user community to ensure that the data warehouse and the available methods of accessing it continue to meet their requirements. Of course, should the organization experience an explosion of requirements for new data and capabilities to be added to the data warehouse, then additional Business Requirements Analyst resources should be added as needed in order to preserve the integrity of the data warehouse and its ability to perform within agreed-upon parameters. However, too much growth can jeopardize the health and stability of the data warehouse environment, leading to an erosion of confidence in the quality and accuracy of the data warehouse; managed growth should be the approach adopted by any organization that has successfully implemented its first iteration of a data warehouse.

If possible, the additional Business Requirements Analysts should be recruited from the target end-user community so that they will continue to enhance the business (not technology) emphasis of the project. Candidates from this group should be able to demonstrate an aptitude for analyzing business problems and using data to answer key business questions; they should have experience working with end users and translating their requirements into workable solutions using the data available. Each additional subject area, source of data, and/or group of users with its own requirements for information may thereafter cause an incremental increase to the staffing requirements to support the management of the data warehouse.

Data Warehouse Architect

After the initial data modeling effort has been completed, the same data modeling resource should continue to flesh out those sections of the conceptual data model to support subsequent subject areas and additional sources of data for implementation, as well as maintaining existing data models to support and reflect enhancements to existing capabilities. There should be no real need to increase the size of this team after the initial implementation (beyond ensuring that a part-time resource person has become full-time).

Data Acquisition Developers

Assuming that a data warehouse development tool is used to facilitate data acquisition, additional subject areas and sources of data will only create a small incremental need to increase the number of Data Acquisition personnel after the introduction of the second subject area. Like business requirements analysis, the second iteration of the data warehouse will result in a significant jump in data acquisition resource personnel required, but not the (virtual) doubling required of Business Requirements

Analysts. Likewise, the more departmental and individual levels required will cause some increase, but not much and only incrementally. However, if the data warehouse is developed "by hand," without a productivity tool, then the requirement for more data acquisition resources increases sharply for each new subject area, source, departmental level, and individual level, additively.

Data Access Developers

All of the factors that affect the aforementioned data acquisition resources will only have an incremental impact on data access requirements. The only exception to this is if an Executive Information System will be developed. Supporting the high-level management users of an EIS should receive appropriate dedicated resources to ensure a high degree of data integrity delivered to management.

Data Quality Analysts

The quality of the data loaded into the data warehouse should be continuously monitored. The frequency of that monitoring will most likely be different for each new iteration, reflecting changes in the organization's requirements and the health of the operational systems providing the data. Eventually, a full-time Data Quality Analyst will probably be required; however, this role may only need to be filled by the Metadata Manager, depending on the factors previously noted.

DATA WAREHOUSE TESTERS

Testing was not listed as a specific role due to the generic need for system and user acceptance testing in any project. Specific resources for system testing are not required in the rapid implementation scenario. The Business Requirements Analysts and DQAs can fulfill this task. Indeed, due to their familiarity with the design and the source systems as a result of their analyses, they are better suited to determine if the resulting data in the warehouse is correct than resource people that have not previously been involved with the project. Of course, disinterested testers may be used if the data warehouse project management wishes to remove those responsible for the development of their own work from testing it.

Likewise, the users of the initial implementation of the data warehouse are the best resource for participating in user-acceptance testing. The determination of whether the data in and capabilities of a data warehouse are acceptable is extremely subjective. As such, those users for whom an iteration has been implemented should be the ones to determine if the goals of that iteration have been met, not a disinterested group of people.

FACTORS AFFECTING GROWTH IN DATA WAREHOUSE STAFFING

Geographic replication of data warehouse capabilities will have an impact on all types of resources. An organization with facilities nationwide will have an increased need for geographic dispersion of its informational capabilities; this is especially true of an organization with worldwide facilities. Since it is often desirable to physically locate data in proximity to either the source of the data or the users of the data warehouse, or both, the effect on staffing to support a nationwide or worldwide implementation of a data warehouse should be carefully considered.

SUMMARY

A data warehouse team should be relatively small so that it can respond in a rapid manner to the constantly evolving requirements for information throughout the organization. As the functional capabilities of the data warehouse grow and evolve, the staff supporting and maintaining it needs to grow as well; however, this growth should be incremental, matching pace with the incremental growth in the capabilities and users of those capabilities.

There is a tendency to staff the data warehouse from outside the organization, trying to identify technical skills for the roles that need to be filled. However, since the purpose of the data warehouse is to facilitate a better understanding of the organization's data and to turn that data into information based on the organization's business requirements, a more effective approach to staffing the data warehouse team is to identify existing resources within the organization with the business skills necessary to fill the specified roles. Technical skills are easier to teach and acquire than an in-depth understanding of the company's business processes and data.

Likewise, since most organizations have some existing means of trying to meet their informational needs prior to implementing a data warehouse, there exists within the company resource people who are currently facilitating those existing informational processes. Their business knowledge as to what users have wanted historically and what has been necessary to try to meet those needs make these existing information workers excellent resources from which to staff the data warehouse team.

14

Data Warehouse End-User Roles and Responsibilities

Like the data warehouse team, the end users of the data warehouse have some specific roles to fulfill as well. These generally break down into two categories: *Support Roles* and *User Types*.

SUPPORT ROLES

Each iteration of the data warehouse must have an Executive Sponsor from the business area of the user community that will be the primary beneficiary of the functionality of that iteration. There are also two important additional roles in the end-user community: Subject Matter Expert and User Support Technician. The responsibility areas of these support roles include the entire data warehouse environment, from a user perspective, as illustrated in Figure 14.1

Iteration Sponsors

Executive sponsors are especially important to a data warehouse. Since the data warehouse is developed iteratively, the executive sponsor for the development of an iteration's functionality will probably change over time as different business requirements for

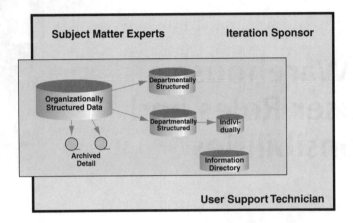

Figure 14.1 End-user support roles responsibility areas.

information are addressed by the data warehouse in each subsequent iteration. Consequently, the executive sponsor for each iteration is referred to as an Iteration Sponsor. Iteration Sponsors should be from as high up in the target user group's management as appropriate. Figure 14.2 depicts the Iteration Sponsor's participation in the data warehouse.

Iteration Sponsor

- Sets scope and business requirements for the iteration or iterations that are intended to meet the informational needs of the department, group, line of business, etc.

- Provides key user resources as required to develop the iteration

- Participates in resolving business issues such as definition of key metrics, standardization, etc.

- May provide funding for development and maintenance of iteration's functional capabilities

Figure 14.2 Iteration sponsor's responsibilities.

It is the Iteration Sponsor's responsibility to ensure that Subject Matter Experts and other user resources are available to the data warehouse team. This may mean that, for the duration of the development of the current iteration of the data warehouse, the Subject Matter Experts' "regular" business responsibilities are reduced or even suspended. Another responsibility of the Iteration Sponsor is to ratify the scope and deliverables of the current iteration of the data warehouse. The Iteration Sponsor must also arbitrate business issues that are discovered by the data warehouse team. For example, if several definitions for a given term or metric are discovered during the analysis phase of an iteration, the Iteration Sponsor is the one who should make the decision as to what the standard should be. In some cases, the Iteration Sponsor cannot make this decision alone, but must take it to other managers or peers within the organization for consensus. It should not be the responsibility of the data warehouse team to make these decisions; the data warehouse team identifies issues that need to be resolved, provides options and recommendations to the Iteration Sponsor for decision or arbitration, and presses forward with the implementation of the data warehouse's functionality.

Once an Iteration Sponsor's business requirements for information are being met by the data warehouse, his or her role changes from one of sponsor to that of supporter and beneficiary of the data warehouse. Since the evolution of the data warehouse is a continuous process, the former sponsor may find him or herself in the role of Iteration Sponsor again as the business requirements for information evolve. At a minimum, the former Iteration Sponsor will continue to be involved in the ongoing use of the data warehouse in that the data warehouse will continue to be an important part of his or her staff's business activities.

Subject Matter Experts

In order to best support the data warehouse, it is necessary to establish a relationship between the user community and the data warehouse development and management team. This relationship should be of a representative fashion; that is, there should be Subject Matter Experts in the various user organizations who can facilitate the communication between the end users and the data warehouse team. These people should be just that: experts on the specific subject areas, source systems, and/or business requirements for information for which they and the organizational groups they represent access the data warehouse. Figure 14.3 demonstrates the responsibilities of these experts on behalf of the user community they represent.

By having a thorough understanding of the business requirements of the department or group that they represent, these experts are able to interpret and communicate the end users' business requirements to the data warehouse team in such a way that they can address these requirements without "guess work." Likewise, they can facilitate clarification of requirements from the data warehouse team to their user community. Subject Matter Experts can (and should) act as a first point of contact for the end users in their department or group for questions on how best to use the data warehouse and other educational issues. They are also excellent resources for helping the data warehouse team to prioritize requests for new enhancements; facilitate the standardization of business metrics, terms, and definitions; and assist with the introduction of new features and capabilities of the data warehouse to their groups.

Subject Matter Experts

- **Provide input to Business Requirements Analysts to define and clarify scope of an iteration of the data warehouse**

- **Participate in the design and review of the data acquisition and data access capabilities**

- **Assist with the training of other users in their functional group, department, line of business, etc.**

- **Act as support resource to other users in their area or of the iteration's capabilities**

Figure 14.3 Subject matter experts' responsibilities.

User Support Technician

In many instances, a departmental or individual level of the data warehouse will be required to support a specific group, department, or person. Often, it is best to implement these levels physically close to the end users who require them. This requires a certain level of technical support for the end-user group in question. In such circumstances it is desirable and advisable that there be a dedicated resource, a User Support Technician, who works in and reports to the management of the group using the departmental or individual level of the data warehouse. The User Support Technician provides on-site technical support for the ongoing management of the physical hardware and database environment of these levels, and ensures that the business priorities of a User Support Technician are closely aligned with the goals and objectives of the department using that level of the data warehouse. Without such user-managed technical support, the departmental and individual user communities will quickly become frustrated with a centralized IS support staff, which has an entire organization's requests and requirements to manage and prioritize. As portrayed in Figure 14.4, the User Support Technician is not only responsible for the end users of departmental and individual levels, but also may be considered for any group that desires

User Support Technician

- Provides overall technical support to users within his or her department, group, line of business, etc.

- Reports and is responsible to the Iteration Sponsor, not IS

- Understands local technical data warehouse environment

- Limited local DBA support

- Technical support for end-user tools used by local users

Figure 14.4 User support technician's responsibilities.

support in accessing any level or entity in the data warehouse architecture.

USER TYPES

Primarily, end users of a data warehouse are categorized as Predefined Application Users, Limited Ad Hoc Access Users, and Unlimited Ad Hoc Access Users.

Unlimited Ad Hoc Access Users

As the name implies, these end users have the greatest technical abilities of all of the end users of the data warehouse. Unlimited Ad Hoc Access Users have the aptitude, training, business knowledge, and ability to access the data in the data warehouse at its most detailed, granular level. These end users typically are either trying to satisfy complex requests from management for detailed analyses or are engaged in *data mining,* attempting to discover previously unknown but suspected events taking place in the organization's data. They can use tools such as interactive SQL to directly access the data warehouse or other, more complex tools such as 3GLs or other procedurally-based reporting languages. Figure 14.5 profiles Unlimited Ad Hoc Access Users.

Unlimited Ad Hoc Access Users primarily access the organizationally structured level of the data warehouse, which includes any archived detail. However, they may also need to access departmentally structured levels in order to take advantage of the pre-categorized data that exists there. Figure 14.6 shows Unlimited Ad Hoc Access Users' access to the data warehouse. The analyses and research that Unlimited Ad Hoc Access Users conduct also provide a basis for building predefined pathways, queries, and other data-access application techniques to support Limited Ad Hoc Access Users.

Limited Ad Hoc Access Users

The majority of data warehouse end users require what is referred to as "limited ad hoc access" to the data warehouse. Limited Ad Hoc Access Users are typically analysts and others from

Unlimited Ad Hoc Access Users

- "Explorers"

- Highly technically skilled in accessing data

- Need powerful, procedural tools, not simple-but-limited tools

- Often develop predefined pathways and applications for use by other user types

- Limited number of users, typically

- Support organizational requirements for complex reporting

Figure 14.5 Unlimited ad hoc access users' profile.

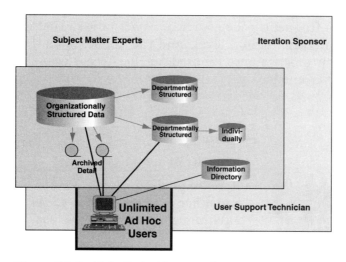

Figure 14.6 Unlimited ad hoc users' access.

whom the Predefined Application User may request a more detailed analysis of a trend or other business information. These end users will use the predefined queries available to Predefined Application Users, but also need access to more detailed information available in the data warehouse. However, they still need to be insulated to some extent from the complexity of the data as it exists in its most granular form at the organizationally structured level. For these end users, a tool that provides access to predefined paths or pre-joined views of logically organized data will enable them to select, filter, and act on those data elements they require without forcing them to understand the complexities of relational database design or interactive SQL. Figure 14.7 profiles Limited Ad Hoc Access Users.

Limited Ad Hoc Access Users may occasionally need to drill down to the organizationally structured level, but should have substantial drill-down capabilities at the departmentally structured level and in the data-access applications available to them to support the majority of their informational requirements. Limited Ad Hoc Access Users will also need to access any individually structured levels in order to support their managers. These are frequently the source of new analyses that can be integrated into individual levels and the applications that access them. Figure 14.8 shows Limited Ad Hoc Access Users' access to the data warehouse.

Limited Ad Hoc Access Users

- "Farmers"
- Majority of analytical users
- Require predefined pathways and other vehicles, such as OLAP environment, to facilitate access
- Significant drill-down and drill-across capabilities required
- Typically support upper management's requests for information

Figure 14.7 Limited ad hoc access users' profile.

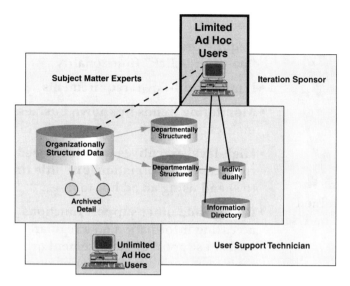

Figure 14.8   Limited ad hoc users' access.

Predefined Application Users

Predefined Application Users do not have a high level of technical expertise, but are typically at a relatively high level within an organization's management structure; they are also frequently administrative assistants or other designees of managers. Executives, managers, and other high-level end users do not require and, indeed, usually do not desire access to the data warehouse at a detailed level. For these types of end users an application front-end should be developed that provides simple, easy-to-navigate, predefined queries that address their typical business requirements for information. These predefined queries provide a strategic (or high-level) view of business information, usually represented as a trend of key metrics or critical success factors necessary to monitor the health and progress of the organization. The data access applications that serve Predefined Application Users need some drill-down capabilities to meet managers' basic requirements for understanding the results and metrics that are presented to them. Ease-of-use, understanding, and rapid response are essential characteristics of any data access application that is developed for Predefined Application

Predefined
Application Users

- "Tourists"

- Require predefined applications with "point-and-click" functionality

- Limited drill-down requirements

- Monitoring trends in known business metrics

- High-level executives with high need for access to information, but little time to spend using an ad hoc tool

- Clerical and other support functions accessing information on a regular basis in support of management or their own periodic informational needs

Figure 14.9   Predefined application users' profile.

Users. Figure 14.9 profiles Predefined Application Users. Figure 14.10 shows the level of the data warehouse that Predefined Application Users typically access.

As depicted in all of the access area diagrams in this chapter, all of the end users of the data warehouse—Predefined Applica-

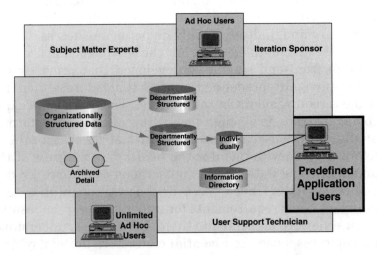

Figure 14.10   Predefined application users' access.

tion Users, Limited Ad Hoc Access Users, and Unlimited Ad Hoc Access Users—need access to the metadata stored in and managed by the Information Directory. Without access to the Information Directory, through either direct means or an application, end users will not be able to understand the content and context of the data in the data warehouse, and therefore will not be able to accurately conduct their analyses. This lack of ability to verify the accuracy and understanding of the data they are accessing will quickly lead to distrust of the accuracy of the data in the data warehouse. This phenomenon is especially true for less technologically sophisticated end users who rely on data-access applications to access, preanalyze and present their information.

DATA WAREHOUSE INITIAL END-USER STAFFING

Table 14.1 gives a brief description of the suggested staffing of user roles for the initial implementation of a typical data warehouse. The following is a more detailed description of some of the resources required to fill the user roles necessary for a successful initial data warehouse implementation.

Subject Matter Experts

An initial implementation of a data warehouse should be an activity with heavy user participation, if not direct sponsorship. It is best to concentrate on a specific business function for each iteration, when possible, rather than trying to serve too many functionally different requirements in a singe shot. Therefore, the user group that is the focus of the initial implementation should make as many Subject Matter Experts available to the data warehouse development team as possible without overwhelming the ability of the Business Requirements Analysts to complete their analysis and design in a reasonable time frame.

User Support Technician

It is usually not necessary to have a User Support Technician for the initial implementation of the data warehouse. The need for

Table 14.1 Suggested End-User Staffing for Initial Data Warehouse Development

Role	Description	Minimum Initial FTEs
Iteration Sponsor	Sets scope and acceptance criteria for the iteration. Provides crucial user resources.	1 (Not a full-time requirement, but a critical role that must be filled.)
Subject Matter Experts	Experts on the specific subject areas, source systems, and/or business requirements for information for the organizational groups they represent.	3 to 5 (minimum of 1) (Not necessarily full-time, depending on the scope of the iteration.)
User Support Technicians	Work in end-user department or group to maintain departmental and individual levels and directly support end users.	None likely for initial iteration.
Unlimited Ad Hoc Access Users	Access data warehouse at most granular level for most complex and undefined analyses.	1 to 3
Limited Ad Hoc Access Users	Typically access data warehouse at the departmental level, requiring substantial drill-down capabilities, in support of upper management.	3 to 5
Predefined Application Users	Require substantial data-access application capabilities to provide simple, rapid access to predefined metrics and trends.	3 to 5 (not required)

this role grows over time and is based directly on the requirements of the departmental groups and the culture of the organization.

ONGOING DATA WAREHOUSE USER ROLES STAFFING

Just as an increase in IS staffing is necessary to support the growing data warehouse, there is also an increase in the end-user resources as represented by the end-user roles and responsibilities. Table 14.2 identifies some of the factors that affect growth in the

Table 14.2 Suggested End-User Staffing for Ongoing Data Warehouse Management

Role	Additional FTEs per Iteration
Iteration Sponsor	1 per iteration (may be same person, therefore not a "new" or "additional" sponsor).
Subject Matter Experts	3 to 5 (not additive)
User Support Technicians	Up to 1 per department
Unlimited Ad Hoc Access Users	1 to 3+
Limited Ad Hoc Access Users	∞
Predefined Application Users	∞

number of end-user resources. The following is a more detailed description of the impact on staffing some of these user roles as the data warehouse increases in functionality, scope, and size.

Subject Matter Experts

Subject Matter expertise will increase steadily with each new subject area and/or source system added, as well as with each new functional user group. These are end-user resources and should not directly impact Information Systems staffing; however, it should be noted that Subject Matter Experts should be in place within user groups to facilitate communication and support between the data warehouse team and the end users. Therefore, end-user management should account for an increase in resources to support this important role.

User Support Technicians

As previously stated, the need for a User Support Technician grows directly out of the requirements of groups within the organization to control *their* departmental and/or individual levels of the data warehouse. As with subject matter experts, these are end-user resources and should not directly impact Information Systems staffing. Likewise, End User groups should plan on staffing these resources as their departmental or individual capabilities grow and their need or desire for direct support grows.

SUMMARY

It may seem unnecessary to identify the key roles that users play in developing and managing a data warehouse. However, many organizations have failed to recognize the importance that users play in data warehouse management and consequently have lost sight of the importance of driving the evolution of the data warehouse from users' business requirements. The result is usually a technology focus to the data warehouse, not a user focus, resulting in an information environment that does not meet the organizations' needs for decision support analysis.

From an iteration's sponsor of business functionality to an executive who needs to monitor the trends in an important business metric; from a subject matter expert to a highly skilled technical user to the occasional browser of corporate information, users have distinct and important roles to play in the evolution of the data warehouse, so that it can continue to meet their business requirements for information. Users also have a significant responsibility as "good corporate citizens" to work with the data warehouse team to ensure that the data warehouse continues to add value to the organization by providing an important strategic and tactical tool for accessing and analyzing information.

Data Warehouse Project Principles

It is now taken for granted that organizations create data warehouses because they want to enable users to make better decisions by gaining insight into corporate data. In a fundamental sense, data warehouses offer the opportunity for users to do their jobs more effectively than ever before. Warehouses are built by Information Systems (IS) for business users. With that perspective in mind, it seems short-sighted to consider the needs of the end user solely during the selection of data retrieval technologies. Rather, it seems preferable to embed the user's perspective during the entire process of building a data warehouse—from design to deployment. This chapter contains some concepts and principles that may help the DWA bring the user perspective to data warehousing projects. It is organized into six sections:

- Setting Project Objectives
- The Project Team
- Anticipating Your Users' Needs
- Implementation Objectives for Tool Selection
- Data Design and Architecture Guidelines
- Project Delivery Tactics
- Key Concept Summary

SETTING PROJECT OBJECTIVES

Before you begin any warehouse project, it is important to know what you expect to achieve and to set reasonable expectations with both users and project management. You will immediately discover that everyone associated with the project has different objectives. To further complicate matters, not all objectives will be expressed in measurable or quantitative items like increasing revenues, reducing backlogs, or reducing costs. Some objectives may be expressed as corporate missions like improving user motivation or making better decisions.

One project actually started because there was an extra database server around and some energetic IS staff figured they might as well use it for something. So they threw data into it and said, "Okay, now we have a warehouse." From there it grew and evolved into a vibrant system over a year or two. Other projects came into being to meet the demands of the CFO. When the CFO says, "We are a billion-dollar-a-year technology company and I'm sick and tired of meetings where three different people have three different numbers and they are all somewhat right. I want one number," data warehouses are built. More frequently, IS organizations are stretched to such limits that they are eager to adopt new technology and systems architectures that will enable them to be more responsive and pro-active to the needs of their end users.

Determine the Type of Organization

Although data warehouses are useful and valuable in almost any environment, the speed of adoption, the degree of resistance, and intensity of support are highly dependent upon the "character" of the IS organization and the role it plays in the organization. Some questions to ask, as indicators of your organization's character, are:

What are your organization's data-access preferences and how do you assess them?

Do you have to tightly control access to data?

Are your end users empowered and encouraged to ask questions?

Is your company generally slow or quick to change?

Is it possible for you to effect change in existing production systems?

Are you an earlier adopter of technology or a later adopter of technology?

Figure 15.1 divides the universe of companies into four quadrants to guide evaluation of an organization's characters. Design the overall warehouse implementation project plan to reflect the answers discovered. If you fundamentally believe that your company is prepared to support the paradigm shift that is required to make optimal use of a data warehouse, then develop an aggressive plan and plan for rapid adoption. If your company is not a technology pioneer, you can still go ahead with a warehouse,

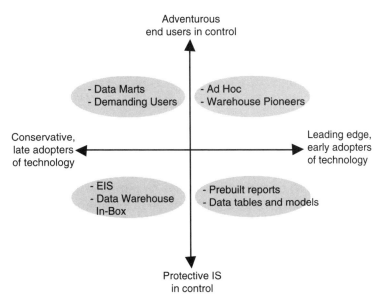

Figure 15.1 Warehouse strategy is determined by two factors: degree of IS control over end users and position along the IS technology adoption curve.

but perhaps it should be on a smaller scale, with a more cautious implementation schedule.

Determine Project Size and Starting Point

Another critical consideration is project size and entry point. The best way to get started is to pick the right set of initial users. Most immediately successful projects started by focusing on the needs of a well-defined user community. Size alone is not an important determiner of success: Small groups can be difficult; large groups can be hugely successful. Successful projects have users who share a common profile.

What determines that common profile? Most important is the data those users work with. Users in the core group must all use the same data. They may use the data to make different types of decisions and reports, but the users must need the data that will be in the warehouse. The second characteristic concerns the type of work being done. Telesales staff and market researchers—although each works with sales data—are unlikely to be satisfied with identical data warehouse solutions. Each group needs data at different levels of detail and needs to perform vastly different forms of analysis. The first group of users of a new data warehouse should be people who are going to use the systems in similar fashion, using common data at manageable levels of detail.

Small Is Beautiful

Data warehousing is a relatively new idea; it is possible that no one in your organization has ever used, much less built, a data warehouse before. There are few books to read (you have one in your hands) and no methodologies to purchase. Experienced consultants are in great demand and educational opportunities are limited. In a new environment such as this, the only way to learn is by trial and error. The "error" part of the trial suggests that you may not get everything right the first time. Logically, it's better to experiment and learn on small systems with not too much data and not too many users, than it is to build the first system with terabytes on the server and thousands of clients.

Some very smart people get hooked on the vision of the great, perfectly integrated "corporate warehouse in the sky," in which all data is clean, related to every other element, is perfectly up-to-date, and responds in seconds to any request. If you want to get there, you can do it in small, incremental steps by building that universal data warehouse one data mart at a time.

Each phase of the phased data warehouse is targetted at a well-defined group of business users and closely related data subject areas. Subsequent phase projects add new business users and new subject areas as necessary. With each new project some of the data tables, fields, and definitions from previous marts can be reused and will therefore link the new data with what is existing. By some estimates, more than 50 percent of the data in all data marts will be shared in common with at least a few other data marts in the organization. Rather than contributing to wanton data proliferation of *stove-pipe* data collections, a well-organized, structured, and planned program of successive data marts will create a virtual enterprise-wide data warehouse. This approach will produce immediate results, reduce risk, shorten implementation cycles, and allow the organization to experience the benefits of data warehousing in a much more cost-effective fashion than the alternatives.

Most successful data warehouses started with a group of users who agreed on fundamentals and needed a manageable amount of data from a limited number of sources. Small projects succeed when large ones fail because small projects can cycle more quickly. They have less inertia so it is easier to move them in the right direction. Small projects also produce results more quickly. It simply takes less time to everything—less time to locate data, transform it, load it, and build indexes; less time to train users and tune performance. A good rule of thumb is to design your warehouse projects to have finished the first cycle within six months.

THE PROJECT TEAM

Although the roles and responsibilities of the data warehouse team was discussed at length in Chapter 12, this section provides a brief and compact review of those roles. The data warehouse project team will typically be composed of 12 to 15 people who will be responsible for building a data warehouse in the organization. Who should be on this team? The ideal team should have representatives from each of the following five categories: Database Designer, Data Archaeologists, Systems Programmers, Users and Trainers, and Data Warehouse Administrator.

Database Designer

Good physical database design is essential because it has more impact on the performance of the system (from the user's perspective) than anything else, even the database server itself. The data warehouse database designer needs to know more than just code and date; he or she needs to understand the principles of dimensional modeling and must be able to apply those principles to the warehouse project. The database designer must understand both business people and analysts— people who can think about the business and present the business of the organization through the data structures of the warehouse. Data designers frequently become metadata managers, so they must be able to communicate in both technical and business terms; they may well become the key users of metadata management tools.

Data Archaeologists

The data archaeologists are the people who know legacy systems inside and out. In many projects, up to 60 percent of the total team effort is spent locating, scrubbing, reconciling, rationalizing, and figuring out what the data means before it reaches the warehouse. You simply can't get the data out of legacy systems unless you have data archaeologists who know what's in the old systems or you're willing to invest staggering amounts of time to uncover the past. Leaving those people off the team and assuming that they will answer the questions when asked is inviting delays and increased costs.

Systems Programmers

Transformation programmers ensure that the data from legacy systems moves cleanly and repetitively into the warehouse. Even commercial tools need programmers to manage them, so don't skimp on this resource.

Users and Trainers

Plan for the deployment of the data warehouse from the beginning of the project. As soon as possible, invite on the team the people who are actually going to be the evangelists of the solution into the user community. A few key power users, any current decision-support service providers, and a key business manager will be essential contributors during data design reviews, the user tools selection, and the implementation planning and deployment. Invite the training organization to participate as well. This ensures a strong connection into the user community and quick access to current business knowledge to balance the technical expertise of the rest of the team.

Data Warehouse Administrator

Most commonly, the DWA is the project team leader who will be responsible for coordinating all aspects of the data warehouse project and for balancing the competing needs and objectives of all the other interests. The DWA can be a technically inclined business manager or a business-needs-oriented technician, so long as the person is able to gather support and mediate between IS and the user community.

ANTICIPATING USER NEEDS

The data warehouse project leader must always remember that the data warehouse is only successful if it is used. It is essential that IS professionals on the data warehouse project break the information technology knowledge barrier. The DWA does more than read report requests and write reports; he or she must understand the nature and context of the business and the users' needs. Only then can the DWA make the design decisions and functionality tradeoffs, and create effective solutions that will work for the organization.

Who Visits the Warehouse?

Understanding users is crucial to meeting their needs. Users of the data warehouse can be categorized into four groups:

- **Report Viewers** are those users who prefer to work with information in structured reports.
- **Data Tourists** want guidance as they tour their data, but can take the initiative to sometimes go off the beaten path and investigate data on their own.
- **Information Surfers** want to look at any data, anytime, anywhere with instant response. They are typically frustrated by the limitations of current systems and frequently have learned SQL, SAS, Nomad, or Focus on their own in order to do the analysis they need.
- **Information Planners** and Data Warehouse staff are also users of the data warehouse. They will visit the warehouse every day, testing, validating, tuning, observing its behavior, and its usage.

Report Viewers typically look for answers in the same location on the same report on a predictable schedule. They could care less about what tool is used to produce the report and they might even prefer to look at the report on paper. Report Viewers typically have no tolerance for a system that requires them to remember how to do something. They may work with systems so infrequently that they will need to be prompted through each step in the process. Report Viewers are candidates for accessing data with browser-type applications that require little set up or ongoing support. The good news about meeting the needs of report viewers is that they usually do not demand instantaneous response to ad hoc requests; they know that they are going to get their report. In access-tool terminology, viewers need EIS solutions, or standard reports.

Contrast the Report Viewer with the Data Tourist. A tourist visiting a new city starts with a guide book that mentions cultural and historic highlights, points of interest, and where to eat. The guide shows where to get started and may include a map. Data Tourists entering the data warehouse want the same kind of assistance; they want recommendations as to interesting places to go. They also want a system that can collect and cluster data together so that it makes sense. Data Tourists typically prefer a structured report to start with, but that report has to have some variability. While they use standard reports with variables, Data Tourists also need to customize their own reports and save a record of the paths they took through their data. Finally, Data Tourists are somewhat less tolerant of delays than are Viewers, so they expect good response during a single session. In access-tool terminology, Data Tourists need a stable managed query environment that allows interactive analysis and variable, customizable reports. Data Tourists are heavily dependent on business metadata to help them locate and assemble the solutions they need.

The Information Surfer is the most demanding but fortunately the smallest percentage of the average population. Surfers constitute, at most, 10 percent of the typical user community. They want the ability to ask any question of any data at any time with instantaneous response. Surfers are rarely satisfied by existing reporting systems because they are always asking an unexpected question. Surfers are the ones who need true interactive multidimensional analysis and may be frustrated by the restrictions of a tightly controlled managed query environment. To answer their questions, Surfers are not afraid of digging into technology and crafting what they need out of what is available. Information Surfers are typically power users of desktop software and some may have even taught themselves SQL or other mainframe programming languages in order to gain access to the corporate data they need to use. Surfers, demanding though they may be, will be the source of many of the ideas for additions and improvements of the data warehouse. Include a few Surfers on the data planning teams of the data warehouse on an ongoing basis for the quality of their ideas and as leading indicators of future requirements.

As system planners, the IS team will interact with the data

	EIS/Fixed Format Reports	Managed Data View	Variable Queries & Reports	Ad Hoc, Interactive Analysis	Live View of Data Structure
Report Viewers	Essential	Essential	Basic	Low	None
Data Tourists	Basic	Essential	Essential	Low	None
Information Surfers	Optional	Low	Basic	Essential	Essential
System Planners	None	None	None	Basic	Essential

Figure 15.2 Tool feature and function requirements based on the type of user.

warehouse every single day as they work through the development cycle. Many data access tools with thick, static semantic layers are unsuitable for the Planner. Upon discovering this, Information Planners have been know to avoid all end-user tools and choose to work in SQL directly. This is an unfortunate outcome that should be avoided because it makes it even harder for IS to understand the needs of the end users. How can IS judge the capabilities of the tools if they themselves do not "walk the walk" with users' tools? If possible, the DWA should equip the warehouse IS team with the tools that are being used by the end-user clients.

The requirements placed on desktop tools by each of these groups are quite different and can be characterized by the chart in Figure 15.2. It is quite a challenge to find a single solution that is acceptable across the board because features that are essential for one group may be almost completely useless for others.

IMPLEMENTATION OBJECTIVES FOR TOOL SELECTION

During the implementation of the data warehouse, many tactical implementation decisions must be made: selecting products, assembling teams, designing the database, and deploying the warehouse to end users. One of the most difficult tactical decisions when building a data warehouse is the selection of the right products. In a client-server environment it seems as though the number of choices to make is becoming exponential, not linear, with the complexity of the systems. Each choice takes time, and there is never be enough time to review everything completely. If it were possible to do a "complete" evaluation, it would probably be out-of-date the day the product was purchased. So the question is, "Where should the DWA spend time?"

Although the database server is a critical decision, it is not covered here because all organizations have experience using and selecting databases. There is little comparable experience selecting end-user tools, yet they are equally important to the success of the data warehouse project. The most frequently made mistakes are to leave the decision about end-user tools to the end of the project or to believe that tool selection is essentially unimportant. Too many companies have selected and deployed software to end users simply because it was free, because it came bundled with another system, or because it was recommended by a current vendor. Cost is usually a factor and compatibility with other components is essential, but the most important factor in the selection of end-user tools is how well the product meets the needs of *your* end users.

To select tools the end users will like, put yourself in the users' shoes, or better yet, allow users to pick their favorite. Remember that the last 10 percent is 90 percent of the perceived value of the project. The users are interacting with the database solely through the medium of the query tools you provide. Much of their sense of the warehouse will be set by these products. It is important, therefore, to find the tools users can work with.

Over time you will fill the users' tool kit with specialized tools that meet specialized needs, but start with the basics and pick at least one product that will fill the essential needs of each type of user, as shown in Figure 15.2.

Report Viewers need push-button, front-end functionality that produces standard format output and EIS systems that allow them to open a spreadsheet, a mail document, or a word processor and push a button labeled "today's report." It is possible to find EIS construction systems that integrate with standard desktop products, are easy to build, and require no special maintenance, setup, or administration.

The tool for a Data Tourist is the classic Managed Query tool that offers protected, predefined views of the database, prebuilt reports, and variable, prompted constraints. You will also need an attractive, easy-to-use, point-and-click graphical user interface. Data Tourists need to be nudged into doing some analysis on the data. It's really comfortable to push the button, get the report, hand it to the boss, and not think about it too much. But the better managed query products contain simple analysis tools with drill-down and multidimensional views, in addition to report-writers, so the users can see a bit more than just the familiar report.

Information Surfers are the hardest to satisfy because they want "more, now." They want to discover things in the data that no one has ever seen before. Typically, they will not be content with prebuilt models of the data, so managed query environments can be frustrating to surfers. They aren't content with only "abstractions" of tables or prebuilt reports. They're going to want to combine elements together that have never been combined before. They do not want to traverse a hierarchy that has been preset by someone else because they are looking for relationships that no one has anticipated. So the key requirements on tools for surfers are that they are completely open-ended, provide a direct connection to the database, and multidimensional capabilities.

The Information Planner needs a tool that provides a direct view of the physical tables and offers control over the modeled layer. With a live view you can actually define tables, load data, and look at the results immediately. You don't have to define additional layers. Planners want to support query tools that have centralized, repository-based administration. If you can find one of those that also provides automatic version control and protection for the user community against the changes you're making, you will have a good solution. Auditing capabilities are also a key requirement so that IS planners can monitor the usage of the system and improve its performance, or educate its users through time.

The category of products called *query tools* are distinguished from other kinds of data-access products because they are versatile objects that can be adapted to many purposes. A *tool* can be used by many people of many different levels of expertise to accomplish very different results. Anyone can use a hammer, but a child will achieve different results with it than will a master carpenter. The best query tools are the hammer of the data warehouse. They can provide a starting point for tourists, integrate into desktop systems for report viewers, and include multidimensional analysis so surfers can go beyond reporting.

DATA DESIGN AND ARCHITECTURE GUIDELINES

Users of a data warehouse actually see the database design and feel the effects of the system architecture decisions. Together with the choice of access tool, the database design is one of the two most important components of the data warehouse.

System Architecture Considerations

If the warehouse is built on a stable, solid system architecture, it will work better and last longer without major revision. A good architecture for the data warehouse is a true client-server model because it most effectively leverages the tremendous compute power in the CPUs on the desktop machines of the users. Whenever possible, design the system so that it spreads the load between the centralized data processing power and the desktop CPUs. Centralized servers are the ideal place to store virtually unlimited amounts of data in highly scalable systems. But it is inevitably the case that no matter how expensive and robust the central server is, that processor still must be shared among all the users of the warehouse.

The database server has lots and lots of storage space, lots and lots of disk space, but proportionally less memory. Desktops typically have restricted disk space, but significant quantities of available memory (Figure 15.3).

The database server should then be required to do the "heavy lifting"—the selecting and aggregating of interesting items into a results set that is delivered to the client machine for further analysis. The processor capabilities of the desktop CPU can be harnessed for more than just display; it should do local analysis

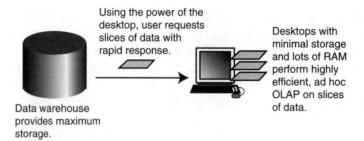

Using the power of the desktop, user requests slices of data with rapid response.

Desktops with minimal storage and lots of RAM perform highly efficient, ad hoc OLAP on slices of data.

Data warehouse provides maximum storage.

Figure 15.3 A highly scalable, cost effective architecture that provides high throughput and rapid response times results from spreading the load between server and local desktops.

and second or third pass processing. This architectural observation has a bearing on the selection of data-access products, metadata repositories, and servers.

Database Design for the Data Warehouse

The design of the data warehouse will be completely different than the data design of transaction sources. If you simply move your transaction system into a separate database and call it a warehouse, it will not work for two reasons: (1) users will not be happy with it because it will be too complex, and (2) they will not be happy because Third Normal Form designed schemas will not respond quickly to typical decision-support queries that may require five or six joins. Several common design techniques that are taught as part of relational theory are *not* appropriate for data warehousing. A common mistake made by many novice design teams is to believe that relational databases only "work" when the data schemas are designed according to relational theory. This is a fallacy and makes about as much sense as believing that #2 pencils only "work" to fill in the circles on standardized tests. A relational database is a remarkably versatile tool for locating information based on its attributes. If you need it to be the backbone of a transaction system, there are appropriate design rules you should follow for optimal performance and data integrity.

There are also appropriate design rules to employ when you are designing a database to support end-user access in a data warehouse. It is just that the rules are different, although the tool is the same. Before you begin, study dimensional modeling techniques, plan on denormalizing whenever possible, reduce the number of tables by a factor of 10 or more, and pre-aggregate to create business data at an appropriate granularity in each dimension. Good designs have these characteristics:

- The design will make sense to users. Users will recognize their business in the data and will generally know which fields and tables they should use without much assistance.
- Most queries will return results rapidly.
- Users will soon ask for more data to be added.

Design Rules for Data Warehouse Databases

Make the logical database understandable for end users.
Data warehouses are meant to be used. If users don't understand it, they will not use it happily and will need constant hand-holding. While some companies who have difficulties with data warehousing claim that bad performance is the reason that their data is not accessed, the majority will admit when pressed that the culprit is an incomprehensible database.

Denormalize the data.
Stand the usual rules of relational theory on their head and denormalize the data. Normalized designs are hard to comprehend. Denormalized designs tend to be more self-explanatory. Most end users seem to understand the concept of a record perfectly well. However, few understand how joins work, even after significant amounts of training. Denormalized tables have longer records that may contain some duplicated data rather than shorter records that require many joins. Typical multi-attribute search-and-scan performance is better on denormalized data because fewer tables are involved than in normalized designs.

Minimize the number of tables.
Fewer tables make the database easier to understand and improves query performance.

Minimize the number of joins.

Fewer joins make the database easier to understand and improve query performance.

Make the physical layout of the database the same as or close as possible to the logical layout.

What purpose is served in keeping a logical model that looks "the way it should" and leaving physical tables in some other state? By making them the same, response time is dramatically improved and the work load of system maintenance is reduced. Sometimes in test systems or for short periods of time you may use logical models to cover for you while you adjust load programs and create the correct physical tables; however, such a state should be avoided in production data warehouses if at all possible.

Design for continuing change.

While transaction databases are usually fairly static, data warehouses tend to change frequently. Because data warehouses are meant to support analysis, they are affected by the same forces that produced the report bottleneck in the first place. Users will ask for more ways to view the data than anyone can anticipate. Regardless of how much time has gone into designing the 'ultimate data warehouse," over time, tables and columns will be added. Many managers of successful data warehouses earn "bragging rights" based on the rate of change in their data warehouses. Planning for this rate of change is a necessity if you wish to avoid a success disaster.

Avoid duplicate metadata.

Metadata is data describing the structure of the data warehouse and its contents. One of the implications of the continuing evolution of the typical data warehouse is that the metadata will need to be changed, too. Currently there are many proprietary metadata formats on the market. Some are more rigid and inflexible than others and some metadata formats cannot be shared between tools or systems. Because the warehouse will change over time, maintaining all the available metadata may involve more work than maintenance of the warehouse itself.

The best advice about metadata is to try to keep it to a minimum at first and to avoid all multiple, incompatible formats.

Star Schema or Dimensional Modeling

One basic data design principle that is easy to implement is to use a *star schema* design (some people call this "tall table" design or a dimensional model in a relational database). Tall Tables mean there are many fields in each table rather than many tables. The notion of a "star" suggests that the basic measurements by which you run your business can be stored in a single table—the *fact table*—and that the significant attributes describing each major dimension of the business can each be stored in tables, one per dimensions. Dimensional models have a distinctive structure as shown in Figure 15.4. Essentially, construct a *star schema* by denormalizing as much as possible until all attributes of similar objects in single tables are combined. Identify the finest granularity that you need to store in the warehouse and the basic independent "dimensions," or entities that describe the data you wish to capture. When combined with the essential measurements of the business, the dimensions and facts can be modeled in a database design that may look, generally, like what is known as a star schema.

Two benefits arise from this type of design. The first is improved query performance. Relational database servers simply do better when there are fewer joins per query. The second rea-

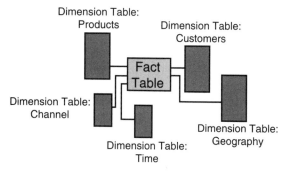

Figure 15.4 A typical star schema design.

son is that users understand their business in those kinds of terms. The average end user doesn't know that in a completely normalized database an address might be stored in several tables, one for each component of an address—city, state, country, and so on. Such a structure allows database designers to enforce integrity on input, but the price is paid when the data is retrieved. When the entire address is requested, then the user and the database server have to join five tables together just to get a single address record back.

Average users don't have a clue what the physical database looks like. They expect to see an address record , so build a table in the warehouse with all elements of the address side-by-side in an address table. Remember, you do not have to enforce update data integrity in a data warehouse. Data integrity is enforced at load time, so it doesn't really matter how redundant the data is in the warehouse.

Although it is possible to hide normalized database designs under thick semantic layers, logical views or other superficial adjustments, each of those techniques only addresses the first problem but has no impact on the second. No matter how understandable you have made the database schema appear, unless the physical schema is optimized for data warehouse style, decision-support queries, performance will suffer. Don't wallpaper over the structural cracks of a bad database design with thick semantic layers; they won't fix the problems with the foundation of the warehouse.

Closely related to the ideas driving a dimensional model is the ideal that every item and every scrap of data in the warehouse may be directly accessed by an end users. Therefore, create the warehouse using business terms for field and table names. You're building the database from scratch, so you can pick names without any legacy baggage left over from years of programmer dominance. In the data warehouse, the needs of the user are paramount; nowhere are those users more important than in the names you place. It is important to link the old names to the new ones; that is an excellent use for business metadata. In the metadata layer, record the fact that the field called "weekly sales" came from QXR1 and that it is, in fact, a weekly aggregate of the field that's called QXR1 in the accounting system. But in the data warehouse, if it represents Weekly Sales, simply name it that.

Data Considerations

One of the unique features of a data warehouse is that every field in the database is potentially visible to its end users. As there is no application control over what users see, the quality of the data must be intrinsic to the data itself and not depend on application logic to be applied on the way out. The data in the data warehouse will be visible to users directly. The applications that gathered data in the OLTP systems from which it was extracted most probably contained rules and logic that rendered user's transactions into semi-meaningful database records. The DWA must remember that those rules and transformation algorithms will *not* be visible to end users. Even the best metadata systems may never be seen by an end user. Therefore, the data has to stand on its own.

Not only is it tremendously inefficient to transform the same item of data the same way to hundreds of users, hundreds of times each day, but that is an unreliable plan. When rules are required to transform data between the data warehouse and the user, there is the potential for trouble. It is always possible for someone to mistakenly skip a required transformation, or fail to link items correctly, or bypass an application or security server. In such instances, users might see data that appears incorrect or inconsistent and the reputation of the warehouse may be damaged.

It is easy to prevent problems like that from occurring. Simply follow the golden rule of data warehouse data design "If it doesn't make sense to the user, it should not be in the warehouse." If you make sure the data goes into the data warehouse correctly—that is, so it will make sense to its users—then you won't have to make sure it gets cleaned up as it goes out to each user's desktop. Clean it up once, remove the inconsistencies, and rationalize it at *load time*, not with decode statements. For example, if you have a field called gender, make sure that it contains Ms and Fs, or some other "readable" value, not a numeric code that must be joined to a look-up table in every query and constraint. Also, make sure that every table that has a field called gender always contains Ms and Fs. Don't let one of them contain zeros and ones, another contain M and F, and yet another table contain "male" and "female."

Where, When, and How to clean up and translate data

There are only three times / places / methods to use to clean up data warehouse data:

1. Clean it up in the source systems as shown in Figure 15.5. This is usually the best place to make changes to data, but sometimes resource limitations and technical difficulties eliminate this option from consideration by the warehouse team.

2. Clean during load and translation as shown in Figure 15.6. The most common form of cleansing is the substitution of one code for another during the load phase. As this effort is solely the responsibility of the warehouse team, resource issues do not come into play and, in fact, the warehouse project team is frequently able to accomplish miracles between the source output files and the target input records. Cleaning data during the extract and transformation step is efficient and is frequently the only feasible option.

3. The data warehouse server itself can be used to clean and translate data files as shown in Figure 15.7. Particularly if the source database is difficult to work with, it can be very ef-

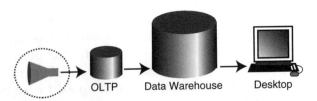

OLTP   Data Warehouse   Desktop

Data is cleaned as it enters OLTP system. Most efficient stage, but requires rewriting existing systems.

Figure 15.5 Cleaning data in the OLTP system.

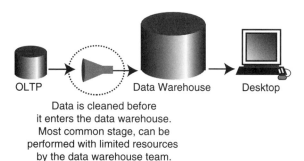

Data is cleaned before
it enters the data warehouse.
Most common stage, can be
performed with limited resources
by the data warehouse team.

Figure 15.6   Cleaning data during the extract and transformation steps.

ficient to download the entire source data file to the data warehouse server. Once there, it is worked on by SQL programmers, as though by a team of makeup artists who slave over their client to transform the actor into something quite unrecognizable. When finished, hierarchies are flattened, dimensions are pulled out and a dimensional schema emerges from a tangle of accounts. With SQL programs, the data can be redesigned and significantly transformed.

Ensure Data Quality

Consistent data and simplicity are more important than 100 percent accuracy. Make certain that the data is internally consistent: It is unlikely to exactly match any of the source systems from which it was derived, but within the warehouse, the data *must* be the same. Do some preparatory work to describe what

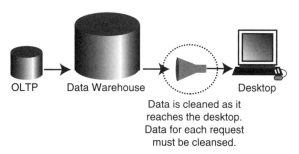

Data is cleaned as it
reaches the desktop.
Data for each request
must be cleansed.

Figure 15.7   Cleaning data in the warehouse with SQL.

assumptions were used when you cleaned up and loaded the data into the warehouse, so that users can conceptually reconcile the two systems. But if the data is internally inconsistent, you may never be able to convince users that it is correct.

Make sure that all data in the warehouse follows the same rules. Don't change them in mid-stream; that means you must reload and restate if that is what it takes. Consider stock tables after a stock splits. If the yearly highs and lows were not adjusted to reflect the effects of the split, the numbers would be worthless. Even though the low happened 9 months ago, and at the time was $20 per share, after a 2 for 1 split, that low would be recorded in the data warehouse as though it had been $10 per share. The person who goes back into transaction database records to see at what price a trade was executed will see $20, which is *not* what it is in the warehouse. But the warehouse is in some sense more correct than history. So, too, historical data in the data warehouse must be adapted to reflect the rules, boundaries, and divisions of the moment. This rule is called "view the past through the prism of today."

What about Aggregates?

Other questions of data design concern aggregates. Where should they go? Do you need them at all? How many should you build and on what values? Can specialized servers or software help? Fortunately, there isn't a single right answer to these questions because there are so many situational dependencies. Due to the fluid nature of data warehouse databases, it is possible to adopt one course, then adjust over time. One example of a project that tried several approaches to aggregates serves as an interesting case study. This warehouse project was designed by a central staff to support many distributed offices throughout the country.

When this team first designed their warehouse, they wrestled with the aggregate question. They had determined the basic granularity of their data, but thought that precomputing summary values for common selections might improve performance. They decided to build some aggregates and store them in separate tables. Users were taught which tables to use for which types of queries. Two years later, after several revisions, extensive research and user observation, they have removed all the precomputed aggregates. They determined that the basic performance of their database, an intelligently denormalized schema managed by a popular RDBMS running on a UNIX server, was good enough that their users could compute all aggregates on-the-fly. Ad hoc aggregates are feasible in this instance because the query tool is easy to use and the server is fast and scalable enough to respond to user demands. An additional benefit of eliminating the aggregate tables was that it reduced the work required of IS as they were spared the task of building, maintaining, recomputing, and reloading those separate tables. The load time has been reduced by one third and average query time has not increased.

PROJECT DELIVERY TACTICS

In a client-centered data warehouse, the success of the delivery of the data warehouse is measured by the actions of the users after the official "launch." A successful warehouse project delivery goes beyond deployment—the DWA's objective is to get user adoption. The fact that many IS managers speak of "deploying" their warehouse is a telling use of language. "Deployment" frequently conveys the image of an involuntary action imposed without regard to the wishes of another. If the users' true needs are met, if the system is approachable and made understandable, then the data warehouse is more likely to be perceived as successful. In fact, it will be adopted and embraced, not deployed.

A common error made in the majority of warehouse projects is to leave deployment to chance, to the last minute, or to ignore it altogether. The delivery of the warehouse project is critical for two reasons: (1) because it is the best time to demonstrate the value of the system, and (2) because you have the benefit of curiosity and the intrinsic appeal of newness only once—the first time a user sits down with query tool in hand ready to explore the data warehouse. It is essential, therefore, that when it comes time to bring the total solution to the users, that the deployment process be managed so as to increase the likelihood of user satisfaction.

First Things First

As with most other components, the ground work for successful delivery of the system is laid much earlier in the project. Before concerning yourself with the process of bringing your data warehouse to the user, you should review the basics of your project. Confirm that these following key ideas are reflected in the system you are about to release. If they are not, postpone the initial training or restrict it to a tiny number of individuals who are predisposed to see the value in what you are trying to accomplish, even if it is not readily apparent. Otherwise, negative reviews will get out and your project will be unfairly evaluated.

- Does the database design make sense to users and allow them to ask and answer critical business questions?
- Is the data in the warehouse useful to the initial users? Is it accurate and consistent?
- Will the database server support the initial number of users and provide reasonable response times?
- Are you providing users with a tool that they will accept? Can they use it effectively?
- Do you have a training process and a follow-up process in place?
- Do you have visibility with high-level user sponsors? Do you have objectives that you can achieve?

Marketing the Project

Assuming that you have answered in the affirmative to the previous questions, it is time to roll-out. After four to six months of difficult technical decisions and project management challenges, the DWA must become a master marketeer and sell this project to the organization. Unfortunately, users will not get all the benefits the first day the software is installed, so it is very important to manage the roll-out process with delicacy and control. Think like a marketing manager and plan to get good press, to have exciting events, and to manage communications, both internal to the team and external with users. If you have not already, this is the time to start understanding the business benefits of the warehouse so that you can articulate them to anyone who asks.

Just as the difference between deployment and adoption can be huge, so too is the difference in focus between a technology-oriented manager and one who is market-driven. To be successful, the DWA will need to adopt some of the tricks of the marketing trade and add them to the warehouse project management.

A simple task, but one that pays significant benefits, is to name the data warehouse project. A simple logo as shown in Figure 15.8, a theme, and a catchy name from the very start will attract and bind people to the team; it will raise awareness of the project internally and externally and give a sense of purpose and mission. Seeing the project's logo on training schedules, in internal white papers, and in presentations creates a sense of legitimacy around the warehouse project.

Launch the warehouse and introduce early phases of potential users at an open launch event. Use food to attract people in the areas that are most likely to have data early, and look to recruit additional protagonists and testers. The event should be as large as you can accommodate and held in an "expo-like" setting

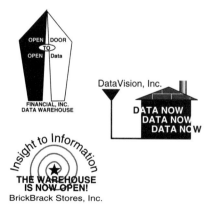

Figure 15.8 Sample data warehouse project logos.

where people can wander, observe, and ask questions of the team, one-on-one. Make sure that the evangelists are present and, if possible, are using the data warehouse at the launch event. As they demonstrate, explain, and showcase their work, they will be a walking, talking advertorial endorsement of the business application of the data warehouse. At the launch event, allow anyone who is interested to sign up for training. You can always deal with logistics and details after the fact, but you never have a better time to capture enthusiasm and curiosity than at the launch.

Adopt a Customer-Focused Orientation

If the project is customer-focused from the start, then the team will include end users who will have had an influential voice. End users will be included in live testing, will participate in database design reviews, and will play central roles in the user tool selection process. If you also iterate often, incorporating user ideas and feedback, users will see and appreciate the role they play in the project and may have more patience and feel more ownership of the result than if they are merely passive recipients of the results.

One of the most effective tactics to employ is to create evangelists inside the user community. Look for evangelists in your Information Surfer community and in the ranks of the Data Tourists who will be working with the first collection of data. Users who have taken the initiative to communicate with IS directly—those who make the most suggestions or seem to be constantly pushing the limit of what is possible with the current systems—are likely to be more easily excited by the potential of the data warehouse. Choose as your evangelists a few opinion leaders due to their seniority, responsibility, or mastery of the old system, as their endorsement will lend the most credibility to the new data warehouse.

Your chosen evangelists will be part of the team, either formally or informally. If they have the time and the inclination to attend meetings, review database designs, draft RFI requirements, and use desktop query tools, then it is wise to include them. But such extensive participation is rare. You can, however, recruit evangelists in a less formal fashion by working with them one-on-one on an off-hours basis. These evangelists will be the first users of everything in the data warehouse and you must be prepared to go out of your way to make them successful. If they don't understand something, make it easier. If they need more data, locate it and add it to the warehouse before you roll it out to the other users. Obviously you must exercise judgment and make certain that you will continue to meet the needs of the larger community; but once you make the commitment to invite early users on board, you must be willing to follow-through and give them what they need. Evangelists can

> review database designs;
>
> learn potential user-access tools;
>
> test and build real applications;
>
> identify data problems;
>
> talk about what they are doing; and
>
> demonstrate to peers.

Visible, communicative, enthusiastic, and supportive evangelists in the user community are an essential component of all successful data warehouses.

Deliver It Well

When the database is complete, the user tools acquired, data loaded, and connections in place, you will be ready to begin the process of delivering your creation. The warehouse delivery tasks are not as technically challenging as those of earlier stages, but they are as critical to the success of the project. There are really only four required elements in the data warehouse delivery plan: Launch, Infrastructure, Training, and Follow-up.

Launch

The purpose of the launch is to expose as many users as possible to the warehouse and show them what it might be able to do for them. It is to inspire ideas and enthusiasm. Leaving the event, users should want to sign up for training to make sure that they are among the first people connected. Some launches have been so successful that users have stayed around or have come back the next day to complete an analysis left in progress at the end. Clearly, a user who needs the data that much should be recruited as an evangelist or at least made into an internal reference as quickly as possible.

Schedule the launch to fall early enough in the process that changes can still be made based on user feedback, but not so early that there is nothing to see. The launch of the warehouse should occur when there is a selection of useful, interesting data in the warehouse, at least one end-user tool, and some preliminary results produced by evangelists and team members.

Infrastructure

Managing the infrastructure consists of two components: ensuring that the client-server connections between the user's machine and the database server are in place and functional, and creating a library of standard reports and documents that are ready to use. To ensure that client machines are correctly configured, that connection software is installed correctly, and that the selected user access tools work, is a project in its own right. The major point to remember is that, in a data warehouse, the client's machine is a part of the data warehouse, so ensure that it works. One organization with very limited IS resources had 200 users to get up in three weeks. They created a shopping list that enumerated the required minimum machines, networks, and assembled client desktop software packs with a quick customized installer. Users with correct machines could run the installer pack and in less than one hour be connected to the data warehouse.

A selection of standard, recognizable reports is an invaluable tool that will help encourage end-user adoption of your data warehouse. Even though the eventual intent is to have the majority of users constructing their own ad hoc questions, few of the users have ever worked with a database that way. As a result, they may be reluctant to dive in and start playing. If you treat them all as Data Tourists and equip them with a guide book of prebuilt reports, they will gain the confidence to move ahead into ad hoc exploration. You do not need to replicate 100 percent of the reports that are currently coming from the transaction systems; if you aim to capture 10 percent as a start, you will be doing well.

Training

Plan some sort of formal education for 30 percent of the users. Close to 80 percent of the users in the first groups will need education, but that percent drops off rapidly as the number of trained people who are available to help answer questions increases over time. There are only two key components to remember when setting up a training plan for the data warehouse:

Offer a variety of training classes for different levels of users.

Teach users the data, not just the tools.

Fear of looking stupid in front of one's peers holds everyone back. For this reason, and to help maintain homogeneous classes, it is wise to develop at least two standard training sessions. The first should be an introduction to the features and functions of the product and will be targeted for data tourists. In this class, spend time introducing the data, the standard reports, and basic concepts of client-server data warehouses. As with a good microscope, users need to learn very little about how to operate the device initially. Rather, the instructor focuses on teaching students how to interpret what appears in the lens of the data-access tool.

The second, more advanced class might include deeper investigation into physical tables, performance characteristics, and the special features of the end-user access tools. Both Information Surfers and IS professionals who will be supporting end users will want to attend this level 2 training.

However, training is not a one-time event that you can do and forget. In the data warehouse it is a continuous process with an initial push to get the first users up to speed and self-sufficient. One successful plan is to do all the basic and introductory training for all users of the first data warehouse up front. Then, users play on their own using standard reports or building as necessary for several weeks or so. One month after first-round training, offer a follow-up session to cover more advanced topics and answer specific questions. As more and more data is added to the data warehouse, and more and more users participate, repeat the training process until a critical mass of knowledge is achieved in the user community.

Follow-up

Part of the successful deployment of a great data warehouse is the creation and administration of a feedback cycle that will provide information about how to make the warehouse even better in the future. You will not be finished simply because there is some data in the warehouse and you have middleware and connectivity. Think of all you don't know at that point. Who are the users? What do they do? How are they going to use the data warehouse? How are they going to learn it? How will you monitor what they're doing with it? How can you know if it works?

Some actions the DWA can take to ensure effective follow-through are presented in the following list. The idea linking all of these ideas is to communicate information that will be helpful to users of the warehouse and to facilitate the collection of information that will be useful for the DWA.

■ Start a user group and schedule monthly meetings.
■ Announce new features in the tools.
■ Introduce new data elements, tables, or subject areas.
■ Conduct usage surveys. Ask and publish "How has the system helped you the most?" Why?
■ Publish a newsletter about the data warehouse. Feature profiles of successful users who can explain how they are using it and why.
■ Monitor or audit database use, produce standard reports, and place the results in public tables in the data warehouse. Graph usage. Allow anyone to see how much the system is being used and by whom.

Data warehousing does require a paradigm shift throughout the organization. As the manager of the project and its visionary, the DWA must help others to change by teaching them how to work, how to play, and how best to take advantage of the system.

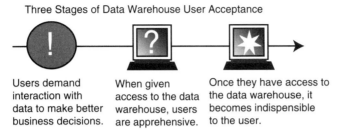

Three Stages of Data Warehouse User Acceptance

Users demand interaction with data to make better business decisions.

When given access to the data warehouse, users are apprehensive.

Once they have access to the data warehouse, it becomes indispensible to the user.

Figure 15.9 It may take a while before users embrace the data warehouse, even when it is the solution they've been requesting.

The wise DWA will anticipate difficulties and will work in advance to minimize the inevitable pushbacks. End users typically go through three phases as they learn data warehousing as shown in Figure 15.9. They start with demands for assistance and for a system with more data, more power, flexibility, and interaction. If users are loud enough and get to the right person, then a data warehouse project is initiated to satisfy the demand. The second stage happens late in the data warehouse project, as some users are asked to participate in the internal beta program. Now their reaction is one of amazement, that "You want me to do it myself?" Be calm and resist the urge to tell them that what they are seeing is exactly what they originally asked for. Instead, help them get into the third phase, during which their attitude will be, "I can't wait to see what I will discover in the data warehouse today."

SUMMARY

Why is a data warehouse project like an iceberg? Because there is so much hidden beneath the surface, yet it is only the tip that is judged. The IS view reveals all those difficult and essential tasks that lie below the surface of the project: SQL optimization, data modeling, legacy extracts and data integrity, schema design, indexes, and load performance. From the users' perspective, the only thing that is visible is the proverbial "tip of the iceberg." Users see only the provided schema—through either a semantic layer or the physical tables—and the tools provided for query, report, and analysis. They also see how quickly the system responds to their requests. Two critical pieces of advice fall from this simple observation:

1. Don't spend 100 percent of your time in that 90 percent below the water that no user is ever going to see. The last 10 percent is bigger than the first 90. The sad truth is that if you neglect the 10 percent above the water, and make bad decisions about tools and design, no one will know how excellent the rest of the project may be. No users will see your beautiful clean data if you've hidden it away behind an impenetrable schema, or if the tools you provide are difficult to use or are unsuitable to the user's tasks.

2. The other corollary of this observation is that you've got to begin your project with the end in mind. Remember that you are building the warehouse for the end users. Throughout the project you must keep in mind that the mission of the warehouse project is to allow end users to access data on their own.

Let's look at a real life example, using a medium-sized insurance company. Prior to the start of the data warehouse project, the IS organization inferred the needs of end users from the reports they requested. The IS organization knew the reports were usually big and complicated, produced many pages of tightly formatted results, and frequently were difficult to write. IS assumed that big, complicated reports were what users wanted. So, when IS began the warehouse project, it started out by trying to replicate the longest and most complicated user-requested reports as "standard reports." The organization built hundreds of reports, wrote governors, and built indexes to maximize the performance of those reports. Users were also given an ad hoc query tool which IS thought was going to be used at most 5 or 10 percent of the time.

Care to guess how many of those reports are in use today? About a dozen are used. What they find today is a lot of little, quick queries hitting the database. A typical query might scan

50,000 rows and return four rows of aggregated results—one row for each quarter. The query returns so little data because that is the answer to a single question. A follow-on question is typically to discover details behind one of those rows. That second query will scan perhaps 10,000 rows and return 100 rows.

What the IS organization discovered was that users didn't really want a multi-page report with M x N x O dimensions and subtotals every which way. Users actually prefer to work sequentially with small collections of data that result from "small questions." Before the warehouse, IS had not known those kinds of reports were even desired because they were never requested.

The lesson to be learned from that story is that data warehousing is a new paradigm. It is only efficient for users to work in their natural "trial-and-error" fashion when they have easy-to-use desktop tools and a reasonably responsive database system. Don't expect the behaviors of today to apply in the new environment. Don't rely upon past experiences with OLTP systems to predict user needs in the warehouse, and don't apply old-style OLTP technologies to warehouse problems.

Write Your Own Rules

One of the joys of data warehouses is that there are no rules. You have a blank slate on which to create. There are no legacy users to preserve and no 20-year-old systems to support. You are not obligated to anyone. The only rule is to do what works. It's just you, your users, a bunch of data, a server, and some tools. Imagine the possibilities.

By all means, use a star schema for the data—performance and usability will improve if you do. If you are in a relational environment, do your best to leverage the search, retrieval, join, and aggregation capabilities of that engine. But don't be afraid to break the old OLTP rules of third or fifth normal form. Those rules are not what make a database. It is such a common mistake, and so easy to avoid, to believe that you should follow the old rules, even when in a data warehouse. Design the data schema that makes sense to your users.

Anticipate Change

It is an interesting characteristic of the data warehouse that it is never complete. Now this may offer lifetime employment for the members of the team, but it also makes it difficult to know when to show it off to management and when to schedule team vacations. Try to avoid speaking of "when the warehouse is done." It will never be done and that is as it should be. It will always be under construction, so plan to live in a construction zone. It's like living in a big city, the streets are never done: As soon as they fix the water pipes, they dig in the same place to upgrade the phones. In the warehouse, as soon as you have one data set complete and one group of users up to speed, another group of users will ask you to load their data too, and the process starts all over again.

In the data warehouse, assume lots of variability and pick tools and technologies that are very modular and use open standards as much as possible. With regard to user tools, tools that require little to no maintenance and that can self-adjust to changes in data schemas or metadata will make your job much, much easier.

Ensure High Performance

The DWA must ensure the performance of the complete data warehouse system. On the surface, the most obvious requirement is that most user queries must run quickly and efficiently. But the DWA typically is also responsible for the performance of data loads, index creation, and metadata maintenance. Most data warehouses reside in database systems that are separate from any significant OLTP application. Data warehouses are most commonly implemented on a separate database with dedicated processor, disk, and memory. This is the most optimal environment because it is certain to alleviate 100 percent of the contention problems, gives the DWA design freedom, and supports specific access structures appropriate solely for a data warehouse database.

Unlock Your Creativity

Satisfying the needs of the end users is key to the success of the project. But you must do more than just give them great tools; you must also inspire them to be creative. Part of the paradigm shift that has happened in the data warehouse is that you may have to teach your users how to take full advantage of the new environment.

Users need help to understand that there are no "stupid" questions of a data warehouse. Teach users to be creative and satisfy their natural curiosity. For people who are accustomed to production reports that come in stacks of paper on the desk, it's going to take a new mind set. It's the responsibility of the entire warehouse team to help users move smoothly into the new paradigm. Choosing tools that are well-designed, easy-to-use, and a little bit fun, will make the job easier and the project more successful. If you do all this—design it well, fill it with clean, well-organized data, and teach users how to use it—users will come to the data warehouse and they will stay.

Appendix

PRISM SOLUTIONS TECH TOPICS

Time-Dependent Data Structures. A discussion of the different types of data structures and their advantages and disadvantages.

Creating the Data Warehouse Data Model from the Corporate Data Model. The steps you need to take to create the data warehouse data model from the corporate data model.

Representing Data Relationships in the Data Warehouse: Artifacts of Data. Design issues for the building of data relationships in the data warehouse.

Snapshots of Data in the Warehouse. A description of the different types of snapshots and the advantages and disadvantages of each.

Defining the System of Record. The design considerations of identifying and defining the system of record.

What Is a Data Warehouse? This Tech Topic defines what a data warehouse is and what its structure looks like. This is a basic discussion appropriate to anyone investigating the world of data warehouse.

Capacity Planning for the Data Warehouse. This Tech Topic discusses the issue of capacity planning and projection for both disk storage and processor resources for the data warehouse environment.

Operational and DSS Processing from a Single Database: Separating Fact and Fiction. An early notion was that a single database should serve as the basis for both operational processing and DSS analytical processing. This Tech Topic explores the issues and describes why data warehouse is the appropriate foundation for DSS informational processing.

Parallel Processing in the Data Warehouse. The management of volumes of data is the first and major challenge facing the data architect. Parallel technology offers the possibility of managing much data. This Tech Topic is on the issues of parallel technology in the data warehouse environment.

Metadata in the Data Warehouse. Metadata is an important component of the data warehouse. This Tech Topic discusses why, and what the different components of metadata are for the data warehouse.

Loading the Data Warehouse. At first glance, loading data into the data warehouse seems to be an easy task. It is not. This discussion is on the many different considerations of loading data from the operational environment into the data warehouse.

Accessing Data Warehouse Data from the Operational Environment. Most flow of data is from the operational environment to the data warehouse environment, but not all. This Tech Topic discusses the "backward" flow of data.

Information Architecture for the 90s: Legacy Systems, Operational Data Stores, Data Warehouses. Describes the role of operational data stores and a description of them, along with a description of the architecture that results when you mix an operational data store and a data warehouse.

Information Engineering and the Data Warehouse. The data warehouse architecture is extremely compatible with the design and modeling practices of information engineering. This Tech Topic describes that relationship.

EIS and Data Warehouse. EIS under a foundation of legacy systems is very shaky, but EIS under a data warehouse foundation is very solid, as detailed in this Tech Topic.

Client-Server and Data Warehouse. Client-server processing is quite able to support data warehouse processing. This Tech Topic addresses the issues of architecture and design.

Data Warehouse and Cost Justification. *A priori* cost justification is a difficult thing to do for a data warehouse. This topic discusses the issues.

Reengineering and the Data Warehouse. Many organizations are not aware of the very strong and very positive relationship between re-engineering and the data warehouse. This topic identifies the relationship and discusses the ramifications.

The Operational Data Store. The operational counterpoint of the data warehouse is the operational data store (ODS). The ODS is defined and described in detail in this Tech Topic.

Security in the Data Warehouse. Security takes on a very different dimension in the data warehouse than in other data processing environment. This Tech Topic describes the issues. Tech Topics are available from PRISM Solutions.

Using the Generic Data Model. Some corporations have a data model as a point of departure for the design of their data warehouse; others do not. The generic data model "jump starts" the data warehouse design and development effort.

Service Level Agreements in the Data Warehouse Environment. One of the cornerstones of online operations is the service level agreement. Service level agreements are applicable to the data warehouse, but are implemented quite differently.

Getting Started. The data warehouse is built iteratively. This Tech Topic describes the first steps, in a detailed manner.

Changed Data Capture. The resources required for repeatedly scanning the operational environment for the purpose of refreshing the data warehouse can be enormous. This briefing addresses an alternative way to accomplish the same thing—changed data capture.

Telling the Difference Between Operational and DSS. In every shop the issue arises, what is operational and what is DSS? This Tech Topic tells you how to tell the difference between the two environments.

Managing Multiple Data Warehouse Development Efforts. When the organization starts to build multiple data warehouse efforts simultaneously, a new set of design and development issues arise. This Tech Topic identifies and addresses those issues.

Performance in the Data Warehouse Environment. Performance is as important in the DSS data warehouse environment as it is in the OLTP environment. However, performance plays a very different role. This Tech Topic is all about performance in the DSS data warehouse environment.

The Data Warehouse Budget. This Tech Topic addresses the different patterns of spending and the rate at which funds are spent. In addition, some suggestions for minimizing expenses are included.

Explaining Metadata to the End User. When the layman first encounters metadata, the first reaction usually is, "What in the world is metadata and why would I ever need it?" This Tech Topic addresses metadata in very plain, straightforward terms.

Summary Data in the Data Warehouse-Operational Data Store. Summary data has its own set of unique considerations. There is, for example, dynamic summary data and static summary data. Both types of summary data require very different treatment from the designer and the end user. This Tech Topic creates a taxonomy for summary data and relates the different types of summary data to the data warehouse and the operational data store.

OLAP and Data Warehouse. Lightly summarized data has always been an integral part of the data warehouse architecture. Today, this construct is known as OLAP or a data mart. This Tech Topic addresses the relationship of OLAP and the detailed data found in the data warehouse.

PRISM Solutions
1000 Hamlin Court
Sunnyvale, CA 94089
1-800-995-2928

Recommended Reading

BOOKS

Inmon, W.H. *Building the Data Warehouse*. New York: John Wiley & Sons, 1993.

Inmon, W.H. *Building the Data Warehouse*. 2d ed. New York: John Wiley & Sons, 1996.

Inmon, W.H. *Building the Operational Data Store*. New York: John Wiley & Sons, 1995.

Inmon, W.H. *Information Systems Architecture: Development in the 90s*. New York: John Wiley & Sons, 1993.

Inmon, W.H. *Rdb/VMS: Developing the Data Warehouse*. New York: John Wiley & Sons, 1993.

Inmon, W.H. *Third Wave Processing: Database Machines and Decision Support Systems*. Wellesley, MA: QED, 1991.

Inmon, W.H. *Using the Data Warehouse*. New York: John Wiley & Sons, 1994.

Kimball, Ralph. *Practical Techniques for Building Dimensional Data Warehouses*. New York: John Wiley & Sons, 1996.

Love, Bruce. *Enterprise Information Technologies*. New York: Van Nostrand Reinhold, 1990.

Parsaye, Kamrank, and Marc Chignell. *Intelligent Database Tools and Applications*. New York: John Wiley & Sons, 1995.

ARTICLES

"An Architecture for a Business and Information System." *IBM Systems Journal* 17, no. 1 (1988). A description of IBM's understanding of the data warehouse.

Ashbrook, Jim. "Information Preservation." *CIO Magazine* (July 1993). An executive's view of the data warehouse.

Bair, John. "It's about Time! Supporting Temporal Data in a Warehouse." *INFODB* 10, no. 1 (February 1996). A good discussion of some of the aspects of time-variant data in the DSS-data warehouse environment.

Ballinger, Carrie. "TPC's Emerging Benchmark for Decision Support." *DBMS* (December 1993). A description of the extension of the TPC benchmark to include DSS.

"Chargeback in the Information Warehouse." *Data Management Review* (March 1993). Chargeback in the data warehouse can be both a blessing and a curse. This article addresses both sides of the issue.

Geiger, John. "Information Management for Competitive Advantage." *Strategic Systems Journal*. ACR (June 1993). A discussion of how the data warehouse and the Zachman framework have advanced the state of the art.

———. "Information Management for Competitive Advantage." *Strategic Systems* (June 1993). A description of the transition from systems to information.

———. "What's in a Name?" *Data Management Review* (June 1996). A discussion on the implications of naming structures in the data warehouse environment.

Gilbreath, Roy. "Health Care Data Repositories: Components and a Model." *Journal of the Healthcare Information and Management Systems Society* 9, no. 1 (Spring 1995). An excellent description of information architecture as it relates to health care.

———. "Informational Processing Architecture for Outcomes Management." Under review: A description of data warehouse as it applies to health care and outcomes analysis.

Gilbreath, Roy, Jill Schilp, and Robert Pickton. "Towards an Outcomes Management Informational Processing Architecture." *HealthCare Information Management* 10, no. 1 (Spring 1996). A discussion of the architected environment as it relates to health care.

Goldberg, Paula, Robert Lambert, and Katherine Powell. "Guidelines for Defining Requirements for Decision Support Systems." *Data Resource Management Journal* (October 1991). A good description of how to define end-user requirements before building the data warehouse.

Graham, Stephen. "The Foundations of Wisdom." *IDC Special Report* (April 1996). International Data Corp. (36 Toronto Street, Toronto, Ontario, Canada M5C 2C5). The definitive study on the return on investment for data warehouse, as well as the measurement of cost effectiveness.

———. "The Financial Impact of Data Warehousing." *Data Management Review* (June 1996). A description of the cost-benefit analysis report done by IDC.

Hackney, Doug. "Vendors Are Our Friends." *Data Management Review* (June 1996). Doug Hackney talks about beneficial relationships with vendors.

Hufford, Duane. "Data Administration Support for Business Process Improvement." *AMS*. Discusses data warehouse and data administration.

———. "A Conceptual Model for Documenting Data Synchronization Requirements. *AMS*. Discusses data synchronization and data warehouse.

―――. "Data Warehouse Quality, Part I." *Data Management Review* (January 1996). A description of data warehouse quality.

―――. "Data Warehouse Quality, Part II." *Data Management Review* (March 1996). A discussion of the proper strategic approach to data warehousing.

Imhoff Claudia and John Geiger. "Data Quality in the Data Warehouse." *Data Management Review* (April 1996). A description of the parameters used to gauge the quality of data warehouse data.

Inmon, W.H. "The Need for Reporting." *Database Programming and Design* (April 1992). The different kinds of reports found throughout the different parts of the architecture.

―――. "Building the Data Bridge." *Database Programming and Design* (April 1992). Ten critical success factors in building the data warehouse.

―――. "Data Warehouse—A Perspective of Data over Time. *370/390 Database Management* (February 1992). A description of the relationship of data warehouse and the management of data over time.

―――. "Data Structures in the Information Warehouse." *Enterprise Systems Journal* (January 1992). A description of the common data structures found in the data warehouse.

―――. "Winds of Change." *Database Programming and Design* (January 1992). Data administration and the data warehouse; a description of how data administration evolved to where it is today.

―――. "The Cabinet Effect." *Database Programming and Design* (May 1991). A description of why the data warehouse-centered architecture does not degenerate into the spider web environment.

―――. "Going Against the Grain." *Database Programming and Design* (July 1990). A description of the granularity issue and how it relates to the data warehouse.

―――. "At the Heart of the Matter." *Database Programming and Design* (July 1988). Primitive and derived data and what the differences are.

―――. "Neat Little Packages." *Database Programming and Design* (August 1992). A description of how data relationships are treated in the data warehouse.

―――. Metadata: A Checkered Past, A Bright Future." *370/390 Database Management* (July 1992). A conversation about metadata and how it relates to the data warehouse.

―――. "EIS and the Data Warehouse." *Database Programming and Design* (November 1992). The relationship between EIS and the data warehouse.

―――. "Data Warehouse Lays Foundation for Bringing Data Investment Forward." *Application Development Trends* (January 1994). A description of data warehouse's relationship to legacy systems.

―――. "The Structure of the Data Warehouse." *Data Management Review* (August 1993). This article addresses the different levels of data found in the data warehouse.

―――. "Untangling the Web." *Database Programming and Design* (May 1993). Exploring the factors that turn data into information.

———. "The Data Warehouse—All Your Data at Your Fingertips." *Communications Week* (August 1994). An overview of data warehouse.

———. "Profiling the DSS Analyst." *Data Management Review* (March 1995). A description of DSS analysts as farmers and explorers.

———. "Multidimensional Databases and Data Warehousing." *Data Management Review* (February 1995). A description of how current detailed data in the data warehouse fits with multi-dimensional DBMS.

———. "EIS and Detail." *Data Management Review* (January 1995). A description of how much detail is needed to support EIS and the role of summarized data in the data warehouse environment.

———. "The Data Warehouse: Managing the Infrastructure." *Data Management Review* (December 1994). A description of the data warehouse infrastructure and the budgets associated with it.

———. "The Anatomy of a Data Warehouse Record." *Data Management Review* (July 1995). A description of the internal structure of a data warehouse record.

———. "Profile/Aggregate Records in the Data Warehouse." *Data Management Review* (July 1995). A description of how profile and aggregate records are created and used in the data warehouse.

———. "The Operational Data Store." *INFOBD* 9, no. 1 (February 1995). A description of the ODS.

———. "Data Warehouse and Contextual Data: Pioneering a New Dimension." *Database Newsletter* 23, no. 4 (July/August 1995). A description of the need for contextual data over time, as found in the data warehouse.

———. "Transformation Complexity." *Data Management Review* (September 1995). Why automating the transformation process is a superior idea to manually programming the transformations that are required in order to build the data warehouse.

———. "The Ladder of Success." *Data Management Review* (November 1995). Building and managing the data warehouse environment entails more than selecting a platform. This article outlines the many necessary steps required to achieve a successful data warehouse environment.

———. "Growth in the Data Warehouse." *Data Management Review* (December 1995). A description of why the data warehouse grows so fast and the phenomenon of increasing amounts of storage while decreasing the percent of storage use.

———. "Monitoring the Data Warehouse Environment." *Data Management Review* (January 1996). Describes a data monitor for the data warehouse environment and why you would need it.

———. "Performance in the Data Warehouse Environment." *Data Warehouse Report* . Issue 3 (Autumn 1995). A description of the different aspects of performance in the data warehouse environment.

———. "Managing the Data Warehouse Environment." *Data Management Review* (February 1996). Defining the position of the data warehouse administrator.

———. "From Transactions to the Operational Data Store." *INFODB* (December 1995). A discussion about how quickly transactions in the operational environment go into the operational data store.

———. "Choosing the Correct Approach to Data Warehousing: Big Bang vs. Iterative." *Data Management Review* (March 1996). A discussion of the proper strategic approach to data warehousing.

———. "Security in the Data Warehouse: Data Privitization." *Enterprise Systems Journal* (March 1996). Data warehouse requires a very different approach to security than the traditional VIEW-based approach offered by DBMS vendors.

———. "Virtual Data Warehouse: The Snake Oil of the '90s." *Data Management Review* (April 1996). A discussion of the virtual data warehouse and how the concept tries to attach itself to the legitimacy of the data warehouse.

———. "Rethinking Data Relationships for Warehouse Design." *Sybase Server* 5, no. 1 (Spring 1996). A discussion of the issues concerning data warehouse data relationships.

———. "Performance in the Data Warehouse Environment, Part II." *Data Warehouse Report* (Winter 1995). A continuation of the prior article on data warehouse performance.

———. "Summary Data: The New Frontier." *Data Management Review* (May 1996). A description of the different types of summary data including dynamic summary data and static summary data, lightly summarized data and highly summarized data, and so forth.

———. "Cost Justification in the Data Warehouse." *Data Management Review* (June 1996). A discussion of how to justify DSS and data warehouse on the cost of reporting.

Inmon, W.H. and Michael Loper. "The Unified Data Architecture: A Systems Integration Solution." Auerbach Publications (1992). The original paper (republished in a revised state) suggesting that a data architecture was in order for future systems development.

Inmon, W.H. and Sue Osterfelt. "Data Patterns Say the Darndest Things." *Computerworld* (February 3, 1992). A description of the use of the data warehouse in the DSS community and how informational processing can be derived from a warehouse.

Inmon, W.H. and Chuck Kelley. "The 12 Rules of Data Warehouse." *Data Management Review* (May 1994). A Description of the defining characteristics of data warehouse.

Inmon, W.H. and Phyliss Koslow. "Commandeering Mainframe Database for Data Warehouse Use." *Application Development Trends* (August 1994). A discussion of optimal data warehouse use inside the mainframe.

"In the Words of Father Inmon." *MIS* (February 1996). An interview with Bill Inmon in November of 1995 in Australia.

Jordan, Arthur. "Data Warehouse Integrity: How Long and Bumpy the Road?" *Data Management Review* (March 1996). A discussion of the issues of data quality inside the data warehouse.

Kador, John. "One on One." An interview with Bill Inmon. *Midrange Systems* (October 27, 1995). A discussion about data warehouse with Bill, including some of the history of data warehouse.

Kimball, Ralph. "The Doctor of DSS." *DBMS Magazine* (July 1994). An interview with Ralph Kimball.

———. "Is ER Modelling Hazardous to DSS?" *Data Warehouse Report* (Winter 1995). A dialogue on dimensional modelling versus ER modelling.

Kimball, Ralph and Kevin Strehlo. "Why Decision Support Fails and How to Fix It." *Datamation* (June 1994). A good description of fact tables and star joins, with a lengthy section about Ralph's approach to data warehouse and decision support.

Konrad, Walecia. "Smoking Out the Elusive Smoker." *BusinessWeek* (March 16, 1992). A description of database marketing in the advertising-restricted marketing environment.

Lambert, Bob. "Data Warehousing Fundamentals: What You Need to Know to Succeed." *Data Management Review* (March 1996). Several significant strategies for data warehousing to guide you through a successful implementation.

———. "Break Old Habits to Define Data Warehousing Requirements." *Data Management Review*. A description of how the end user should be approached to determine DSS requirements.

"Liberate Your Data." *Forbes* (March 7, 1994). An interesting and naive article about data warehouse as viewed from the uninformed business person.

Myer, Andrea. "An Interview with Bill Inmon." *Inside Decisions* (March 1996). An interview discussing the start of data warehousing, use of data warehousing for competitive advantage, the origins of PRISM Solutions, building the first data warehouse, etc.

"Now Which Is Data, Which Is Information." *Database Programming and Design* (May 1993). The difference between data and information.

O'Mahoney, Michael. "Revolutionary Breakthrough in Client/Server Data Warehouse Development." *Data Management Review* (July 1995). A description of older legacy development methodologies versus modern iterative methodologies.

"Retail Technology Charges Up at KMart." *Discount Store News* (February 17, 1992). A description of the technology employed by KMart for its data warehouse ODS environment.

Sloan, Robert and Hal Green. "An Information Architecture for the Global Manufacturing Enterprise." Auerbach Publications (1993). A description of information architecture in the large-scale manufacturing environment.

Tanler, Richard. "Data Warehouses and Data Marts: Choose Your Weapon." *Data Management Review* (February 1996). A description of the differences between data marts and the current level of detail of the data warehouse.

———. "Taking Your Data Warehouse to a New Dimension on the Intranet." *Data Management Review* (May 1996). A discussion of the different components of the data warehouse as they relate to the intranet.

Thiessen, Mark. "Proving the Data Warehouse to Management and Customers: Where Are the Savings?" A presentation at the 1994 Data Warehouse Conference. Foils and handouts.

"A Trillion-Byte Weapon." *BusinessWeek* (July 31, 1995). A description of some of the larger data warehouses that have been built and how they play a role in business competition.

Wahl, Dan and Duane Hufford. "A Case Study: Implementing and Operating an Atomic Database." *Data Resource Management Journal* (April 1992). A description of the U.S. Army DSS architecture.

Welch, J.D. "Providing Customized Decision Support Capabilities: Defining Architectures." Auerbach Publications (1990). Decision support systems and architecture (based on the PacTel Cellular DSS architecture).

Glossary

access   the operation of seeking, reading, or writing data on a storage unit.

access method   a technique used to transfer a physical record from or to a mass storage device.

access mode   a technique in which a specific logical record is obtained from or placed onto a file assigned to a mass storage device.

access pattern   the general sequence by which the data structure is accessed (e.g. from tuple to tuple, from record to record, from segment to segment, etc.).

access plan   the control structure produced during program preparation and used by a Database Manager to process SQL statements during application execution.

access time   the time interval between the instant an instruction initiates a request for data and the instant the first of the data satisfying the request is delivered. Note that there is a difference—sometimes large—between the time data is first delivered and the time when ALL the data is delivered.

accuracy   a qualitative assessment of freedom from error or a quantitative measure of the magnitude of error, expressed as a function of relative error.

active data dictionary   a data dictionary that is the sole source for an application program insofar as metadata is concerned.

activity   (1) the lowest-level function on an activity chart (sometimes called the "atomic level"). (2) a logical description of a function performed by an enterprise. (3) a procedure (automated or not) designed for the fulfillment of an activity.

activity ratio   the fraction of records in a database which have activity or are otherwise accessed in a given period of time or in a given batch run.

ad hoc processing one time only, casual access and manipulation of data on parameters never before used.

address an identification (e.g., number, name, storage location, byte offset, etc.) for a location where data is stored.

addressing the means of assigning data to storage locations, and locating the data upon subsequent retrieval, on the basis of the key of the data.

after image the snapshot of data placed on a log upon the completion of a transaction.

agent of change a motivating force large enough to not be denied—usually aging of systems, changes in technology, radical changes in requirements, etc.

AIX Advanced Interactive eXecutive—IBM's version of the UNIX operating system.

algorithm a set of statements organized to solve a problem in a finite number of steps.

alias an alternative label used to refer to a data element.

alphabetic a representation of data using letters—upper and/or lower case—only.

alphanumeric a representation of data using numbers and/or letters, and punctuation.

ANSI American National Standards Institute.

analytical processing the usage of the computer to produce a analysis for management decision, usually involving trend analysis, drill-down analysis, demographic analysis, profiling, etc.

anticipatory staging the technique of moving blocks of data from one storage device to another with a shorter access time, in anticipation of their being needed by a program in execution or a program soon to go into execution.

API (Application Program Interface) the common set of parameters needed to connect the communications between programs.

application a group of algorithms and data interlinked to support an organizational requirement.

application blocking of data the grouping into the same physical unit of storage multiple occurrences of data controlled at the application level.

application database a collection of data organized to support a specific application.

archival database a collection of data of a historical nature. As a rule, archival data cannot be updated. Each unit of archival data is related to a moment in time, now passed.

area in network databases, a named collection of records that can contain occurrences of one or more record types. A record type can occur in more than one area.

artifact a design technique used to represent referential integrity in the DSS environment.

artificial intelligence the capability of a system to perform functions typically associated with human intelligence and reasoning.

association a relationship between two entities that is represented in a data model.

associative storage (1) a storage device whose records are identified by a specific part of their contents rather than their name or physical position in the database. (2) content addressable memory. *See* also parallel search storage.

atomic (1) data stored in a data warehouse. (2) the lowest level of process analysis.

atomic database a database made up of primarily atomic data; a data warehouse; a DSS foundation database.

atomicity the property where a group of actions is invisible to other actions executing concurrently; yielding the effect of serial execution. It is recoverable with successful completion (i.e., commit) or total backout (i.e., rollback) of previous changes associated with that group.

atomic level data data with the lowest level of granularity. Atomic level data sits in a data warehouse and is time variant (i.e., accurate as of some moment in time now passed).

attribute a property that can assume values for entities or relationships. Entities can be assigned several attributes (e.g., a tuple in a relationship consists of values). Some systems also allow relationships to have attributes as well.

audit trail data that is available to trace activity, usually update activity.

authorization identifier a character string that designates a set of privilege descriptors.

availability a measure of the reliability of a system, indicating the fraction of time the system is up and available divided by the amount of time the system should be up and available. Note that there is a difference between a piece of hardware being available and the systems running on that hardware also being available.

back end processor a database machine or an intelligent disk controller.

back up to restore the database to its state at some previous moment in time.

backup a file serving as a basis for backing up a database. Usually a snapshot of a database at some previous moment in time.

Backus-Naur Form (BNF) a metalanguage used to specify or describe the syntax of a language. In BNF, each symbol on the left side of the forms can be replaced by the symbol strings on the right side of the forms to develop sentences in the grammar of the defined language. Synonymous with Backus—Normal Form.

backward recovery a recovery technique that restores a database to an earlier state by applying previous images.

base relation a relation that is not derivable from other relations in the database.

batch computer environment in which programs (usually long running, sequentially oriented) access data exclusively, and user interaction is not allowed while the activity is occurring.

batch environment a sequentially dominated mode of processing; in batch, input is collected and stored for later processing. Once collected, the batch input is transacted sequentially against one or more databases.

batch window   the time at which the online system is available for batch or sequential processing. The batch window occurs during nonpeak processing hours.

before image   a snapshot of a record prior to update, usually placed on an activity log.

bill of materials   a listing of the parts used in a manufacturing process along with the relation of one part to another insofar as assembly of the final product is concerned. The bill of materials is a classical recursive structure.

binary element   a constituent element of data that exists as either of two values or states—either true or false, or one or zero.

binary search   a dichotomizing search with steps where the sets of remaining items are partitioned into two equal parts.

bind   (1) to assign a value to a data element, variable, or parameter. (2) the attachment of a data definition to a program prior to the execution of the program.

binding time   the moment when the data description known to the dictionary is assigned to or bound to the procedural code.

bit—(b)inary digi(t)   the lowest level of storage. A bit can be in a 1 state or a 0 state.

bit map   a specialized form of an index indicating the existence or nonexistence of a condition for a group of blocks or records. Bit maps are expensive to build and maintain, but provide very fast comparison and access facilities.

block   (1) a basic unit of structuring storage. (2) the physical unit of transport and storage. A block usually contains one or more records (or contains the space for one or more records). In some DBMS, a block is called a page.

blocking   combining of two or more physical records so that they are physically colocated together. The result of their physical colocation is that the records can be accessed and fetched by execution of a single machine instruction.

block splitting   the data management activity where data in a filled block is written into two unfilled blocks, leaving space for future insertions and updates in the two partially filled blocks.

B-tree   a binary storage structure and access method that maintains order in a database by continually dividing possible choices into two equal parts and reestablishing pointers to the respective sets, while not allowing more than two levels of difference to exist concurrently.

buffer   an area of storage that holds data temporarily in main memory while data is being transmitted, received, read, or written. A buffer is often used to compensate for the differences in the timing of the transmission and execution of devices. Buffers are used in terminals, peripheral devices, storage units, and CPUs.

bus   the hardware connection that allows data to flow from one component to another (e.g., from the CPU to the line printer).

byte   a basic unit of storage—made up of 8 bits.

C a programming language.

cache a buffer usually built and maintained at the device level. Retrieving data out of a cache is much quicker than retrieving data out of a cylinder.

call to invoke the execution of a module.

canonical model a data model that represents the inherent structure of data without regard to its individual use or hardware or software implementation.

cardinality (of a relation) the number of tuples (i.e., rows) in a relation. *See also* degree of a relation.

CASE Computer Aided Software Engineering.

catalog a directory of all files available to the computer.

chain an organization where records or other items of data are strung together.

chain list a list where the items cannot be located in sequence but where each item contains an identifier (i.e., pointer) for finding the next item.

channel a subsystem for input to and output from the computer. Data from storage units, for example, flows into the computer by way of a channel.

character a member of the standard set of elements used to represent data in the database.

character type the characters that can represent the value of an attribute.

checkpoint an identified snapshot of the database, or a point at which the transactions against the database have been frozen or have been quiesced.

checkpoint/restart a means of restarting a program at some point other than the beginning—for example, when a failure or interruption has occurred. N checkpoints may be used at intervals throughout an application program. At each of these points sufficient information is stored to permit the program to be restored to the moment when checkpoint was established.

child a unit of data existing in a 1:n relationship with another unit of data called a parent; where the parent must exist before the child can exist, but the parent can exist even when no child unit of data exists.

CIO (chief information officer) the manager of all the information processing functions in an organization.

circular file (queue) an organization of data where a finite number of units of data are allocated. Data is then loaded into those units. Upon reaching the end of the allocated units, new data is written over older data at the beginning of the queue. Sometimes called a "wrap-around" queue.

CICS (Customer Information Control System) an IBM teleprocessing monitor.

"CLDS" the facetious name of the system development life cycle of analytical, DSS systems. CLDS is so named because it is the reverse of the name of the classical systems development life cycle—SDLC.

claimed block a second or subsequent physical block of data designated to store table data, after the originally allocated block has run out of space.

class (of entities) all possible entities held by a given proposition.

cluster (1) in Teradata, a group of physical devices controlled by the same

AMP. (2) in DB2 and Oracle, the practice of physically colocating data in the same block based on its content.

cluster key the key around which data is clustered in a block (DB2/Oracle).

coalesce to combine two or more sets of items into a single set.

COBOL (COmmon Business Oriented Language) computer language for the business world. A very common language.

CODASYL model a network database model that was originally defined by the Database Task Group (DBTG) of the COnference on DAta SYstem Language (CODASYL) organization.

code (1) to represent data or a computer program in a form that can be accepted by a data processor. (2) to transform data so that it cannot be understood by anyone who does not have the algorithm necessary to decode the data prior to presentation (sometimes called "encode").

collision the event that occurs when two or more records of data are assigned to the same physical location. Collisions are associated with randomizers or hashers.

column a vertical table where values are selected from the same domain. A row is made up of one or more columns.

command (1) the specification of an activity by the programmer. (2) the actual execution of the specification.

commit a condition raised by the programmer signalling to the DBMS that all update activity done by the program should be executed against a database. Prior to the commit, all update activity can be rolled back or cancelled with no adverse effects on the contents of the database.

commit protocol an algorithm to ensure that a transaction is successfully completed.

commonality of data similar or identical data that occurs in different applications or systems. The recognition and management of commonality of data is one of the foundations of conceptual and physical database design.

communication network the collection of transmission facilities, network processors, and so on, which provides for data movement among terminals and information processors.

compaction a technique for reducing the number of bits required to represent data without losing the contents of the data. With compaction, repetitive data is represented very concisely.

component a data item or array of data items whose component type defines a collection of occurrences with the same data type.

compound index an index spanning multiple columns.

concatenate to link or connect two strings of characters, generally for the purpose of using them as a single value.

conceptual schema a consistent collection of data structures expressing the data needs of the organization. This schema is a comprehensive, base level, and logical description of the environment where an organization exists; free of physical structure and application system considerations.

concurrent operations activities executed simultaneously, or during the same time interval.

condensation the process of reducing the volume of data managed without reducing the logical consistency of the data. Condensation is essentially different than compaction.

connect to forge a relationship between two entities, particularly in a network system.

connector a symbol used to indicate that one occurrence of data has a relationship to another occurrence of data. Connectors are used in conceptual database design and can be implemented hierarchically, relationally, in an inverted fashion, or by a network.

content addressable memory main storage that can be addressed by the contents of the data in the memory, as opposed to conventional location addressable memory.

contention the condition that occurs when two or more programs try to access the same data simultaneously.

continuous time span data data organized so that a continuous definition of data over a period of time is represented by one or more records.

control character a character whose occurrence in a particular context initiates, modifies, or stops an operation.

control database a utilitarian database containing data not directly related to the application being built. Typical control databases are audit databases, terminal databases, security databases, etc.

cooperative processing the ability to distribute resources (programs, files, and databases) across the network.

coordinator the two phase commit protocol defines one database management system as coordinator for the commit process. The coordinator is responsible for communicating with the other database manager involved in a unit of work.

CPU central processing unit.

CPU-bound the state of processing where the computer cannot produce more output, because the CPU portion of the processor is being used at 100 percent capacity. When the computer is CPU-bound, typically the memory and storage processing units are less than 100 percent utilized. With modern DBMS, it is much more likely that the computer is I/O-bound, rather than CPU-bound.

CSP (Cross System Product) an IBM application generator.

CUA (Common User Access) specifies the ways in which the user interface to systems will be constructed.

current value data data whose accuracy is valid as of the moment of execution, as opposed to time variant data.

cursor (1) an indicator that designates a current position on a screen (2) a system facility that allows the programmer to thumb from one record to the next after the system has retrieved a set of records.

cursor stability an option that enables data to move under the cursor. Once the program has used the data examined by the cursor, it is released. As opposed to repeatable read.

cylinder the storage area of DASD that can be read without movement of the arm. The term originated with disk files, in which a cylinder consisted of one track on each disk surface so that each of these tracks could have a read/write head positioned over it simultaneously.

DASD *see* direct access storage device.

data a recording of facts, concepts, or instructions on a storage medium for communication, retrieval, and processing by automatic means and presentation as information that is understandable by human beings.

data administrator (DA) the individual or organization responsible for the specification, acquisition, and maintenance of data management software and the design, validation, and security of files or databases. The data model and the data dictionary are usually the responsibility of the DA.

data aggregate a collection of data items.

database a collection of interrelated data stored (often with controlled, limited redundancy) according to a schema. A database can serve single or multiple applications.

database Administrator (DBA) the organizational function charged with the day-to-day monitoring and care of the databases. The DBA is more closely associated with physical database design than the DA is.

database key a unique value that exists for each record in a database. The value is often indexed, although it can be randomized or hashed.

database machine a dedicated-purpose computer that provides data access and management through total control of the access method, physical storage, and data organization. Often called a "back end processor." Data is usually managed in parallel by a database machine.

database management system (DBMS) a computer-based software system used to establish and manage data.

database record a physical root and all of its dependents (in IMS).

DatacomDB a database management system created by CA.

data definition the specification of the data entities, their attributes, and their relationships in a coherent database structure to create a schema.

data definition language (DDL)—also called a data description language— the language used to define the database schema and additional data features that allows the DBMS to generate and manage the internal tables, indexes, buffers, and storage necessary for database processing.

data description language *see* data definition language.

data dictionary a software tool for recording the definition of data, the relationship of one category of data to another, the attributes and keys of groups of data, and so forth.

data division (COBOL) the section of a COBOL program that consists of entries used to define the nature and characteristics of the data to be processed by the program.

data driven development the approach to development that centers around identifying the commonality of data through a data model and building programs that have a broader scope than the immediate application. Data driven development differs from traditional application oriented development.

data driven process a process whose resource consumption depends on the data by which it operates. For example, a hierarchical root has a dependent.

For one occurrence there are two dependents for the root. For another occurrence of the root there may be 1,000 occurrences of the dependent. The same program that accesses the root and all its dependents will use very different amounts of resources when operating against the two roots although the code will be exactly the same.

data element (1) an attribute of an entity. (2) a uniquely named and well defined category of data that consists of data items, and that is included in the record of an activity.

data engineering (*see* information engineering) the planning and building of data structures according to accepted mathematical models on the basis of the inherent characteristics of the data itself, and independent of hardware and software systems.

data independence the property of being able to modify the overall logical and physical structure of data without changing any of the application code supporting the data.

data item a discrete representation having the properties that define the data element to which it belongs. *See* data element.

data item set (dis) a grouping of data items, each of which directly relates to the key of the grouping of data in which the data items reside. The data item set is found in the midlevel model.

data manipulation language (DML) (1) a programming language that is supported by a DBMS and used to access a database. (2) language constructs added to a higher-order language (e.g., COBOL) for the purpose of database manipulation.

data model (1) the logical data structures, including operations and constraints provided by a DBMS for effective database processing. (2) the system used for the representation of data (e.g., the ERD or relational model).

data record an identifiable set of data values treated as a unit, an occurrence of a schema in a database, or a collection of atomic data items describing a specific object, event, or tuple.

data security the protection of the data in a database against unauthorized disclosure, alteration, or destruction. There are different levels of security.

data set a named collection of logically related data items, arranged in a prescribed manner, and described by control information; to which the programming systems has access.

data storage description language (DSDL) a language to define the organization of stored data in terms of an operating system and device independent storage environment. *See also* device media control language.

data structure a logical relationship among data elements that is designed to support specific data manipulation functions (e.g., trees, lists, and tables).

data type the definition of a set of representable values that is primitive and without meaningful logical subdivision.

data view *see* user view.

data volatility the rate of change of the contents of data.

data warehouse a collection of integrated subject-oriented databases designed to support the DSS function; where each unit of data is relevant to some moment in time. The data warehouse contains atomic data and lightly summarized data.

DB2   a database management system created by IBM.

DB/DC   database/data communications.

dBase III   a micro processor DBMS (by Ashton-Tate).

DBMS language interface (DB I/O module)   software that applications invoke in order to access a database. The module in turn has direct access with the DBMS. Standard enforcement and standard error checking are often features of an I/O module.

deadlock   *see* deadly embrace.

deadly embrace   the event that occurs when transaction A desires to access data currently protected by transaction B, while at the same time transaction B desires to access data that is currently being protected by transaction A. The deadly embrace condition is a serious impediment to performance.

decision support system (DSS)   a system used to support managerial decisions. Usually DSS involves the analysis of many units of data in a heuristic fashion. As a rule, DSS processing does not involve the update of data.

decompaction   the opposite of compaction; once data is stored in a compacted form, it must be decompacted to be used.

decryption   the opposite of encryption. Once data is stored in an encrypted fashion, it must be decrypted to be used.

degree (of a relation)   the number of attributes or columns of a relation. *See* cardinality of a relation.

delimiter   a flag, symbol, or convention used to mark the boundaries of a record, field, or other unit of storage.

demand staging   the movement of blocks of data from one storage device to another device with a shorter access time, when programs request the blocks and the blocks are not already in the faster access storage.

denormalization   the technique of placing normalized data in a physical location that optimizes the performance of the system.

derived data   data whose existence depends on two or more occurrences of a major subject of the enterprise.

derived data element   a data element that is not necessarily stored, but that can be generated when needed (e.g., age as of current date, and date of birth).

derived relation   a relation that can be obtained from previously defined relations by applying some sequence of retrieval and derivation operations (e.g., a table that is the combination of others and some projections). *See* a virtual relation.

design review   the quality assurance process where all aspects of a system are reviewed publicly prior to the striking of code.

device media control language (DMCL)   a language used to define the mapping of the data onto the physical storage media. *See* data storage description language.

direct access   retrieval or storage of data by reference to its location on a volume. The access mechanism goes directly to the data in question, as is generally required with online use of data. Also called random access or hashed access.

direct access storage device (DASD) a data storage unit where data can be accessed directly without having to progress through a serial file such as a magnetic tape file. A disk unit is a direct access storage device.

directory a table specifying the relationships between items of data. Sometimes it is a table or index giving the addresses of data.

distributed catalog a distributed catalog is needed to achieve site autonomy. The catalog at each site maintains information about objects in the local databases. The distributed catalog keeps information on replicated and distributed tables stored at that site and on remote tables located at another site that cannot be accessed locally.

distributed database a database controlled by a central DBMS; but where the storage devices are geographically dispersed or not attached to the same processor. *See* parallel I/O.

distributed environment a set of related data processing systems, where each system has capacity to operate autonomously, but where applications can execute at multiple sites. Some of the systems may be connected with teleprocessing links into a network in which each system is a node.

distributed free space space left empty at intervals in a data layout, to permit insertion of new data.

distributed request a transaction across multiple nodes.

distributed unit of work the work done by a transaction that operates against multiple nodes.

division an operation that partitions a relation on the basis of the contents of data found in the relation.

DL/1 IBM's Data Language One, used for describing logical and physical data structures.

domain the set of legal values from which actual values are derived for an attribute or a data element.

download the stripping of data from one database to another, based on the content of data found in the first database.

drill down analysis the type of analysis where examination of a summary number leads to the exploration of the components of the sum.

dual database the practice of separating high performance, transaction oriented data from decision support data.

dual database management systems the practice of using multiple database management systems to control different aspects of the database environment.

dumb terminal a device used to interact directly with the end user, where all processing is done on a remote computer. A dumb terminal acts as a device that gathers data and displays data only.

dynamic SQL SQL statements that are prepared and executed within a program, while the program is executing. In dynamic SQL, the SQL source is contained in host language variables rather than being coded into the application program.

dynamic storage allocation a technique where the storage areas assigned to computer programs are determined during processing.

dynamic subset of data a subset of data selected by a program and operated on only by the program, and released by the program once it ceases execution.

EDI Electronic Data Interchange.

EIS (Executive Information Systems) systems designed for the top executives, featuring drill-down analysis and trend analysis.

embedded pointer a record pointer (i.e., a means of internally linking related records) that is not available to an external index or directory. Embedded pointers are used to reduce search time, but also require maintenance overhead.

encoding a shortening or abbreviation of the physical representation of a data value (e.g., male = "M", female = "F").

encryption the transformation of data from a recognizable form to a form unrecognizable without the algorithm used for the encryption. Encryption is usually done for the purpose of security.

enterprise the generic term for the company, corporation, agency, or business unit. Usually associated with data modelling.

entity a person, place or thing of interest to the data modeller at the highest level of abstraction.

entity-relationship attribute (ERA) model a data model that defines entities, the relationship between the entities, and the attributes that have values to describe the properties of entities and/or relationships.

entity-relationship diagram (ERD) a high-level data model—the schematic showing all the entities within the scope of integration and the direct relationship between those entities.

event a signal that an activity of significance has occurred. An event is noted by the information system.

event discrete datas data relating to the measurement or description of an event.

expert system a system that captures and automates the usage of human experience and intelligence.

extent (1) a list of unsigned integers that specifies an array. (2) a physical unit of disk storage attached to a data set after the initial allocation of data has been made.

external data (1) data originating from other than the operational systems of a corporation. (2) data residing outside the central processing complex.

external schema a logical description of a user's method of organizing and structuring data. Some attributes or relationships can be omitted from the corresponding conceptual schema or can be renamed or otherwise transformed. *See* view.

extract the process of selecting data from one environment and transporting it to another environment.

field *See*s data item.

file a set of related records treated as a unit and stored under a single logical file name.

first in first out (FIFO) a fundamental ordering of processing in a queue.

first in last out (FILO) a standard order of processing in a stack.

flag an indicator or character that signals the occurrence of some condition.

flat file a collection of records containing no data aggregates, nested repeated data items, or groups of data items.

floppy disk a device for storing data on a personal computer.

foreign key an attribute that is not a primary key in a relational system, but whose values are the values of the primary key of another relation.

format the arrangement or layout of data in or on a data medium or in a program definition.

forward recovery a recovery technique that restores a database by reapplying all transactions using a before image from a specified point in time to a copy of the database taken at that moment in time.

fourth generation language language or technology designed to allow the end user unfettered access to data.

functional decomposition the division of operations into hierarchical functions (i.e., activities) that form the basis for procedures.

graphic a symbol produced on a screen representing an object or a process in the real world.

granularity the level of detail contained in a unit of data. The more detail there is, the lower the level of granularity. The less detail there is, the higher the level of granularity.

hash to convert the value of the key of a record into a location on DASD.

hash total a total of the values of one or more fields, used for the purposes of auditability and control.

header record or header table a record containing common, constant, or identifying information for a group of records that follow.

heuristic the mode of analysis in which the next step is determined by the results of the current step of analysis. Used for decision support processing.

hierarchical model a data model providing a tree structure for relating data elements or groups of data elements. Each node in the structure represents a group of data elements or a record type. There can be only one root node at the start of the hierarchical structure.

hit an occurrence of data that satisfies some search criteria.

hit ratio a measure of the number of records in a file expected to be accessed in a given run. Usually expressed as a percentage—number of input transactions/number of records in the file × 100 = hit ratio.

homonyms identical names that refer to different attributes.

horizontal distribution the splitting of a table across different sites by rows. With horizontal distribution rows of a single table reside at different sites in a distributed database network.

host the processor receiving and processing a transaction.

Huffman code a code for data compaction in which frequently used characters are encoded with fewer bits than infrequently used characters.

IDMS a network DBMS from CA.

IEEE Institute of Electrical and Electronics Engineers.

IMS Information Management System—an operational DBMS by IBM.

image copy   a procedure in which a database is physically copied to another medium for the purposes of backup.

index   the portion of the storage structure maintained to provide efficient access to a record when its index key item is known.

index chains   chains of data within an index.

index sequential access method (ISAM)   a file structure and access method in which records can be processed sequentially (e.g., in order, by key) or by directly looking up their locations on a table, thus making it unnecessary to process previously inserted records.

index point   a hardware reference mark on a disk or drum; used for timing purposes.

indirect addressing   any method of specifying or locating a record through calculation (e.g., locating a record through the scan of an index).

information   data that human beings assimilate and evaluate to solve problems or make decisions.

information engineering (IE)   the discipline of creating a data driven development environment.

information center   the organizational unit charged with identifying and accessing information needed in DSS processing.

input/output (I/O)   the means by which data is stored and/or retrieved on DASD. I/O is measured in milliseconds (i.e., mechanical speeds) whereas computer processing is measured in nanoseconds (i.e., electronic speeds).

instances   a set of values representing a specific entity belonging to a particular entity type. A single value is also the instance of a data item.

integrity   the property of a database that ensures that the data contained in the database is as accurate and consistent as possible.

intelligent database   a database that contains shared logic as well as shared data and automatically invokes that logic when the data is accessed. Logic, constraints, and controls relating to the use of the data are represented in an intelligent data model.

interactive   a mode of processing that combines some of the characteristics of online transaction processing and batch processing. In interactive processing the end user interacts with data over which he/she has exclusive control. In addition, the end user can initiate background activity to be run against the data.

interleaved data   data from different tables mixed into a simple table space, where there is commonality of physical colocation based on a common key value.

internal schema   the schema that describes logical structures of the data and the physical media over which physical storage is mapped.

interpretive   a mode of data manipulation in which the commands to the DBMS are translated as the user enters them (as opposed to the programmed mode of process manipulation).

intersection data   data that is associated with the junction of two or more record types or entities, but which has no meaning when disassociated with any records or entities forming the junction.

inverted file   a file structure that uses an inverted index, where entries are grouped according to the content of the key being referenced. Inverted files provide for the fast spontaneous searching of files.

inverted index   an index structure organized by means of a nonunique key, to speed the search for data by content.

inverted list   a list organized around a secondary index instead of around a primary key.

I/O (Input/Output Operation)   Input/output operations are the key to performance because they operate at mechanical speeds, not at electronic speeds.

I/O bound   the point after which no more processing can be done because the I/O subsystem is saturated.

ISAM   *see* Indexed Sequential Access Method.

"is a type of"   an analytical tool used in abstracting data during the process of conceptual database design (e.g., a cocker spaniel is a type of dog).

ISDN (Integrated Services Digital Network)   telecommunications technology that enables companies to transfer data and voice through the same phone lines.

ISO   International Standards Organization.

item   *see* data item.

item type   a classification of an item according to its domain, generally in a gross sense.

iterative analysis   the mode of processing in which the next step of processing depends on the results obtained by the existing step in execution; heuristic processing.

jad (Joint Application Design)   an organization of people—usually end users—to create and refine application system requirements.

join   an operation that takes two relations as operands and produces a new relation by concatenating the tuples and matching the corresponding columns when a stated condition holds between the two.

judgment sample   a sample of data where it is accepted or rejected for the sample based on one or more parameters.

junction   from the network environment, an occurrence of data that has two or more parent segments. For example, an order for supplies must have a supplier parent and a part parent.

justify   to adjust the value representation in a character field to the right or to the left, ignoring blanks encountered.

keeplist   a sequence of database keys maintained by the DBMS for the duration of the session.

key   a data item or combination of data items used to identify or locate a record instance (or other similar data groupings).

key compression   a technique for reducing the number of bits in keys; used in making indexes occupy less space.

key, primary   a unique attribute used to identify a single record in a database.

key, secondary   a nonunique attribute used to identify a class of records in a database.

label   a set of symbols used to identify or describe an item, record, message, or file. Occasionally, a label may be the same as the address of the record in storage.

language   a set of characters, conventions, and rules used to convey information, and consisting of syntax and semantics.

latency   the time taken by a DASD device to position the read arm over the physical storage medium. For general purposes, average latency time is used.

least frequently used (LFU)   a replacement strategy in which new data must replace existing data in an area of storage; the least frequently used items are replaced.

least recently used (LRU)   a replacement strategy in which new data must replace existing data in an area of storage; the least recently used items are replaced.

level of abstraction   the level of abstraction appropriate to a dimension. The level of abstraction that is appropriate is entirely dependent on the ultimate user of the system.

line   the hardware by which data flows to or from the processor. Lines typically go to terminals, printers, and other processors.

line polling   the activity of the teleprocessing monitor in which different lines are queried to determine whether they have data and/or transactions that need to be transmitted.

line time   the length of time required for a transaction to go either from the terminal to the processor or the processor to the terminal. Typically line time is the single largest component of online response time.

linkage   the ability to relate one unit of data to another.

linked list   set of records in which each record contains a pointer to the next record on the list. *See* chain.

list   an ordered set of data items.

living sample   a representative database typically used for heuristic statistical analytical processing in place of a large database. Periodically the very large database is selectively stripped of data so that the resulting living sample database represents a cross section of the very large database at some moment in time.

load   to insert data values into a database that was previously empty.

local site support   within a distributed unit of work, a local site update allows a process to perform SQL update statements referring to the local site.

local transaction   in a distributed DBMS, a transaction that requires reference only to data that is stored at the site where the transaction originated.

locality of processing   in distributed database, the design of processing so that remote access of data is eliminated or reduced substantively.

lockup   the event that occurs when update is done against a database record, and the transaction has not yet reached a commit point. The online transaction needs to prevent other transactions from accessing the data while update is occurring.

log   a journal of activity.

logging the automatic recording of data with regard to the access of the data, the updates to the data, etc.

logical representation a data view or description that does not depend on a physical storage device or a computer program.

loss of identity when data is brought in from an external source and the identity of the external source is discarded, loss of identity occurs. A common practice with microprocessor data.

LU6.2 (Logical Unit Type 6.2) peer-to-peer data stream with network operating system for program to program communication. LU6.2 allows mid-range machines to talk to one another without the involvement of the mainframe.

machine learning the ability of a machine to improve its performance automatically, based on past performance.

magnetic tape (1) the storage medium most closely associated with sequential processing. (2) a large ribbon on which magnetic images are stored and retrieved.

main storage database (MSDB) a database that resides entirely in main storage. Such databases are very fast to access, but require special handling at the time of update. Another limitation of MSDBs are that they can only manage small amounts of data.

master file a file that holds the system of record for a given set of data (usually bound by an application).

maximum transaction arrival rate (MTAR) the rate of arrival of transactions at the moment of peak period processing.

message (1) the data input by the user in the online environment that is used to drive a transaction. (2) the output of a transaction.

metadata (1) data about data. (2) the description of the structure, content, keys, indexes, etc. of data.

metalanguage a language used to specify other languages.

microprocessor a small processor serving the needs of a single user.

migration the process by which frequently used items of data are moved to more readily accessible areas of storage, and infrequently used items of data are moved to less readily accessible areas of storage.

mips (million instructions per second) the standard measurement of processor speed for minicomputers and mainframe computers.

mode of operation a classification for systems that execute in a similar fashion and share distinctive operational characteristics. Some modes of operation are: operational, DSS, online, interactive, etc.

modulo an arithmetic term describing the remainder of a division process. 10 modulo 7 is 3. Modulo is usually associated with the randomization process.

multilist organization a chained file organization in which the chains are divided into fragments and each fragment is indexed. This organization of data permits faster access to the data.

multiple key retrieval that requires searches of data on the basis of the values of several key fields (some or all of which are secondary keys).

MVS (Multiple Virtual Storage) IBM's mainline operating system for mainframe processors. There are several extensions of MVS.

Named Pipes program to program protocol with Microsoft's LAN Manager. The Named Pipes API supports intra and inter machine process to process communications.

natural forms first normal form—data that has been organized into two dimensional flat files without repeating groups. Second normal form—data that functionally depends on the entire candidate key. Third normal form—data that has had all transitive dependencies on data items other than the candidate key removed. Fourth normal form—data whose candidate key is related to all data items in the record, and that contains no more than one nontrivial multivalued dependency on the candidate key.

natural join a join in which the redundant logic components generated by the join are removed.

natural language a language generally spoken, whose rules are based on current usage and not explicitly defined by a grammar.

navigate to steer a course through a database, from record to record, by means of an algorithm which examines the content of data.

network a computer network consists of a collection of circuits, data switching elements, and computing systems. The switching devices in the network are called communication processors. A network provides a configuration for computer systems and communication facilities within which data can be stored and accessed, and within which DBMS can operate.

network model a data model that provides data relationships on the basis of records, and groups of records (i.e., sets) in which one record is designated as the set owner, and a single member record can belong to one or more sets.

nine's complement transformation of a numeric field calculated by subtracting the initial value from a field consisting of all nines.

node a point in the network at which data is switched.

nonprocedural language syntax that directs the computer as to what to do, not how to do it. Typical nonprocedural languages include RAMIS, FOCUS, NOMAD, and SQL.

normalize to decompose complex data structures into natural structures.

null an item or record for which no value currently exists or possibly may ever exist.

numeric a representation using only numbers and the decimal point.

occurrence *see* instance.

offset pointer an indirect pointer. An offset pointer exists inside a block, and the index points to the offset. If data must be moved, only the offset pointer in the block must be altered; the index entry remains untouched.

online storage storage devices and storage mediums where data can be accessed in a direct fashion.

operating system software that enables a computer to supervise its own operations and automatically call in programs, routines, languages, and data as needed for continuous operation throughout the execution of different types of jobs.

operational data   data used to support the daily processing a company does.

operations   the department charged with the running of the computer.

optical disk   a storage medium using lasers as opposed to magnetic devices. Optical disk is typically write only, is much less expensive per byte than magnetic storage, and is highly reliable.

ORACLE   a DBMS by ORACLE Corp.

order   to place items in an arrangement specified by rules such as numeric or alphabetic order. *See* sort.

OS/2   the operating system for IBM's Personal System.

OSF   Open Software Foundation.

OSI   Open Systems Interconnection overflow   (1) the condition in which a record or a segment cannot be stored in its home address because the address is already occupied. In this case, the data is placed in another location referred to as overflow. (2) the area of DASD where data is sent when the overflow condition is triggered.

ownership   the responsibility for updating for operational data.

padding   a technique used to fill a field, record, or block with default data (e.g., blanks or zeros).

page   (1) a basic unit of data on DASD. (2) a basic unit of storage in main memory.

page fault   a program interruption that occurs when a page that is referred to is not in main memory and must be read in from external storage.

page fixed   the state in which programs or data cannot be removed from main storage. Only a limited amount of storage can be page fixed.

paging   in virtual storage systems, the technique of making memory appear to be larger than it really is by transferring blocks (pages) of data or programs into external memory.

parallel data organization   an arrangement of data in which the data is spread over independent storage devices and is managed independently.

parallel I/O   the process of accessing or storing data on multiple physical data devices.

parallel search storage   a storage device in which one or more parts of all storage locations are queried simultaneously for a certain condition or under certain parameters. *See* associative storage.

parameter   an elementary data value used as a criteria for qualification, usually of searches of data or in the control of modules.

parent   a unit of data in a 1:n relationship with another unit of data called a child, where the parent can exist independently, but the child cannot exist unless there is a parent.

parsing   the algorithm that translates syntax into meaningful machine instructions. Parsing determines the meaning of statements issued in the data manipulation language.

partition   a segmentation technique in which data is divided into physically different units. Partitioning can be done at the application or the system level.

path length   the number of instructions executed for a given program or instruction.

peak period   the time when the most transactions arrive at the computer with the expectation of execution.

performance   the length of time from the moment a request is issued until the first of the results of the request are received.

periodic discrete data   a measurement or description of data taken at a regular time interval.

physical representation   (1) the representation and storage of data on a medium such as magnetic storage. (2) the description of data that depends on such physical factors as length of elements, records, pointers, etc.

pipes   vehicles for passing data from one application to another.

plex or network structure   a relationship between records or other groupings of data in which a child record can have more than one parent record.

plug compatible manufacturer (PCM)   a manufacturer of equipment that functionally is identical to that of another manufacturer (usually IBM).

pointer   the address of a record, or other groupings of data contained in another record, so that a program may access the former record when it has retrieved the latter record. The address can be absolute, relative, or symbolic, and hence the pointer is referred to as absolute, relative, or symbolic.

pools   the buffers made available to the online controller.

populate   to place occurrences of data values in a previously empty database. *See* load.

precision   the degree of discrimination with which a quantity is stated. For example, a three digit numeral discriminates among 1,000 possibilities, from 000 to 999.

precompilation   the processing of source text prior to compilation. In an SQL environment, SQL statements are replaced with statements that will be recognized by the host language compiler.

prefix data   data in a segment or a record used exclusively for system control; usually unavailable to the user.

primary key   an attribute that contains values that uniquely identify the record in which the key exists.

primitive data   data whose existence depends on only a single occurrence of a major subject area of the enterprise.

privacy   the prevention of unauthorized access and manipulation of data.

privilege descriptor   a persistent object used by a DBMS to enforce constraints on operations.

problems database   the component of a DSS application where previously defined decision parameters are stored. A problems database is consulted to review characteristics of past decisions, and to determine ways to meet current decision-making needs.

processor   the hardware at the center of execution of computer programs. Generally speaking processors are divided into three categories—mainframes, minicomputers, and microcomputers.

processor cycles   the hardware's internal cycles that drive the computer (e.g., initiate I/O, perform logic, move data, perform arithmetic functions, etc.).

production environment   the environment where operational, high performance processing is run.

program area   the portion of main memory in which application programs are executed.

progressive overflow   a method of handling overflow in a randomly organized file that does not require the use of pointers. An overflow record is stored in the first available space and is retrieved by a forward serial search from the home address.

projection   an operation that takes one relation as an operand and returns a second relation that consists of only the selected attributes or columns, with duplicate rows eliminated.

proposition   a statement about entities that asserts or denies that some condition holds for those entities.

protocol   the call format used by a teleprocessing monitor.

punched cards   an early storage medium on which data and input were stored. Today punched cards are rare.

purge data   the data on or after which a storage area may be overwritten. Used in conjunction with a file label, it is a means of protecting file data until an agreed upon release date is reached.

query language   a language that enables an end user to interact directly with a DBMS to retrieve and possibly modify data managed under the DBMS.

record   an aggregation of values of data organized by their relation to a common key.

record-at-a-time processing   the access of data a record at a time, a tuple at a time, etc.

recovery   the restoration of the database to an original position or condition, often after major damage to the physical medium.

redundancy   the practice of storing more than one occurrence of data. In the case where data can be updated, redundancy poses serious problems. In the case where data is not updated, redundancy is often a valuable and necessary design tool.

referential integrity   the facility of a DBMS to ensure the validity of a predefined relationship.

reorganization   the process of unloading data in a poorly organized state and reloading the data in a well organized state. Reorganization in some DBMS is used to restructure data. Reorganization is often called—"reorg" or an "unload/reload" process.

repeating groups   a collection of data that can occur several times within a given record occurrence.

rolling summary   a form of storing archival data where the most recent data has the lowest level of detail stored and the older data has higher levels of detail stored.

scope of integration   the formal definition of the boundaries of the system being modelled.

SDLC (System Development Life Cycle)   the classical operational system development life cycle that typically includes requirements gathering, analysis, design, programming, testing, integration, and implementation. Sometimes called a "waterfall" development life cycle.

sequential file a file in which records are ordered according to the values of one or more key fields. The records can be processed in this sequence starting from the first record in the file, and continuing to the last record in the file.

serial file a sequential file in which the records are physically adjacent, in sequential order.

set-at-a-time processing access of data by groups, each member of which satisfies some selection criteria.

snapshot a database dump or the archiving of data as of some one moment in time.

storage hierarchy storage units linked to form a storage subsystem, in which some units are fast to access and consume small amounts of storage, but which are expensive, and other units are slow to access and are large, but are inexpensive to store.

subject database a database organized around a major subject of the corporation. Classical subject databases are for customer, transaction, product, part, vendor, etc.

system log an audit trail of relevant system events (for example, transaction entries, database changes, etc.).

system of record the definitive and singular source of operational data. If data element abc has a value of 25 in a database record, but a value of 45 in the system of record, by definition the first value must be incorrect. The system of record is useful for the management of redundancy of data.

table a relation that consists of a set of columns with a heading and a set of rows (i.e., tuples).

time stamping the practice of tagging each record with some moment in time, usually when the record was created or when the record was passed from one environment to another.

time variant data data whose accuracy is relevant to some moment in time. The three common forms of time variant data are continuous time span data, event discrete data, and periodic discrete data. *See* current value data.

transition data data possessing both primitive and derived characteristics; usually very sensitive to the running of the business. Typical transition data include interest rates for a bank, policy rates for an insurance company, retail sale prices for a manufacturer/distributor, etc.

trend analysis the process of looking at homogeneous data over a spectrum of time.

true archival data data at the lowest level of granularity in the current level detail database.

update to change, add, delete, or replace values in all or selected entries, groups, or attributes stored in a database.

user a person or process issuing commands or messages and receiving stimuli from the information system.

Index*

---

*DW = data warehouse